DOCTRINAL TRACTS

OF THE

Presbyterian Publication Committee.

VOL. I.

The Presbyterian Publication Committee.

DEPOSITORIES:

PHILADELPHIA: PRESBYTERIAN HOUSE, 386 CHESTNUT STREET.
NEW YORK: IVISON & PHINNEY, 178 FULTON ST.

No. 1.

EXTENT OF THE ATONEMENT.

WHETHER Christ died for *all* men, or for a *part* only? is a question which has been much agitated, since the Reformation, though, according to Milner, the Church, from the earliest ages, rested in the opinion that Christ *died for all.* He does not except even Augustine, whom Prosper, his admirer and follower, and a strict Predestinarian, represents as maintaining that Christ gave himself a ransom for all;* so far at least as to make provision for their salvation, by removing an impediment which would otherwise have proved fatal. The early Christians seemed to go upon the principle, that as salvation was indiscriminately tendered to all, it must have been provided for all, and thus made *physically possible* to all where the gospel comes; otherwise, the Deity would be represented as tendering *that* to his creatures which was in no sense within their reach, and which they could not possibly attain, whatever might be their dispositions.

Among those who leaned strongly to what are called the doctrines of grace, the maxim was adopted, "*That Christ's death was sufficient for all, and efficient for the elect.*" By which they seem to have intended, that while Christ's death

---

* Vol. II. page 445.

opened the door for the salvation of all, so far as an expiatory sacrifice was concerned, it was *designed*, and by the sovereign grace of God made *effectual*, to the salvation of the elect. Their belief was, that Christ died *intentionally* to save those who were given to him in the covenant of redemption; but it does not appear that they supposed his death, considered merely as an *expiatory offering*, had any virtue in it, in relation to the elect, which it had not in relation to the rest of mankind. With respect to the *ultimate design* of this sacrifice, or the application which God would make of it, they doubtless supposed there was a difference; but in the *sacrifice itself*, or in its *immediate end*, the *demonstration of God's righteousness*, they could see no difference. In this view, it was precisely the same thing, as it stood related to the *elect* and to the *non-elect*. The sacrificial service was one and the same, appointed by the same authority, and for the same immediate purpose, and performed by the same glorious Personage, at the very same time. It wanted nothing to constitute it a true and perfect sacrifice for sin, as it stood related to the whole world; it was but this true and perfect sacrifice, as it stood related to the elect. Any other view would have overturned its sufficiency for all mankind; for it was not the sufficiency of Christ *to be* a sacrifice, but his sufficiency *as a sacrifice* for the whole world, that they maintained. And in perfect accordance with this, they held that this most perfect sacrifice was *efficient* for the elect. But how was it *efficient?* Not by its having in it any thing in regard to the *elect* which it had not in regard to others; for, *intrinsically* considered, it was the same to both, *a true and perfect sacrifice for sin;* but it was the purpose of God, in appointing it, that it should issue in the salvation of his chosen. This was the use he intended to make of it; nay, it was a part of the covenant of redemption, that if the Mediator performed the sacrificial service required, he should see of the travail of his soul, and be satisfied. There was, therefore, an infallible connection between the death of Christ and the salvation of his people; and, of course, his death *was efficient* in procuring their salvation, it being the great medium through which the saving mercy of God flowed, and connected both by the purpose and promise of God with the bestowment of that mercy.

But even all this does not suppose that the death of Christ, considered simply as a *sacrifice for sin,* had any thing in it peculiar to the elect, or that in and of itself it did any thing for them which it did not do for the rest of mankind. The intention of God, as to its application, or the use he designed to make of it, is a thing perfectly distinct from the sacrifice itself, and so considered, as we believe, by the Church antecedent to the Reformation. In no other way, can we see, how their language is either *intelligible* or *consistent.*

Whether the *Reformers,* as they are called, were exactly of one mind on this subject, is not quite so certain. But that *Luther, Melancthon, Osiander, Brentius, Œcolampadius, Zwinglius,* and *Bucer* held the doctrine of a general atonement, there is no reason to doubt. We might infer it from their Confession at *Marpurge,* signed A. D. 1529, as the expressions they employ on this subject are of a comprehensive character, and best agree with this sentiment. From their subsequent writings, however, it is manifest that these men, and the German Reformers generally, embraced the doctrine of a *universal propitiation.* Thus, also, it was with their immediate successors, as the language of the Psalgrave Confession testifies. This Confession is entitled, "A Full Declaration of the Faith and Ceremonies professed in the dominions of the most illustrious and noble Prince Frederick V., Prince

Elector Palatine." It was translated by John Rolte, and published in London, A. D. 1614.

"Of the power and death of Christ, believe we," say these German Christians, "that the death of Christ (whilst he being not a bare man, but the Son of God, died,) *is a full, all-sufficient payment, not only for our sins, but for the sins of the whole world;* and that he by his death hath purchased not only forgiveness of sins, but also the new birth by the Holy Ghost, and lastly everlasting life. But we believe therewith, that no man shall be made partaker of such a benefit, but only he that believeth on him. For the Scripture is plain where it saith, '*He that believeth not shall be damned.*' "

It would be unnecessary to take up time to show that the Lutheran Divines, with scarcely a single exception, from that period to the present, have declared in favour of a universal atonement. It could scarcely be otherwise when we consider the great reverence in which they held their distinguished leader, who, on various occasions, expressed himself most decidedly upon this subject. To give but a single instance. While speaking of the blood of Christ, the inestimable price paid for our redemption, (in his commentary on 1 Peter i. 18,) he remarks that no understanding or reason of man can comprehend it: so valuable was it, "that a single drop of this most innocent and precious blood, was abundantly sufficient for the sins of the whole world. But it pleased the Father so largely to bestow his grace upon us, and to make such abundant provision for our salvation, that he willed that Christ his Son should pour forth all his blood, and at the same time to give this whole treasure to us."

We know what the opinion of the Church of England was, by the language of her thirty-first article, which is in these words: "The offering of Christ once made, is that *perfect redemption, propitiation,* and *satisfaction for all the sins of the whole world, both original and actual;* and there is none other satisfaction for sin, but that alone;" and with this agree the words of the Heidelberg Catechism, in the thirty-seventh question, which state that "Christ bore, both in body and mind, the weight of the wrath of God, for the sins of *all mankind,* to the end that by his sufferings as a propitiatory sacrifice, he might redeem our bodies and souls from eternal damnation, and acquire for us the grace of God, justification and eternal life."

We are well aware that many who have expounded this catechism, have adopted more limited views; and that toward the close of the sixteenth century, there was not a little zeal displayed, in some of the Reformed Churches, in Germany and Holland, and other parts of Europe, in defence of what was called particular redemption. Yet, in the Synod of Dort, there were many able advocates for the doctrine that *Christ died for all,* in the only sense in which it is contended for now, by that part of the Calvinistic school who plead for a *general propitiation.* The delegates from England, *Hesse,* and *Bremen* were explicit in their declaration to this effect. But all were not of the same mind; and, therefore, though they agreed upon a *form of words,* under which every man might take shelter, still it wears the appearance of a compromise, and is not sufficiently definite to satisfy the rigid inquirer.

But some may be curious to know in what light this subject was viewed by *Calvin,* a man who, from the *extent* of his *erudition,* and the *vigour* of his faculties, exerted a mighty influence over his contemporaries, and the generations which succeeded him. Seldom, indeed, has the world seen such a man. Fearless as he was able, he examined every subject with care, and penetrated farther into the great doctrines of the gospel, probably, than any other divine of that or of preceding ages. What did *he* think of the doctrine of atonement? Did he consider it in the light of a universal provision for the whole human race, or did he suppose it restricted in its very nature to the elect? In his *Institutes,* which he wrote in early life, and which display an astonishing measure both of talent and research, some have supposed that he favoured the doctrine of a particular or limited atonement. The truth, however, is, so far as I can judge, that he carefully avoids committing himself on this point, and uses language on all occasions of such a general and indeterminate character, that it is not easy to discover what were his real sentiments. The probability is, that the subject had not then been much agitated, and that he thought it enough to keep to the language which was generally adopted by the Church. He often asserts that the death of Christ was a full and perfect sacrifice for sin—that it *takes away* sin—that he died for us—and that we are *purged by his blood;* but he does not teach that any man's sins are put away until he believes, but he plainly teaches the contrary. Having occasion to quote these words of the apostle, "Being justified freely by his grace, through the redemption that is in Christ Jesus; whom God hath set forth to be a propitiation through faith in his blood," he remarks, "Here Paul celebrates the grace of God, because he has given the price of our redemption in the death of Christ; and then enjoins us to betake ourselves to his blood, that we may obtain righteousness, and may stand secure before the judgment of God." But why betake ourselves to his blood, that we may obtain righteousness or justification, if his death, considered simply as a sin-offering, actually took away our sin, and reconciled us to God? For myself, I have no doubt that he considered the *sprinkling* of Christ's blood as essential to a *real* and *effective* propitiation as the shedding of it. *His blood shed* was the meritorious cause of our reconciliation, or the grand means by which it was effected; but this effect was never actually produced except in cases where his blood was sprinkled or applied, and that this blood is applied in no case antecedent to faith, and without faith. His doctrine, then, appears to me to be this: That Christ's death was the only full and perfect sacrifice for sin; that as such, it laid the foundation for God to be propitious to a world of sinners, even the whole human family; but that it actually reconciled him to none, so as to take away their sin and entitle them to life, till they repented and believed; but that to all such there is an *actual propitiation*, an *effective reconcilement* or at-one-ment, because by faith they lay their hands upon the head of the bleeding victim, and his blood is sprinkled upon them or applied to their souls. But whatever might have been his opinions in early life, his commentaries, which were the labours of his riper years, demonstrate in the most unequivocal manner that he received and taught the doctrine of a *general* or *universal* atonement. This is distinctly asserted by Dr. Watts, and several striking examples of his interpretation given. But having examined for myself, I am prepared to say that he takes the ground of a universal atonement in almost every controverted text on this subject in the New Testament. Hear him on Matthew xxvi. 28: "This is my blood of the New Testament, which is shed for *many*, for the remission of sins." "Under the name of *many*," says Calvin, "he designates not a part of the world only, but the whole human race. For he opposes many to one, as if he should say he would be the Redeemer, not of one man, but would suffer death that he might liberate many from the guilt of the curse. Nor is it to be doubted that Christ, in addressing the few, designed to make his doctrine common to the many. Nevertheless, it is at the same time to be noted, that in distinctly addressing his disciples in Luke, he exhorts all the faithful to appropriate the shedding of his blood to their own use. While, therefore, we approach the sacred table, not only this general thought should come into the mind, *that the world is redeemed by Christ's blood*, but that every one for himself should reckon his own sins to be expiated." He expounds John iii. 16 in accordance with the same views. "*God so loved the world that he gave his only begotten Son, that whosoever believeth on him should not perish, but have eternal life.*" By the *world*, according to him, we are to understand "*genus humanum*," the human race collectively, and not the elect as a distinct portion of the world. "God hath *affixed*," saith he, "a *mark of universality* to his words on this occasion, both that he might invite all promiscuously to the participation of life, and that he might cut off excuse to the unbelieving;" and this universality is indicated, he tells us, not only by the term *whosoever*, but by the term *world*. "For though God finds nothing in the world worthy of his favour, nevertheless he shows himself *propitious to the whole world*, since he calls all men without exception to *faith* in Christ, which is nothing else than an entrance into life."

His remarks on 1 Corinthians viii. 11, 12, are still more decisive. "And through thy knowledge shall thy *weak brother perish for whom Christ died.*" Here the question is, what is meant by the weak brother *perishing?* Calvin's paraphrase is, "If the soul of every weak person was the purchase of the blood of Christ, he that for the sake of a little meat plunges his *brother again into death* who was *redeemed by Christ*, shows at how mean a rate he esteems the blood of Christ." His observations on Hebrews x. 26, are of the same decisive character. Paul declares "*that if we sin wilfully after that we have received the knowledge of the truth, there remaineth no more sacrifice for sins.*" This Calvin interpreted of those who openly apostatize from the truth and renounce their Christian profession—and to such, he says, there is no more a *sacrifice* for sins, because they have departed from the death of Christ and treated it with sacrilegious contempt—but to sinners of any other description, even to lapsed Christians, "Christ daily offers himself, so that no other sacrifice need to be sought for the expiation of their sins."

It is obvious that Calvin considered *apostates* as standing in a different relation to the death of Christ from what they once did, and different from that of other sinners under the dispensation of the gospel. That *once* his death might be regarded as a *sacrifice* for sin, available for them, but now it was otherwise; having despised him and being rejected of God, there remained to them neither this sacrifice nor any other, but only a fearful looking for of judgment and fiery indignation which shall consume the adversaries.

Again, on 1 John ii. 2, "He is the propitiation for our sins, and not for ours only, but for the sins of the whole world." "Here," says Calvin, "a question is raised, how the sins of the whole world were atoned for? Some have said *that Christ suffered for the whole world sufficiently, but for the elect alone efficaciously. This is the common solution of the schools,* and though I confess *this is a truth,* yet I do not think it agrees to this place."

See also on 2 Peter ii. 1, "There shall be false teachers among you who privily shall bring in damnable heresies, even denying *the Lord that bought them,* and bring upon themselves swift destruction." Upon this, Calvin remarks, "Though Christ is denied in various ways, yet, in my opinion, Peter means the same thing here that Jude expresses, namely, that the grace of God is turned into lasciviousness. For Christ has redeemed us that he might have a people free from the defilements of the world, and devoted to holiness and innocence. Whoever, therefore, shake off the yoke and throw themselves into all licentiousness, are justly said to deny Christ, by whom they *were redeemed.*"

To the same purpose are his remarks on Jude, verse fourth: "Turning the grace of God into lasciviousness, and denying the only Lord God, and our Lord Jesus Christ." "His meaning is," says Calvin, "that Christ is really denied when those who *were redeemed by his blood* again enslave themselves to the devil, and as far as in them lies, make that incomparable price vain and ineffectual."

It is but candid, however, to allow that in some passages where the word *all* is brought into question, this writer supposes that it signifies all of *every kind*, or all sorts, rather than all, *every one.* But this he might easily do and consistently maintain as the doctrine of the New Testament, that the death of Christ was a full and perfect sacrifice for the sins of all men absolutely. This doctrine he most certainly did maintain, as several of the extracts from his writings now presented clearly evince. We need not be afraid, therefore, that our *Calvinism* will be essentially marred by holding the doctrine of a *general propitiation*, unless we wish to be more Calvinistic than John Calvin himself. But as we should call no man master, upon earth, but examine for ourselves, and take our opinions from the living oracles, let us hear what the Scriptures say upon this subject.

To facilitate our inquiries, I propose to consider the truth of the following *positions:*

First. That the death of Christ was a true and proper sacrifice for sin.

Second. That though his death was of *vicarious import*, as were the ancient sin-offerings, yet it was not *strictly* vicarious.

Third. That this sacrifice bore such a relation to the *sins of men*, that a way was thereby opened for the restoration of the whole human family to the favour of God.

Should these propositions turn out to be true, we shall be at no loss how to answer the question which stands at the head of this lecture.

First. As to the first position, *that Christ's death was a true and proper sacrifice for sin*, there will be no dispute, as this is common ground to all Calvinists, and to all, indeed, who do not virtually give up the doctrine of atonement. Still it may be well to remark that the language of Scripture, on this subject, is clear and precise. Christ is called *the Lamb of God, which taketh away the sins of the world.* He is said *to have given himself for us, an offering and a sacrifice to God.* It is affirmed *that he needed not, like the high priests under the law, to offer up sacrifice daily, first for his own sins, and then for the sins of the people; for this he did once when he offered up himself.* He is expressly called *the propitiation for our sins*, and God is said to have sent him into the world for the purpose of *making propitiation*, and of making it by his death. The whole system of Jewish sacrifices, as well as Patriarchal, were but types of his one great sacrifice when he offered up himself, and demonstrate his death to be a true and proper *expiatory offering.* But this is a point on all hands conceded.

Second. Was his death, then, of *vicarious import* simply? or was it strictly *vicarious?*

That it was of *vicarious import* cannot reasonably be

denied, if we compare it with the legal sacrifices, or attend to the express language of Scripture on the subject.

The victims under the law were vicarious offerings; they suffered in the room and stead of the offerer, and thus far there was a *transfer*, not of *sin* or *guilt*, strictly speaking, but of its *penal effects;* suffering and death, only, were transferred, and this is what is meant by putting the iniquities of the sinner upon the head of the victim, and of the victim's bearing the iniquities of the sinner.

To suppose a literal transfer, either of *sin* or of *punishment*, would be to suppose something which is entirely unauthorized by the language of Scripture, and at the same time to involve the absurdity of making a man and even a beast guilty by proxy. *Sin, guilt, ill-desert* are in the very nature of things *personal;* and *punishment* presupposes guilt, and guilt in the subject; neither the one nor the other is properly transferable. Or, to use the language of Magee: "*Guilt* and *punishment* cannot be conceived but with reference to *consciousness*, which cannot be transferred."

While we would maintain, therefore, that the sufferings of Christ were of *vicarious import*, because he suffered in the room of sinners, and bore the indications of Divine wrath for their sakes, we cannot subscribe to the opinion that they were *strictly vicarious*, if by this is meant that the *sins* of those for whom he suffered, their *personal desert* and *their punishment*, were literally transferred to him. We maintain the doctrine of substitution, but not such a substitution as implies a transfer of character, and consequently of *desert* and *punishment*. This we think to be impossible; and *unnecessary*, if not impossible. It was enough that there should be a transfer of *sufferings*, and *these*, not exactly in *kind*, *degree*, or *duration*, but in all their circumstances amounting to a full equivalent in their moral effect upon the government of God. We hold that Jesus died in the room of the guilty; that though innocent himself, he *was made sin for us*, or treated as a sinner on our account, and in our stead; that the Lord laid on him the iniquities of us all; and that he bore our sins in his own body on the tree, by suffering what was a full equivalent to the punishment due to our offences. But this, we think, is all the substitution which the Scriptures teach, all that the nature of things will admit, and all that was *necessary* to effect the same moral ends in the government of God which would have been effected by inflicting on the transgressor the penal sanctions of his law. This brings us to our third position.

Third. That the sacrifice of Christ bore such a relation to the *sins of men*—that a way was thereby opened for the restoration of the whole human family to the favour of God.

I say the *sins of men*, for it does not appear that his sacrifice bore any specific relation to the sins of the rebel angels. For them no sacrifice was appointed, but justice seized at once upon its victims, and thrust them down to hell, where they are reserved in chains under darkness unto the judgment of the great day. And but for a sacrifice, which did honour to the Divine Law, and rendered it consistent for a holy God to treat with rebellious man, it is not easy to see why the arm of justice was not uplifted to avenge its insulted rights, in the immediate and interminable punishment of our apostate race. Be this, however, as it may, it is an undeniable fact, that Jesus took not on him the nature of angels, but the seed of Abraham, and was in all things made like unto his brethren of the human family. In that very nature in which the law of God had been broken and dishonoured, did Jesus appear to put away sin, by the sacrifice of himself. But this, it will be said, it behooved him to do, if he were to expiate the sins of his people only, and if his death had not the remotest reference to the sins of the finally lost. Granted: but must it not also be allowed, that if he had intended to make provision for the whole human family by pouring out his blood, it behooved him neither to be nor to do any thing more than he actually did? As a Person of infinite dignity, he accomplished that *very service* in that *very nature*, and in all *those circumstances* of *touching interest*, which alone would have been requisite had he intended to make atonement for the whole world absolutely. This is so obvious as generally to be admitted. It is allowed on all hands, that he atoned for all sorts of persons, of all nations and all ages of the world; and that the sacrifice he offered was of sufficient value to have redeemed the whole human race. But how did he atone for any, but by obeying the law in *that very nature* in which they had disobeyed it, and by suffering in that *very nature*, a moral equivalent to *the evil* which they had deserved to suffer, as the just award of the same righteous law? But this nature, let it be remembered, is the common nature of man, and if rendering a service in *this nature* would amount to an atonement for *one*, why not for *another*, and *another*, until the whole were included? That such might be the case, it is easy to see; and that such, in fact, was the case, it would be very natural to presume.

The leading circumstance which constitutes the connection between Christ and those for whom his sacrifice is available, is that he obeyed the law in their nature, and in the same nature suffered its penalty, or that which was equivalent. All had reproached or dishonoured God alike, by trampling upon the authority of his law; Christ assumes their nature, and by his obedience and sufferings magnifies the law and makes it honourable. They with one voice had proclaimed that the law was not good, nor God worthy to be obeyed. Christ reverses this statement, and proclaims in the ears of the universe the purity of God's character, and the excellence and importance of his law. Nay, he condemns sin, vindicates God's holiness, and shows his unalterable determination to uphold the authority of his government; since, in the very expedient he has adopted for dispensing mercy, he will not forgive sin, without an adequate satisfaction to the right of his injured majesty, considered as the moral head of the universe. All this Christ did in man's nature, and with reference to the sins of men, and more than this he need not do, and could not do, by offering himself a sacrifice for sin. What is there, let me ask, in the nature and circumstances of this great sacrifice, which should limit its availableness to a *part* of the human race? Did it not bear sufficiently upon the conduct of the *whole?* Did it not condemn sin—all sin—the sin of one man as much as the sin of another? Did it not vindicate the Divine holiness, and the purity and excellence of that law which man had broken? Did it not evince God's determination to sustain the authority of that law, while it exhibited his boundless compassion toward a world of rebels? What more would we have in it, or what other or greater moral influence would we have it exert, had it been designed as a sacrifice of expiation for the whole human family? As for ourselves, we regard the whole scheme of atonement in the light of a remedial law; that it was adapted to counteract the ruins of the fall—and that in its very nature it contained a provision coextensive with those ruins—though in its application, for wise and holy purposes, an important difference will be made. But here we shall be told, that if we have not left out of our statement, we have not sufficiently exhibited *one* all-controlling circumstance, to wit, the *actual substitution* of Christ for, and in behalf of, those for whom he suffered; that to constitute his sufferings an *available sacrifice,* it was necessary not only that he should die in the *nature,* but in the *room* of sinners; and that he might die in their *nature* without dying in their *stead.*

Our reply is, that we consider the death of Christ as a vicarious sacrifice, and offered in behalf of all men; because, from the very nature of the case, it could scarcely be otherwise, he dying in their nature, and in circumstances equally fitted to make him the substitute of all. He did and suffered what he must have done, had he been the substitute of all, and so far as we can discern, nothing less or more; what he did and suffered bore the same relation to sin and holiness, to the law and government of God, as it would have done, had he offered himself for all; nay, we consider it impossible that he should, by his obedience and death, have *condemned sin* and *magnified the law,* and this in man's nature, without doing it with reference to every man's sin, and the dishonour which every man had cast upon the law. His sacrificial service was *open* and *public,* performed in the face of the universe, and gave out a testimony which was heard through all worlds, and a testimony which bore as strongly upon one man's sin as another's, and upon the righteousness of God, in his condemnation. Nay, whatever was the language of this solemn transaction concerning God or man, equally respected all men, and God in relation to all. We could not doubt, therefore, that so far as Christ was the substitute of any man, he was the substitute of all men, were we to look only at the nature of his sacrifice, and the purposes it was immediately designed to answer in the moral administration of God. But the Bible has not left us to general principles here; it has furnished us with facts and declarations upon the subject which we think ought for ever to put this matter to rest.

Look a moment at the doctrine of sacrifice taught from the beginning, but with more explicitness under the dispensation of Moses. For certain transgressions, and some of them of a moral character, every sinner among the Israelites was required to bring a victim, over whose head he was to confess his sin. This victim was afterward to be slain, and offered by the priest as a sin-offering unto the Lord, for the purpose of making an atonement for the soul. The life of the victim was accepted for the life of the sinner, the victim being always regarded as his *substitute.* Where the service was performed, agreeably to God's appointment, an atonement was made, and sin forgiven, so far, at least, as to release the sinner from the penalties and disabilities incurred under the Jewish law. But the victims slain on these occasions were *types* of *Christ,* a nobler victim hereafter to come into the world. This, so far as I know, is universally admitted. But what follows? Why, most certainly, unless the Jewish law was deceptive, the type being the substitute of the sinner, the antitype must be his substitute also; for it looked to him, and derived all its significancy and efficacy from him. A typical offering would be but a mere mockery of the Divine justice and holiness, considered in any other light than as a prefiguration of the glorious Antitype. Of necessity, therefore, they must be regarded as closely conjoined. Admit, then, that every man in the Jewish nation, good or bad, elect or non-elect, when he brought his sin or trespass offering to the Lord, was taught, by the very nature of the institution, that his *offering* or *victim* was his substitute, could he avoid the conclusion that a greater and infinitely more precious victim was his substitute also? Could he understand the nature of this sacrificial service, without perceiving that the type pointed to the *Antitype*, and that, by the appointment of God, both stood in the same relation to him, as a gracious medium through which pardon was to be obtained, and the Divine favour secured?

Now let me ask, whether it is reasonable to suppose that such a doctrine as this should be held forth in the Jewish sacrifices, if, in truth and in fact, Christ is the appointed substitute for the elect only? I know it is sometimes said, that the Jewish people were a typical nation, and that they properly prefigured the true Church of God, or the whole body of the elect, and, therefore, that their sacrifices for themselves typified Christ's sacrifice for his people. But this by no means avoids the difficulty. The Jewish sacrifices had a language which was distinct and appropriate, and that language was, that every man's victim brought by God's appointment, was a vicarious offering, accepted in behalf of the guilty offerer; that this offering was a type of Christ, and of his great sacrifice, to be made once in the end of the world; and consequently that Christ, thus prefigured, stood in the same relation to the offerer as did the prefiguring victim, to wit, as his substitute, and the only piacular sacrifice on which his faith ought ultimately to rest. This, we have no doubt, is the true state of the case. But to show how perfectly futile the attempt to escape from this argument is, by resorting to the notion that the Jewish nation typified the Church, let us look back to the patriarchal ages, where no such refuge will be found.

It is the common belief of Christians, supported by the clear indications of Holy Writ, that sacrifices were instituted by God immediately after the fall; that these sacrifices were expiatory, resembling, in all important particulars, the sin-offerings under the law. But if these early sacrifices were of God's appointment, it will not be doubted that they were obligatory upon the whole human family during the patriarchal ages, nor that they were *typical*, bearing the same relation to the promised seed of the woman, and to *his sacrifice*, which the Mosaic sacrifices afterward bore. What then do we find in this ancient sacrificial service? Why that God required every man, as he did Cain and Abel, to bring their victims, at the appointed time, and sacrifice them at his altars. Were these victims, then, the substitutes of the offerers, life being accepted for life? There is no room to doubt. Did these victims typify the Saviour, and his sacrifice of expiation? Most certainly they did, or they were an unmeaning and unprofitable service. But if typical of Christ, and the substitutes of the *offerers*, then Christ himself was exhibited as the substitute of the offerers, unless you break up the connection between type and antitype. To him these offerings pointed, and the worshippers were directed, through the medium of these emblems, to the great sacrifice which he was to accomplish, when he should come to break the head of the serpent, and procure the means of deliverance to a ruined world.

Here was instruction which God himself imparted, and it exhibits, with the light of a sunbeam, two important facts, to wit, that the *victims* employed in animal sacrifice were the appointed substitutes of their respective offerers, and that, being types of Christ, they show him to be the substitute of the offerers also. Now, as the rite of sacrifice was universal—instituted for the whole family of man—how can we escape the conclusion, that a foundation was laid for this universality, by appointing the Mediator to appear in human nature, and to offer a sacrifice in behalf of the whole human family? Allow a substitution thus universal, and all appears plain; say, with the apostle, that Christ is a Mediator between *God* and *men*, and that he, by the grace of God, tasted death for *every man;* give these expressions their full and unrestricted import, and there is no difficulty in allowing that the ancient victims were the real substitutes of those who offered them, and at the same time types of the Lord Jesus, who, in his sacrificial character, sustained an important relation to the entire family of man. But deny a substitution thus universal, and you are plunged into impenetrable darkness.

We have dwelt the longer on this point, because it is vital to the controversy. If Christ were a substitute for all men, or died in the room of all, then it cannot be denied that his sacrifice bore such a relation to the sins of men, that a way was thereby opened for the restoration of the whole human race to the favour of God. And on the other hand, if no substitution of this universal character existed, I do not see but that we must restrict the availableness of Christ's death to the elect only. But our brethren of the opposite school will probably rejoin: "If Christ died in the room of all, why are not all saved? And again, if he died *for*, or in reference to all, why the *specialty* sometimes indicated in regard to the object of his death? He is said to lay down his life for his sheep, for his friends, for the Church."

The first of these inquiries we answer by saying, that if Christ did die for all, so as to make his death available to their salvation, it will not follow as a consequence that all will actually be saved; and as to the indication of *specialty* in regard to the object of Christ's death, such as that he died for his sheep, his Church, his friends, these are all explained by a reference to the *ultimate* object of his death. Doubtless, he died with an intention of saving those who were given him in the covenant of redemption; they were the seed to serve him, promised as a reward for his agony and bloody sweat, and he looked to their salvation as the fruit of his sufferings, and as the joy set before him. But such an ultimate design of his death, which included the application which should be made of it by the sovereign and discriminating grace of God, hinders not the availableness of his sacrifice in relation to all, nor throws the slightest suspicion upon the doctrine which we have advocated in this lecture. Because he died with the declared design of saving his people, does it follow that he had no other design? Because this was an ultimate end sought in his death, is it a just consequence that he could have had no other end, either immediate or ultimate? Doubtless, whatever follows as the proper result of his atoning sacrifice, he sought more immediately or remotely as an end of his undertaking in this infinitely solemn and amazing tragedy.

But we have not done with this article; *that the sacrifice of Christ stood in such a relation to the sins of men, as to open a way for the salvation of all.*

We argue this from the parable of the marriage supper, where it is expressly said, *all things are ready*, and *ready* too, for those who, it seems, in the event never came. * * * We argue it from the indefinite tender of salvation made to all men where the gospel comes. To us, no maxim appears more certain, *than that a salvation offered, implies a salvation provided;* for God will not tantalize his creatures by tendering them that which is not in his hand to bestow. We argue it from the declared purpose of God in sending his Son into the world, and which he has expressed in such a manner as to leave no reasonable doubt that provision is made for all. "For God so loved the world, that he gave his only begotten

Son, that whosoever believeth in him should not perish, but have everlasting life."

By the *world* here, must be intended either the chosen vessels of mercy, sometimes called the elect world,—or the *world* of mankind at large, without discrimination. Suppose we interpret it of the *elect world*. Then the sentiment will run thus: God so loved the *elect world*, that *whosoever* of the *elect world* shall believe in him, &c.

But such language is absurd upon the very face of it, and cannot be supposed to proceed from the lips of unerring wisdom. Besides, what follows fixes the sense, and demands a different interpretation. "For God sent not his Son into the world to condemn the world, but that the world through him *might be* saved." And again, "This is the condemnation, that light has come into the world, and men loved darkness rather than light." It is utterly contrary to the *usus loquendi*, to interpret the phrase, *the world* of God's chosen people. It signifies often, mankind at large; sometimes the wicked part of mankind, as distinguished from God's people; and not unfrequently the earth itself, with all that pertains to it. (Nor is it doubted that it is sometimes taken for a *part* of mankind, instead of the whole, as when it is said, "*the world is gone after him.*") But it is nowhere used, that we have discovered, for the *elect*, the *Church*, or God's *redeemed ones*, in distinction from others. Interpret this passage, then, according to its most obvious signification, and what do we find but a declaration of God's love to the human race collectively in the gift of his Son, which gift involved in it the means of their salvation. He sent his Son that *they might be saved*, not that they should infallibly be saved. His love was expressed in providing the *means*, and their destiny he has made to turn upon the use which they shall make of this inestimable provision of his mercy.

And hence Christ himself says in the words immediately following: "He that believeth not is condemned already; *because* he hath not believed in the name of the only begotten Son of God." Not because a way of salvation was not provided through means of this Son, (for *that* he had asserted in a verse or two preceding,) but because he had not believed in the name of the only begotten Son, but despised and rejected him.

Here he assigns the true and only cause of condemnation to sinners under the light of the gospel, namely, their *unbelief*. But how could unbelief be the *cause*, at least the principal cause, if no sacrifice has been offered for them, and no means of salvation provided? There would then be another reason for their condemnation, a reason far deeper and more controlling, to wit, *no atonement*, nor the means of one.

We call not your attention to the universal terms so often employed upon this subject, as that Christ is the *Saviour of all men*, that he tasted *death for every man*, and *gave himself a ransom for all*, &c., not because we suppose these terms ought not to be understood in the widest sense of universality, but because this ground has been trodden over by the parties in this controversy. We ask you to consider some passages which we think far more decisive. Look at Hebrews x. 26, 27: "For if we sin wilfully, after that we have received the knowledge of the truth, there remaineth no more sacrifice for sins; but a certain fearful looking for of judgment, and fiery indignation which shall devour the adversaries." It is agreed, on all hands, that the apostle here describes such as openly and deliberately apostatize from the truth, and set themselves vigorously to oppose Christianity—men who are given up of God, and irrevocably sealed over to destruction, as a just judgment for their wickedness. Now, with respect to these men he said, *there remaineth no more sacrifice for sins.* The original is peculiarly strong and determinate. Οὐκ ἔτι περὶ ἁμαρτιῶν ἀπολείπεται θυσία—a sacrifice for sin no more, or no longer *remains.* What does this imply, but that antecedent to this apostasy, there was a sacrifice which might have availed to take away their sins? But now there is none. They are left without hope, because cut off, by the just judgment of God, from any connection with the only sacrifice which can take away sin. They have trampled under foot the blood of the covenant; and now, instead of pleading for mercy, it pleads for vengeance. But what propriety in this statement, if the blood of Christ was never an available sacrifice for them, and they never stood in any other relation to it than the apostate angels—it having, in no sense, ever been shed for them? Surely, it must be strange language, to say there remaineth no more a sacrifice to those for whom there never was a sacrifice. If this passage stood alone, on the subject before us, I should consider it as settling the question for ever, that the death of Christ bore such a relation to the sins of men, as to open a way for the restoration of the whole human family to the favour of God. For, if it bore such a relation to any one soul who is finally lost, with what reason could it be denied with respect to others?

Look, again, at 1 Cor. viii. 11: "And through thy knowledge shall thy weak brother perish, *for whom Christ died.*" But how shall he *perish?* Why, by being emboldened to eat those things which are offered unto idols, as the apostle teaches us in the preceding verse, he shall be guilty of renouncing the living and true God, or which is equally fatal, confounding him with idols. The apostle does not say he shall be injured, greatly injured, but he shall *perish;* using the very same word which Christ does, when he says that God gave his only begotten Son, that men *need not perish*, but have everlasting life; and the same word which Jude uses, when he speaks of those who *perished* in the *gainsaying of Core*. It is perfectly idle to attempt to explain away the solemn and awful import of this word; and yet if it be allowed its proper signification —if to *perish* is to lose one's soul—then men may be *lost* for whom Christ died; which concludes unanswerably in favour of our doctrine, that Christ died for all, or that his sacrifice bore a solemn and important relation to all.

We draw the same conclusion from 2 Peter ii. 1, where the apostle speaks of some who privily bring in damnable heresies, *denying the Lord that bought them*, and bring upon themselves swift destruction. You have already heard the opinion of Calvin upon this text. And though our brethren of another school have often nibbled at it, and applied to it the various arts of criticism, still it stands as firm as the pillars of Hercules against the sentiment that Christ died for his people only.

If wicked men deny the Lord that bought them, doubtless they were *bought*, and bought by the price of that blood which alone is an adequate ransom for the soul.

But we are told that the *Lord* that bought them was not Jesus Christ, and of course, that they were not bought with his blood. Who, then, was this *Lord*, and how did he buy these wicked men? "Why, the Lord is God the Father, the Sovereign Ruler of the world, and he bought these men as Jehovah bought the Israelites, when he delivered them from the bondage of Egypt." But when was this interpretation first introduced? Can it be found in any of the ancient scholiasts or glossaries? No. Its modern date shows its origin; that it has been resorted to, not from its obvious agreement with the words, but from the necessity of the case. It has been seen that the old interpretation would be fatal to a certain theory; the words of the apostle, therefore, must speak something else than what the Church from the beginning has supposed them to speak.

But let us hear the defence of this novel interpretation. The word in the original, translated Lord, is δεσπότης, and not Κυριος, the more common appellation of Jesus Christ. This word, it is said, signifies Supreme Ruler, and is thus applied to God in several places in the New Testament. True; but is it not also applied to Christ, and even to men who sustain the relation of *master* to others as their servants? Whom does the apostle mean by δεσπότης in 2 Tim. ii. 21, where he says, "If a man purge himself from these, he shall be a vessel unto honour, sanctified and meet for the *master's* use?" Whom does Jude mean by δεσπότης in a passage strikingly parallel with that under consideration, where he speaks of "certain men crept in unawares, who were of old ordained to this condemnation, ungodly men, turning the grace of God into lasciviousness, and *denying the only Lord God, even our Lord Jesus Christ*," as it should be rendered. The best lexicographers tells us that this word has the force of *dominus* among the Latins, and may be applied to God as the Supreme Ruler, to Jesus Christ as the great Head of his Church, or to any head or master of a family. Nothing is therefore more futile than the attempt to escape the obvious construction of this passage, by a criticism upon the word δεσπότης, which in this very place, Schleusner tells us, is applied to Jesus Christ. But if God, the Supreme Ruler of the world, is here designated by δεσπότης, I should like to know a little more definitely *how* he has bought these wicked men, who privily bring in damnable heresies? Will you say he delivered them from the bondage of corruption? This neither the text nor the context declares. But if it were so, what was the price which he paid for their deliverance? When he bought the Israelites, he paid a price for them, and a heavy price it was; he gave Egypt for them—Ethiopia and Sheba for a ransom. Was there any thing to correspond with this, when he bought the false prophets and false teachers spoken of in this text? According to our judgment, there was never a harder shift to blunt the edge of plain and pointed Scripture testimony. But we need not wonder, because as long as this text stands in the Bible, unperverted, it is entirely fatal to that scheme which contends that Jesus Christ was a sacrifice for the elect only.

Let me draw your attention to a single remark more. This important passage has always been considered as parallel with that in Jude, already mentioned. There is a striking resemblance in all the important points of character, attributed to these wicked men by the two sacred writers, and an equally striking analogy in their doom. But what did they do, besides turning the grace of God into lasciviousness, and leading a life of brutal sensuality? What did they do which in a peculiar manner irrevocably sealed them to perdition? Why, they denied the δεσποτης, and by δεσπότης Jude manifestly intends the Lord Jesus Christ.

THE HIDING-PLACE.

Hail, Sov'reign love, that first began
The scheme to rescue fallen man!
Hail, matchless, free, eternal grace,
That gave my soul *a hiding-place.*

Against the God who rules the sky
I fought with hands uplifted high;
Despised the offers of his grace,
Too proud to seek *a hiding-place.*

Vindictive justice stood in view:
To Sinai's fiery mount I flew;
But justice cried with frowning face—
"This mountain is *no hiding-place.*"

But lo! a heavenly voice is heard—
Mercy's bright angel then appear'd;
Who led me on a pleasing pace,
To Jesus Christ, *my hiding-place.*

On him Almighty vengeance fell,
Which must have sunk a world to hell:
He bore it for our guilty race,
And now, *He is my hiding-place.*

Brewer.

No. 2.

THE

PERSEVERANCE OF THE SAINTS.

The doctrine of the infallible perseverance of the saints is not, in my opinion, a *fundamental* doctrine of the gospel. Of course, people may hold different sentiments respecting it, and be saved; yet I cannot but regard it as a *very important* doctrine, and one which is clearly and strongly taught in the word of God—one which is, in a measure, essential to Christian *comfort*, and greatly conducive to the *glory* of God.

In offering a few remarks on it, the design of the writer is not to awaken controversy, or to condemn those Christians who do not believe it. He is far from doubting the *piety* of those individuals and churches who hold views on the point different from those which this tract is intended to exhibit. Nay, he is persuaded that in those churches there are some of the most consistent Christians on earth, and, perhaps, as many real saints as in our own, or any other section of the church. His aim, is simply to state the ground on which the doctrine of our church is built, and to answer the objections which are usually urged against it.

A mere *outline* of the argument, however, is all that is proposed. And if a large space should be allotted to the *objections* which are to be noticed, or if some of these should be regarded as trivial, let it be remembered that great stress is often laid on them, and that to pass them by unnoticed might be construed as inability to remove them. A free use of *italics* has been indulged, on account of the brevity of the argument, to show to the most careless reader the hinge on which the controversy between Calvinists and Arminians turns. I will

I. State and explain the DOCTRINE;

II. Offer some ARGUMENTS in proof of it; and,

III. Notice some OBJECTIONS.

A few words will *explain* what is meant by the expression, "the perseverance of the saints."

1. By a "saint" is not meant a *perfectly holy person*, for there is not such a one on earth. Nor, running to the other extreme, do we consider every *awakened* and *convicted* sinner a saint, for many are alarmed, excited, and partially reformed, who are never thoroughly converted. Nor do we mean *mere professional* Christianity, for outward profession often covers hearts at enmity with God. But by a *saint* is understood *a real Christian*—one who has been *born again*, John iii. 7—one who has become *a new creature*, 2 Cor. v. 17; or, to use a favourite expression of our opponents, one who has "been soundly and thoroughly converted." It is *certain* that such a person will not perish.

2. When we say that a saint will not fall away and be lost, we do not mean that this arises from any thing *in the Christian himself*, but from the *immutability* of the *purpose* and *promise* of God. If left to himself, the Christian would fall in a moment; and hence arises the propriety of those cautions, exhortations, and warnings against falling, which abound in the word of God.

3. When we say a Christian will not *fall from grace*, we do not mean that it is impossible to lose *many degrees of grace*, or to be backsliders to a considerable extent; for this we admit is a frequent occurrence; but that such will not fall *entirely away*, so as to lose *all* grace and *perish* eternally. Dr. Emmons and some other New England divines admit a *total*, though they deny a *final* falling from grace. Our church, in my opinion, very properly denies both; but the latter is the more important of the two, and it is to this I shall principally direct attention.

Our doctrine, therefore, is,

"*That no real Christian—no one who has been truly regenerated and made a new creature in Christ Jesus,* WILL EVER BE SUFFERED TO PERISH ETERNALLY."

ARGUMENTS FOR PERSEVERANCE.

My first arguments shall be founded on the *general principles* of the gospel; after which express passages of Scripture shall be adduced.

I. The doctrine of *Election* proves perseverance. I shall not here enter fully into this most unpopular subject, but shall content myself with observing that *saints* are elected unto salvation—of course to *perseverance.* 2 Thess. ii. 13: "We are bound to give thanks to God always for you, brethren, beloved of the Lord, because *God hath from the beginning chosen you to salvation, through sanctification of the Spirit and belief of the truth.*" "God hath *chosen,*"—here is election—"chosen *from the beginning,*"—here is the *eternity* of that election,—"chosen to *salvation,*"—here is the *end* of that election—"*through sanctification* and *belief of the truth,*"—here is *perseverance* in grace. See, also, Eph. i. 4–12, 1 Pet. i. 1–4: "According as he hath chosen us in him before the foundation of the world, that we should be holy," &c.; "Elect according to the foreknowledge of God the Father, through sanctification of the Spirit, unto obedience and the sprinkling of the blood of Jesus Christ,"—"to an inheritance incorruptible," &c. Saints, therefore, are *chosen* or *elected* to salvation. The only question is, whether this election *secures* salvation? That it does, is evident from two considerations.

1. The elect can *never be deceived or led fatally astray.* Matt. xxiv. 24: "Insomuch that, if *it were possible,* they should deceive the very elect." Does not this teach that it is *impossible* to "deceive" them, so as to ruin them? This *impossibility* arises, however, not from the *wisdom* of Christians, but from the *immutable purpose* of God to bring them to salvation.

2. Because at the day of judgment *nothing shall be laid to their charge.* Rom. viii. 33: "*Who* shall lay *any thing* to the charge of God's elect?" The apostle challenges any one to name an *accuser,* or a *charge,* which should appear against them. Now, the apostles, in the texts I have quoted, address all *saints* as *elected,* and, of course, teach that all saints will *persevere.*

II. The doctrine of *Efficacious Grace* proves perseverance.

The manner in which a man becomes a Christian makes it probable that when once converted, he will never cease to be a Christian. His conversion is not *of himself:* if it were, he might *of himself* go back again; but his conversion is an act of *Almighty power* and *sovereign grace.* Eph. i. 18, 19, and ii. 4, 8. The doctrine of the Bible is that all mankind are by nature at *enmity* with God, Rom. vii. 6, 7; that, in order to be Christians, we must be *born again,* John iii. 7; that those who are born, are born not of the will of *man,* nor of the will of the *flesh,* but of *God,* John i. 13; that those who are willing to serve him become willing in consequence of his *power,* Ps. cx. 3, (and hence our opponents so often call on God to "come down with *power;*") that those who are called are called not of *works,* but of *grace* given in Christ Jesus before the world began. 2 Tim. 1. 9.

From all which we are taught that the cause of a sinner's coming to Christ is not in himself, but *wholly in God.* Now, if God glorifies his power and grace in thus bringing a sinner to himself, what good reason can be assigned for his ever casting him off? The sinner can never be *worse* than he was when he was called; and, if God *loved* him then, why should he ever after *change* and hate him?

I will illustrate my argument by a single text, John vi. 44: *"No man can come unto me, except the Father which has sent me draw him, and I will raise him up at the last day."*

Observe, 1. This is a universal proposition, applying to *every man,—"No man* can come," &c. 2. The cause of the sinner's coming to Christ is not *in himself.* He never *will* come, unless converted by *Divine influence.* 3. When he does come, his conversion is to be attributed not to himself, but to God alone—to the "drawing of the Father." 4. What shall become of him when he is thus *drawn* and has come to Christ? Shall he be suffered to go back? or shall he be saved? Our Lord answers the question, *"I will raise him up at the last day."* This is certainly a *promise,* and not a *curse,* and therefore the *resurrection* is used in a good sense for a resurrection to *life.* As the term "life" in the New Testament does not mean mere *existence,* but *happiness,* so the *"resurrection"* generally means the resurrection of the righteous. Therefore Paul was so anxious to "attain unto the *resurrection* of the dead." Phil. iii. 11.

Our Lord, therefore, promises, in this text, that he *will grant eternal salvation* to those who are thus drawn to him by the Father. And, as *all saints* are thus drawn, it is evident they will *persevere* till "the last day."

III. The *nature of the Covenant of Grace*, and the *character of our Surety*. From the 5th chapter of Romans, it is evident God hath made *two covenants* with man, the first with *Adam*, for himself and all his posterity; the second with *Christ*, for himself and all his people.

The design of the *second* covenant was to remedy the *defects* of the *first*. Heb. viii. 6–13.

Our *surety* in the first covenant was frail and fallible; our *surety* in the present, *infallible*. Under the first covenant the *conditions were never performed, and the blessings were lost.* Had Adam fulfilled the conditions, he would have been confirmed and all his posterity with him in happiness for ever. But our second surety *has fulfilled the conditions* and secured the blessings of the covenant for himself and all his people. He has been admitted into heaven, and there can be no doubt his people will all be admitted also. If the atonement was *yet* to be offered; if the righteousness by which they are to be justified was *yet* to be provided; if the conditions of the covenant were *yet* to be fulfilled; if salvation depended on *their* faithfulness,—there would, indeed, be great uncertainty as to the salvation of saints. But since our surety has performed all the conditions, the Father will not break his covenant with the Son by refusing to save every individual of his people. Ps. lxxxix. 34.

In short, the whole comes to this:—your salvation, O Christian, depends on *Christ's* faithfulness, or on *your* faithfulness, or on *both*. If it depends on *your* faithfulness, you are lost; if on Christ's, you are *safe*, for "he is faithful who has promised." If he has promised to be faithful to you *only so long as you are faithful to* him, then the whole depends on *your* faithfulness at last! And in this case you are worse off than before the fall, for then you had a surety in Adam who was *perfect*, and not likely to fall; but now you have *yourself* for a surety, and are *sure* to come short and perish.

But, if *Christ* be the surety of saints, they are certain to *persevere.*

Thus far I have argued from the general principles of the gospel, because, as *they* are admitted, they will have their force in proving the doctrine of perseverance. But, if I were arguing with an "Arminian," I would *waive* all these principles, which he would either wholly or in part deny, and would argue with him from the following *plain passages of Scripture.* ☞ Please refer to the Bible for the texts in full.

IV. Because *none become saints but those who have been previously* GIVEN *to Christ, and such can never be lost.* John vi. 37, 39: "*All* that the Father *giveth* me *shall come to me;* and him that cometh unto me *I will in no wise cast out.* This is the Father's will who hath sent me, that of *all* which he hath *given* me I should *lose nothing,* but should raise it up at the last day." Observe the terms "*given*" to Christ—"*coming*" to Christ—"in no wise cast out"—and "*lose nothing*"—all cover precisely the *same extent.* So that if one who was *given* to Christ should not *come* to Christ, or one who came should be *cast out or lost,* the whole would be falsified. ☞ See the text.

Suppose, for instance, the number given to Christ be a *thousand millions,* (though we hope ten thousand times that number will be saved,) then it is evident,

1. *Every individual* of these thousand millions given to Christ, *shall come* to Christ, or become a Christian. Can you doubt? Suppose, then, *one* of them should be overlooked, and should not come to Christ, do you not perceive the declaration would be *false*—for "*all*" who were given to Christ would not have come to him! It is absolutely *certain,* therefore, *all will come* to Christ. Suppose them come. Shall they *persevere?* Yes, for

2. Not one of these thousand millions can be *cast out* or *lost,* without breaking this *absolute promise* of Christ. Suppose only *one* individual, after coming to Christ, should *on some wise* be cast out—only one—would not this break the promise as effectually as though a *million* were cast out! *This single text, therefore, secures the infallible per-*

severance of every saint that ever lived, or ever will live, on earth.

"Ah, but," says an objector, "though *Christ* will not cast him out, he may *cast himself out.*" Ans. Would he not then be *lost?* But Christ says, "I should *lose nothing,*" and adds the positive promise before explained, "*And I will raise him up at the last day.*"

Now, if you would duly appreciate the weight of this argument, bring up all the OBJECTIONS you have ever heard,—"Perseverance is inconsistent with *free agency*—tends to *licentiousness*—inconsistent with *cautions, warnings,* falls of Christians, apostacies, &c.,"—bring them all to bear on this single text, and you will find them "like snow-balls pelting a wall of brass," or like noisy waves dashing and breaking on a rock!

This text, too, will confirm all that I have said about election, &c.

Obj. "*Coming* to Christ is a *condition* of their salvation." Ans. Call it "condition," or what you please, it is *sure to take place,* for Christ has promised "all that the Father giveth me *shall come to me.*" Their coming, therefore, and their salvation, are just as *certain* as though there were no such "condition" in the case.

V. Saints are Christ's SHEEP, and *shall never perish.* John x. 11–29: "I am the good Shepherd: the good Shepherd giveth his life for the sheep. As the Father knoweth me, even so know I the Father, and I lay down my life for the sheep. And other sheep I have, which are not of this fold: them also I must bring, and they shall hear my voice, and there shall be one fold and one shepherd. My sheep hear my voice, and I know them, and they follow me: and I give unto them eternal life, and they shall never perish; neither shall any pluck them out of my hand. My Father which gave them me is greater than all, and none is able to pluck them out of my Father's hand. I and my Father are one."

NOTE 1. Christ knows his people *before* their conversion, and calls them his *sheep.* Speaking of the yet *unconverted* Gentiles, he says, (16,) "Other sheep I have which are not of this fold, them also I must *bring.*" (They were, therefore, *not yet* brought.) Just so our Lord told Paul of the unconverted Corinthians, "I have much *people* in this city." Acts xviii. 10. 2. The conversion of his people is *certain* and *infallible.* "Them also I *must* bring, and they *shall* hear my voice." Their calling, therefore, is absolutely fixed. Well, suppose they are called and have become Christians, will they *persevere,* or shall they be left to perish? Hearken—3. Christ *secures to them eternal life.* 28, 29 : "My sheep hear my voice and they follow me, (he takes that for granted,) and I *give unto them eternal life.*" Observe, he does not say "*will* give, if you persevere," &c.; but "I *give*" now, immediately. And what does he give? Mere *temporary* favour, so long as they are faithful? No, he gives unto them "*eternal life.*" And, lest some one should say, though you now favour them, they will by and by perish, he adds, "and they shall NEVER perish;" and lest some one should say, Satan or wicked men will pluck some of them out of your hand, he adds, "neither shall any pluck them out of my hand;" and lest some caviller should still object, Thou art but a man, and cannot guard thy people in all quarters of the world, he rises still higher, "my Father which *gave* them me is greater than all, and none is able to pluck them out of my Father's hand!" and lest an obstinate believer in falling from grace should still object, "Your Father may be of a *different* mind," our Lord declares, "I and my Father are *one!*"

Thus, by *five* things as "immutable" as the word of Christ, those who have heard Christ and followed him may be perfectly sure of *perseverance* to the end, and of everlasting life, as the result.

Obj. "Hearing Christ and following him are *conditions* of becoming his sheep." Ans. No, for they were his *sheep before* they heard and followed him. (16.) And call them "conditions," or what you will, they do not make perseverance doubtful; because these will *certainly* take place, for Christ has promised they "*shall* hear" and *be brought.* Of course, they do not oppose the doctrine of the *certain* perseverance of every saint. Bring all the OBJECTIONS to bear against this also, and you will find the wall as solid here as before.

VI. THE PRAYER OF CHRIST for all saints secures their salvation. John xvii. 9, 20 : "I pray for them : I pray not for the world, but *for them which thou hast given me.* Neither pray I for these alone, but *for them also which shall believe on me through their word.*"

Obj. "Christ here alludes to his *apostles.*" Granted; he does allude to them *principally*, and some things in the chapter may allude to them only; but the burden of the chapter manifestly refers to *all his people* in every age.

1. Because he speaks of *power given him over all flesh*, that he should give eternal life to as many as his Father had given him, (verse 2.) It seems to be narrowing this text too much to suppose he alludes *only* to the twelve apostles. But supposing him to have had in his eye *all his future people*, the sentiment is sublime and grand. 2. But whether he *here* alluded to all his saints or not, it is evident, in the 20th verse, he had in view the *whole* of his future church. "Neither pray I for these (apostles) alone, but *for* ALL *them which shall believe on me through their word.*" Now, not only all the early converts believed on Christ *through the word* of the apostles, but all Christians since have believed through the same word *written;* and all future saints will be brought to Christ through the same word of these apostles. Hence it follows that, in this prayer, the Mediator actually interceded for *every individual believer.* The only question, therefore, is,—*Will his prayer be heard?* or will some one for whom he prayed be lost? He shall answer it himself, xi. 41: "Father, I thank thee, that thou hast heard me. *And I knew that* THOU HEAREST ME ALWAYS, but because of the people which stand by I said it," &c.

Before this argument can be destroyed, one of these two things must be proved—either that Christ *did not pray for all* his people, or that his prayer was *rejected* by the Father!

VII. The CHAIN OF SALVATION proves it. Rom. viii. 30: "Whom he did predestinate, them he also called; and whom he called, them he also justified; and whom he justified, them he also glorified." Here Predestination, Calling, Justification, and Glorification, are represented as so many links of an Almighty chain. If there be any meaning in the apostle's argument, the *predestination* of a person *insures* his *calling;* (i. e. his *effectual* calling, or *conversion;*) his calling insures his *justification;* and his justification insures his *glorification.* Do you doubt? Suppose the contrary,—break the chain, and see what will be the consequence. God *predestinates* Peter and John; but, in the event, it appears Peter and John are *not called!* Does not this falsify the declaration of the text—"*whom* he did *predestinate, them* he also *called?*" Or suppose Peter and John are *called,* but God refuses or neglects to *justify* them,—would not this contradict the word of God, "whom he called, them he also *justified?*" Again, suppose Peter and John are predestinated, called, and justified, but after all they do not *persevere,* are never *glorified!* What a fall is here!—not of two immortal souls only, but of what is far greater, the TRUTH OF GOD! And yet we are told of Saul, Solomon, Judas, &c., that they were *called* and *justified,* and yet not *glorified!* Which will you believe, the apostle or them? We are told that the *cautions* and *warnings* of Scripture prove it *possible* to fall away; but here the Holy Spirit declares it *impossible.* Whose word shall stand, the Lord's or theirs?

Here, then, is a STRONG TOWER, into which the Calvinist runs and is safe. Men may *rail,* but no argument formed against it can prosper.

VIII. Because NOTHING SHALL SEPARATE CHRISTIANS FROM THE LOVE OF GOD IN JESUS CHRIST. Rom. viii. 35–38: "*What* shall separate us from the love of Christ?" The apostle challenges to name *any thing* which shall prevent final salvation; and then adds, "For I am *persuaded* that neither death, nor life, nor angels, nor principalities, nor powers, nor *things present,* nor *things to come,* shall ever separate us from the love of God which is *in Christ Jesus our Lord.*"

From which it is evident, 1. God loves his people with an *unchangeable love.* 2. One reason why Christians are never separated from his love, is that they are loved, and not for their own sakes, (not chosen for their merits, nor rejected for their sins,) but for the sake of *Christ Jesus their Lord.* 3. Therefore the apostle had a *full assurance* (for this is the meaning of the word *persuaded*) not only for himself, but for every saint, that no *temptations* of the world, the flesh or the devil, should ever prevent their eternal salvation.

Obj. "He does not mention *Sin.*"

Ans. 1. Neither does he *except* it, and those who say he does except it, should *prove* their assertion. 2. *Sin* was the *only thing* which he or his brethren were *afraid* of—the only reason for dreading persecution, famine, peril, death, devils, &c., was lest these should lead them into *sin*. This was *the only way* in which these things could possibly separate saints from the Saviour; and, therefore, when he expresses his firm persuasion that none of these things should separate them from the love of God, it is the same thing as saying, *these shall never influence us to sin.* God will give us grace equal to our day. Hence he says in another place, "God is faithful, who will not suffer you to be tempted above that ye are able; but will with the temptation also make a way to escape, that ye may be able to bear it." 1 Cor. x. 13. 3. *Sin* is certainly included in the phrase "things present or things to come." And if neither things present nor things to come shall separate, it will be difficult for an objector, unless wiser than the inspired apostle, to name any thing that *shall* separate from the love of God which is in Christ Jesus the Lord!

IX. Because God hath made the decree of salvation IMMUTABLE for this *very purpose,* that his saints may have STRONG CONSOLATION and an ANCHOR to their souls. Heb. vi. 17, 18: "Wherein God, willing more abundantly to show unto the heirs of promise the *immutability* of his counsel, confirmed it by an *oath;* that by two immutable things, (his word and his oath,) in which it was impossible for God to lie, *we might have strong consolation,* who have fled for refuge to lay hold on the hope set before us, which hope we have as an *anchor of the soul,* both sure and steadfast," &c.

Now, 1. *Saints* are the persons who have "fled for refuge to the hope set before them." 2. To these God wishes to give *strong consolation,* an *anchor* to their souls, by which they may ride in safety, however boisterous the storm or terrible the temptation. 3. How does he accomplish this? By giving them an *immutable promise,* and confirming it by an *oath,* that nothing shall ever separate them from his love!

What could be stronger? It appears to me, that if a man be *conscious* of having fled to the hope set before him in the gospel—as many a Christian is, and *every* Christian *ought* to be—for him, under such circumstances, to doubt his infallible salvation, is to suspect God capable of *falsehood* and *perjury!*

Obj. "He only promises to be faithful *in case we are faithful.*" Ans. Not to say that *Christ,* our surety, *secures our faithfulness,* so that we should be in no danger even on that supposition,—the Arminian idea that the faithfulness of God to us depends on our faithfulness to him, would completely overset this cup of *consolation,* and render our strong *anchor* of no use; for a sinner, even after his conversion, is as unable to stand or to persevere, in his own strength, as a stone unsupported to remain balanced in the air. And Christ might just as well take us up in the air and tell us, "If you remain here without falling, I give you my *word* and *oath* to save you," as to tell us "My faithfulness shall continue as long as yours!" What *strong* consolation could there be if salvation were promised upon *such* conditions? The cup of strong "consolation" would be emptied at once. We should carry the water of life in a sieve, or draw it from the well of truth in a bucket full of holes! The anchor might be strong as Omnipotence, and made fast as the everlasting hills, but we should hold it only by a *cobweb cable!*

X. Because saints are KEPT BY THE POWER OF GOD THROUGH FAITH UNTO SALVATION. 1 Pet. i. 5: "Who are kept by the power of God, through faith unto salvation, ready to be revealed in the last time."

Note, 1. The saint's safety, "who are *kept.*" The original word signifies to *guard,* or to *keep with a garrison.* Thus 2 Cor. xi. 32: "In Damascus, the governor *kept* the city of the Damascenes *with a garrison,* to apprehend me, and through a window, in a basket, was I let down by the wall, and escaped his hands." Christians, therefore, are represented as in a garrison or castle guarded on every side, lest the enemy should come in to destroy, or the soul should escape and be destroyed. God guards his people on every side, and there is not even a "window in the wall" through which he will let them escape. They are thus "*kept*" as in a garrison. 2. *Who* keeps the garrison? How strong is the *power* employed in keeping them? The text informs us, "who are kept by the POWER OF GOD." 3. *How long* are they kept?—"*Unto salvation*, ready to be revealed in the last time;" and all this "*through faith*," or in a state of perseverance in grace.

Now, unless the garrison of the saints is too feeble to preserve them—unless the power of God is insufficient to keep them—and unless, after they have attained "salvation at the last time," they can fall from heaven, I do not see how it is possible for any of the saints to fail of everlasting life. Those who suppose the saints *keep themselves*, may well doubt their infallible perseverance; but those who believe that they are "kept by the power of God encamping round about them that fear Him," must be excused from any distrust.

XI. Because GRACE ABIDETH IN BELIEVERS and makes it impossible to sin fatally or unto death. 1 John iii. 9: "Whosoever is born of God doth not commit sin; for his seed *remaineth* in him; and he cannot sin, because he is born of God."

Observe, 1. This is a *universal* proposition, applying to all Christians. "*Whosoever* is born of God." What is said of one is said of *all*. 2. It is *impossible* for such to *commit sin;* "he *cannot* sin." Now, we must evidently except sins of *infirmity*, *deficiency*, and *partial* captivities to the law of sin, or we contradict the whole Bible, and make the apostle contradict what he said just before, "If any man say I *have no sin*, he deceiveth himself," &c. (i. 8.) The *sin*, therefore, of which the apostle here speaks, is of a different kind; either the *unpardonable sin*, (as some suppose,) or a *wilful*, *deliberate*, *habitual course of sin*, which appears to me to be the meaning of the Holy Spirit. "Committing" sin (ποιῶν αμαρτίαν) is here opposed to "doing righteousness," (ποιῶν δικαιοσύνην) and as "doing righteousness" is an habitual course of righteousness, so "doing sin" is an habitual course of sin. The argument will be the same whether the *sin* here referred to be the *unpardonable sin*, or such a *course of sin* as implies the person has no grace. To one of these the text *must* refer. And it is expressly said that this sin the real saint *cannot commit*—of course he *cannot fall from grace.* 3. We have the *reason* assigned *why* the Christian cannot fall: "for, or because *his seed remaineth in him.*" So far from *sin driving grace* from the heart, as our opponents so frequently assert, it appears from this that *grace* is the conqueror, and *drives sin* from the heart, and thus makes the believer's fall impossible. His seed REMAINETH in him.

Obj. "The argument proves too much, even that believers have *no sin of any kind.*" Ans. "No; it only proves that they do not live in a *course of sin*, that they do not *follow sin* as a trade, nor *work evil.*" 3 John 11.

Obj. "The text simply means we *should* not sin." Ans. Where then is the force of the *reason* assigned for not committing sin, "for his seed *remaineth* in him?" The apostle evidently meant to assert the *impossibility* of a saint ever falling from grace, so as to be *entirely devoted* to sin.

XII. Because saints are SEALED BY THE HOLY SPIRIT UNTO THE DAY OF REDEMPTION. 2 Cor. i. 22, 23: "Now, he which *establisheth* us with you in Christ and hath *anointed* us, is God: who hath also *sealed* us and given us the *earnest* of the Spirit in our hearts." An "earnest" is a part given as a *pledge* of hereafter bestowing the remainder. Eph. i. 13, 14: "In whom also after that ye believed, ye were SEALED with that Holy Spirit of promise, which is the *earnest* of our *inheritance*," &c. Eph. iv. 30: "Grieve not the Holy Spirit of God, whereby ye are SEALED unto the day of redemption."

2 Tim. ii. 19: "The foundation of God standeth *sure*, having this *seal*, the Lord knoweth them that are his." The object of a *seal* is to *distinguish* property, and thus the Lord distinguisheth or marketh "them that are his;" it is also to *confirm* or *establish*. Thus we set our seal to a bond, and kings set their seal to decrees; and thus God makes his foundation *sure*. It is to preserve *inviolate*, thus we seal a letter, a cabinet; and, I may add, it denotes *secrecy* and *value*. In whatever sense you understand the word here, it denotes God's *special care* and *value* of his people. It is set on them to *save them from destruction*. It was said to the destroying angels—"Hurt not the earth, neither the sea, nor the trees, till we have *sealed* the servants of God in their foreheads." Rev. vii. 3.

Now, after the saints have been thus *sealed*, shall they *not* be *known* of God?—shall they *not* be *established?*—shall they *not stand sure* and be saved from *destruction?*

And, after they have received this seal as an *earnest* of heaven, shall they be disappointed of the *remainder?* This would be to make the seal of *God* less security than the *seal* of his creatures. We receive, therefore, the Spirit as the *seal* of salvation, and God's *earnest* of heaven. And this seal is to secure the saints "*unto the day of redemption,*" after which they will be in no danger.

XIII. Because *believing is a proof that the believer has been ordained to eternal life.* Acts xiii. 48: "As many as were ordained to eternal life believed." This teaches,

1. That *some are ordained to eternal life*—of course to *perseverance* unto the end. 2. That their ordination or election to eternal life *preceded* their faith in Christ; and that therefore they were not ordained to life *on account of their faith,* but for some other reason—even for the sake of Christ, in whom they were chosen. 3. That this *faith* was an *evidence* of their having been ordained to eternal life.

The argument needs no application. Show me one who has believed, and I will show you one who has been ordained to eternal life. Hence our Saviour's solemn declaration, John vi. 47, "Verily, verily, I say unto you, He that believeth on me HATH (not shall have) everlasting life." Also, John iii. 36.

XIV. Christians are safe because *their life is not in their own keeping, but is hid with Christ in God.* Col. iii. 3, 4: "Ye are dead, and *your life is hid with Christ in God.* When Christ who is our life shall appear, then shall ye also appear with him in glory."

Note, 1. Christians are *dead*—that is, to the world, the flesh, and the devil; and yet they have *life,* i. e. spiritual and eternal life. 2. This life is not left to themselves to keep, lest it be lost; but the support, continuance, and security of their life are in God. "Your life is hid with Christ in God." It is *hid,* kept as a *secret treasure*—hidden from Satan, from the world, and in some measure from the believer himself. 3. Christ is sure to keep it *unto the end.* "When Christ who is our life shall appear, *then shall ye also appear with him in glory.*" It is in view of salvation as a treasure kept by Christ we hear such expressions as these: "Unto him who is *able to keep you from falling,* and to present you faultless before the presence of his glory."

Jude 24: "I know whom I have believed, and that *he is able to keep that which I have committed unto him* until that day." 2 Tim. i. 12. On this account saints are said to be "*preserved in Jesus Christ.*" Jude 1. And it is this consideration which gives such force to that promise, "*Because I live, ye shall live also.*" John xiv. 19. Until the Lord of Life *dies again*, therefore, the life of his people is divinely secured.

XV. Because *though God may suffer his children to fall in part, he will not suffer them to perish utterly.* Ps. lxxxix. 30–34: "If his children forsake my law, and walk not in my judgments; if they break my statutes, and keep not my commandments; then will I visit their transgression with the rod, and their iniquity with stripes. Nevertheless, my loving-kindness will I *not utterly* take from Him, nor suffer my faithfulness to fail." These words, with the greater part of the psalm from which they are taken, though spoken originally of David himself and his natural seed, have also a manifest reference to *Messiah* (the true David) and *his seed.* They show,

1. That Christians sometimes wander and fall into sin—"they forsake his law and walk not in his judgments." 2. These sins bring *suffering.* "I will visit their transgression with the *rod*, and their iniquity with *stripes.*" 3. Yet he will *not utterly forsake.* "Nevertheless, my loving-kindness will I *not utterly* take from him, nor suffer my faithfulness to fail." 4. It is intimated that to take away mercy from *his people* would be to take it from *Christ*, whose people they are; and that such conduct on the part of God the Father would be unfaithfulness to his Son, and a breach of their mutual *covenant.* "My loving-kindness will I not utterly take from *Him*, nor suffer my *faithfulness* to fail; my *covenant* will I not break; once have I sworn unto David, his seed shall endure for ever," &c.

For similar promises of *unchangeable* love, see Isa. xli., xliii., xlv., liv.; in short, the greater part of that prophecy, from the 40th chapter to the end.

These general promises we see fulfilled in *particular* instances; as in *David*, who fell, but soon rose again higher than ever; in *Solomon*, who, though he fell *far*, did not fall *utterly;* in *Peter*, who, though he was suffered to be "sifted by Satan as wheat," was not left in the power of his enemy. Just so of *all his people*,—he may suffer them to be tempted, but "God is *faithful*, who will not suffer them to be tempted above what they are able, and will, with the temptation, also provide a way of escape." 1 Cor. x. 13. If, then, GOD IS FAITHFUL, saints are safe.

XVI. Because the Bible *takes it for granted of all apostates that they never were Christians.* 1 John ii. 19: "They went out from us, but they were not of us; for if they had been of us, they would no doubt have continued with us; but they went out from us that it might be made manifest they were not all of us."

Note, 1. Here were some apostates, or, as some would say, persons that "fell from grace." "They went out from us." But what does the apostle say of them? 2. That they *never were real Christians:* "they were not *of us.*" He does not say "*are* not," but "*were* not of us." They never were genuine saints—never had real grace. 3. *He takes it for granted that, if they had been Christians, they would have remained so, and would have never fallen.* "For, *if* they had been of us, they would, *no doubt*, have continued with us." Observe how *positively* he denies of apostates that they ever were Christians; and with what confidence he asserts that, if they had been saints, they would never have fallen! He does not even *argue* on the subject; but, as if the matter would not admit of a *question*—as if there was no *possibility of its being otherwise*—he takes it for granted, "if they had been of us, they would, *no doubt*, have continued with us."

So we say of Judas, Saul, Hymeneus, and apostates now-a-days, "if they had been saints, they would have continued saints." If they had been "once in grace, they would have been always in grace." And we think it unnecessary to *doubt* upon a subject on which the inspired apostle speaks with so much *confidence*. If men will still assert that our doctrines were first preached by *Satan*, that they came from *hell*, and will stake their soul's salvation that men may fall from grace, we can only wonder at them, and weep over them! We will not render railing for railing, but contrariwise blessing. They may talk of their having been once Calvinists, and of their having tried our system and rejected it. We say of these as the apostle said of errorists in his day, "They were not of us; for, *if* they had been of us, they would, *no doubt*, have continued with us." They undoubtedly held (or they would not assert it) *what they thought* Calvinism; just as the persons mentioned by John possessed *what they thought* Christianity; but the apostle decided that they were mistaken.

In all this I mean not to call in question the real piety of my brethren. Would I were half as holy as some who affirm that they "abhor Calvinism!" But this I say, when they speak against Calvinism, "they know not what they do;" and peradventure they "will be found fighting against God!"

Apostates are generally spoken of as those who *never had grace.* 1 John iii. 6: "Whosoever sinneth *hath not seen* Him, neither known Him." Observe, it is not said, "*does* not *now see* Him," but "*hath* not seen Him;" i. e. never saw Him. So 3 John 11, "He that doeth evil *hath not seen* God." Show me a man, then, who now lives in a course of habitual sin, who has no grace, and I will show you one that *never had grace,* whatever he might have professed. Thus our Lord says of certain self-deceivers, "I *never* knew you," Matt. vii. 23; that is, I not only do not know and own you *now,* but I never knew and owned you as my true disciples. Thus the *stony ground* hearers had "*no root* in themselves." Matt. xiii. 21. The foolish virgins had "*no oil* in their vessels." Matt. xv. 3. Thus the apostates in Peter (ii. 20–22) are compared to the *swine* whose nature was not changed. All these are intimations to us, I think sufficiently clear, that those who fall away from their profession are to be considered as *having never had grace.* Yet you will hear men appealing to *their own experience,* and ministers appealing to the *experience* of their hearers, that *they themselves* have fallen from grace, and even pointing to "*swine* now wallowing" in sin, as instances of those who were once of the number and *nature* of Christ's *sheep!*

That those who teach such doctrines sincerely believe them, I have no more question than that I sincerely believe my own; but I ask, how can such doctrines be reconciled with the general tenor of the word of God, which everywhere teaches that "*if they had been of us, they would, no doubt, have continued with us?*"

XVII. Lastly, because the contrary opinion leads to many ABSURDITIES. It appears to me to follow from the doctrine of our opponents,

1. That, in respect of the *covenant* under which we are, *we are worse off than before the fall.* Our state was dangerous enough then, when we had a perfect man for our surety; but infinitely more so now, when we wretched sinners are our own sureties! And yet the apostle says of Christ that "he is the mediator of a *better covenant,* which was established upon *better promises.*" Heb. viii. 6. If better than the Sinai Covenant, (which contained some promises of grace,) infinitely better than the covenant of works. 2. A man may *fall from grace twenty times a day, and twenty times a day rise into grace again!* Thus that marvellous *change* which requires Almighty power to effect—that renovation of nature which is called a *new birth,* a *new creation,* a *resurrection* from the dead, becomes a mere trifle! . . . Thus the Holy Spirit, so far from *dwelling* in the believer's heart in peace, is liable to be dispossessed every day, hour, and moment; to have his temple turned into Satan's castle, according to the sinner's caprice! 3. Upon this principle, there is nothing in the word of God to authorize *an assurance of salvation for ourselves.* Nay, more: there can be no *certainty* of our continuance in grace for one hour or moment! For, if our perseverance depends upon ourselves, and there be no promise that a saint *shall* persevere, then there is no promise that *you* or *I* shall persevere; and, therefore, if on our dying bed, and within five minutes of our end, though we are now full of grace and love and joy, we cannot be *sure* but we shall *yet* sink to hell. For, if God has made no promise to keep us from falling, he may let us fall at one moment as well as at another, and even while the breath is leaving the body Satan may assault, our faithfulness may fail, and from the very verge of heaven, with GLORY full in view, and angels waiting to receive and bid us welcome, we may drop—for ever! 4. For the same reason there can be no such thing as *assurance for others,* and we can have little comfort in the death of our pious relatives and friends. Though they may have served God from child-

hood, and brought forth the fruits of holiness till they are threescore years and ten, and have been burning and shining lights in their day and generation, we cannot be sure but they will yet perish! And should they die far from home, on the ocean, in a strange land, in a delirium, or in any way in which we could not have evidence of their being in grace at their *last moment,* we can have no certain or comfortable hope. In fact, if I believed that the perseverance of a saint depended on his own faithfulness, with my present views of human nature, I do not know how I could even *hope* for a single friend on earth; and, as to *confidence* of their salvation, it would be impossible until I saw them pass the gate of heaven. If there be no *absolute* promise to the believer to *keep* him to salvation; then, though the apostle Paul were within five minutes of eternity, and entering the heavenly harbour under the full sail of a perfect assurance, we could not be SURE, but that in the very article of death, in the very entrance to the harbour, he might slip his cable, lose his anchor, or strike on some hidden rock and sink to perdition! Who could tell, in reference to our dying Christian friends, but that, in the last hour, when heart and flesh were failing them, Satan might take advantage of their feebleness, and, by a violent assault, make them *let go their hold,* and then drag them down to hell! This is *not* the consolation of the gospel. The infallible promise of God makes us confident that he who hath begun a good work in us will perform it (or carry it on) unto the day of Jesus Christ.

"Grace will complete what grace begins,
To save from sorrows and from sins;
The work that wisdom undertakes,
Eternal mercy ne'er forsakes."

5. It is absurd to *pray to God for perseverance,* or to *thank him* for the same. For, if God cannot cause us to persevere without destroying our free agency, and if our perseverance depends upon ourselves, I do not know why we should pray to God for influence which he cannot consistently grant, or ask assistance from anybody but *ourselves.*

The psalmist might say, (Ps. cxix. 117,) "*Hold thou me up,* and I shall be safe;" for *he* did not believe that "holding up" destroyed his free agency. But those who think they must *hold themselves up* or fall, cannot, according to my views of propriety, offer this prayer. If we persevere, I cannot see the propriety of *thanking God* for that for which we are chiefly, if not wholly, indebted to ourselves. The *apostle* might say, (Acts xxvi. 22,) "Having obtained *help of God,* I continue until this time;" but *we* ought to say, "Having been *faithful* to *ourselves,* we have come thus far."

The above appear to me legitimate inferences from the doctrine of our opponents. I am aware, however, that these inferences are some of them in fact denied; and I do not think it fair to charge on any church inferences from their doctrine, which they themselves reject. I am persuaded that many who reject our doctrine, rely as entirely upon *grace* for perseverance, and give to God the glory of salvation as entirely as ourselves. There is sometimes "a happy inconsistency between men's heads and hearts," so that the absurdity of their *doctrines* is not always discoverable in their *lives.* But it is fair to draw what you think reasonable inferences from a scheme, provided you do not represent *your* inferences as *theirs* when they disown them, and to show what you think the natural tendency of a doctrine, although the advocates of that doctrine may deny that such are always its actual effects. This is a liberty which very few hesitate to take with *us,* making inferences which we deny, and attributing to our doctrines a tendency which we abhor. To this proceeding we have no objection, provided they will call their children by their own names.

Whether the inferences I have drawn are reasonable or not, and how far they are practically adopted by those who oppose the "perseverance of the saints," I shall not attempt to decide; but they appear to me to be the inevitable consequences of their scheme.

OBJECTIONS.

To the foregoing doctrine some of our Christian brethren object,

I. That "*it destroys free agency.* God cannot decree the infallible perseverance of a saint without infringing his liberty as a moral agent." And they say a great deal about *necessity* being inconsistent with *liberty,* &c.

To which we answer,

1. We grant that *physical* necessity or *force* is inconsistent with liberty; but *moral* necessity or *certainty*, which is all we plead for, does not interfere with liberty in the least. 2. We do not suppose any *other* or *greater* influence necessary to *keep* us in a state of grace than to *bring us into* that state at first. In a word, if *conversion* by divine power does not destroy free agency, *preservation* by the *same* power will not. Nothing but divine grace *upholds* a Christian for a moment; and, if this upholding for a *moment* does not destroy free agency, why should upholding for an *hour*, or a *day*, or a year, or a lifetime, destroy free agency? 3. If God cannot decree the infallible perseverance of a saint without destroying his free agency, then our Lord *Jesus Christ* was not a free agent, for his infallible perseverance was *certain* and fixed. Isa. xlii. 1–4. The same may be said of *angels*, whose perseverance depends entirely upon God, and yet they are free agents. And the same is true, also, of *glorified saints*, of whom Christ says, "because I live, ye *shall* live also." Their perseverance, therefore, throughout eternity, is as certain as the perseverance of Christ himself; and yet are they not free? WE wish no higher freedom. See Rom. xiv. 4: "Yea, he shall be holden up: for God is able to make him stand."

OBJ. II. *"It tends to licentiousness."*

ANS. We cannot always judge accurately of the tendency of a doctrine, especially if it be one which we do not rightly *understand*, which is generally true of doctrines *we do not hold*. The safest rule is to judge of the tendency by the *actual effects*. *We* think the doctrines of our Methodist brethren, for instance, to be of dangerous tendency. They think otherwise; and the actual effects prove that we do not understand the true nature or tendency of their peculiar tenets. Let them make the same allowance for us. We are quite sure they do not understand the tendency of our faith; for we *know* it tends to purify our hearts. The *certainty* of their salvation did not tempt the primitive believers to licentiousness; why should it have a different effect on us? They could say, (1 John iii. 2, 3,) "WE *know* that when he shall appear we *shall* be like him, for we shall see him as he is. *And every man that hath this hope purifieth himself even as he is pure.*" Why should the certainty of *our* perseverance have a different effect? Especially as we can have no *hope*, much less *certainty* of salvation, unless conscious of *present* holiness. Besides, this objection has been brought in every age against the doctrine of Justification by Faith, and the whole system of Salvation by *Grace*. Rom. iii. 7 and 31; vi. 1; ix. 19, &c. The apostolic answer should suffice.

Obj. III. "The certainty of their salvation is inconsistent with the *efforts* and *labours* of saints to save themselves."

The whole force of this objection lies here, that, unless there be some *uncertainty* of success, a person *will not labour* for success; and, if there was a *perfect certainty* of salvation, a Christian would not trouble himself to use the means.

Ans. 1. *Christ* had a *perfect certainty* of success and salvation, and yet he used the means, and laboured with "strong crying and tears." 2. *Paul* had a *perfect certainty* of escape from shipwreck, and yet he used the means. Acts xxvii. In a *desperate* case, like that of a condemned and helpless sinner, *uncertainty* of escape, so far from being a stimulus, deadens every effort! Let there be a glimmering *hope*, and he will do something; let there be a *certainty* of a blessing *on his efforts*, and he will strive with all his might. And Christians can have no certainty of salvation except *through their own efforts.* How can they expect to *run* the race *without running*, or *fight* the battle *without fighting?*

Obj. IV. "The *exhortations, cautions,* and *warnings* of the New Testament prove the *possibility* and the *danger* of saints falling away."

Ans. 1. There *is* a possibility and a danger of saints "falling away;" i. e. to a *considerable extent.* They are in continual "danger" of complying with temptation, of conforming to the world, of sitting down in indolence, and of falling into sin. Hence the propriety of all these *moral stimulants* to activity and watchfulness. If a soldier, from the known character of his captain, were sure of winning the battle, and of the life of every soldier being preserved, he would, nevertheless, fight, knowing that he would otherwise be knocked down, trodden under foot, wounded, and disgraced, even though he escaped with life. Just so; though Christ has promised that every soldier shall escape with life, he has not promised he shall escape with *honour* and receive the crown of victory, unless he fight valiantly. He may, and often does, leave the indolent and the cowardly to be wounded, disgraced, and maimed for life. As the *present comfort* of a Christian, therefore, depends on his activity and holiness, and as his *future reward* will be *measured* by his attainments here, there is the utmost propriety and kindness in administering these cautions and holding out these encouragements. 2. Viewed *in himself*, as I have hinted before, there is a possibility and danger, yea, a *certainty* of his falling *entirely away*, unless he strives and labours. But there is neither certainty, possibility, nor danger of God's breaking an *absolute promise* to save all who come to Christ.

Obj. V. "Facts of acknowledged saints falling into sin —such as *David*, *Solomon*, and *Peter*." As great reliance is placed on this argument, I will notice it more particularly.

David. 1. That he *died* a saint, and is *now* in heaven, I believe nobody questions. 2 Sam. xxiii. Of course he did not *finally* fall from grace, and his example, therefore, is nothing to the point. They must bring an instance of a saint who *actually perished*. 2. That he fell into *sin*, and into a great and complicated sin, is lamentably true. That his conscience was stunned by his fall, and his spiritual comfort entirely destroyed, I have no question. But that he fell *entirely* from grace, when there are so many clear declarations of God to the contrary in regard to *every* saint, I will not admit, except on one condition—that those who assert it will produce some *express declaration* of God to that effect.

That the Lord was *displeased* with David, as he is with every Christian when he sins, is not denied; but that he *wholly cast him off* is nowhere said, and never can be proved. That the Holy Spirit took away the "joys of his salvation" is admitted, but that the Spirit *entirely* left him cannot be proved, and the contrary is implied in Ps. li. 11. A flame may be damped without being quenched; a seed may be buried deep without being killed; a man may be very sick and nigh unto death, and yet not dead; a saint may fall very far, and yet not be lost; God may *chastise*, but will "not utterly" destroy; may "*hide* his face for a moment, but with *everlasting* kindness will he have mercy" on his people. Ps. lxxxix. 30–34; Isa. liv. 8. It remains, therefore, for them to prove that David became spiritually dead and was "born again" a second time.

SOLOMON is another instance of a saint supposed to have fallen from grace. My reasons for believing that Solomon neither totally nor finally fell from Divine favour are—

1. The *circumstances of his birth and infancy.* "Before he had done either good or evil," in his infancy, it is said "*the Lord loved him,*" 2 Sam. xii. 24; the same expression which is used of Jacob, Rom. ix. 13, and denotes his choice to salvation. 2. The *name* which the Lord then gave him, "*Jedediah,*" or beloved of the Lord. I do not think an instance can be brought of a person thus honoured with a divine name, who was afterward rejected. 2. The *Promise* concerning him. 2 Sam. vii. 14, 15. Where the Lord promises to be a father to him, to *chasten* but not *disinherit* him; and expressly distinguishes the favour intended for *him* from the mere temporary favour granted to *Saul.* 4. The *reserve* expressed, 1 Kings xi. 4, 6: "And his heart was *not perfect* with the Lord his God, as was the heart of David his father. And Solomon did evil in the sight of the Lord, and went NOT FULLY after the Lord, as did David his father." This is spoken of him at the time of his greatest wickedness, even "when his wives turned away his heart after other gods." (Verse 4.) 5. *Commendation* after his death. 2 Chron. xi. 17; Neh. xiii. 26. 6. He wrote the book of *Ecclesiastes* (i. 1) when he was an *old man,* and confesses the very sins of which the objectors suppose he did not repent. And the apostle says of the Scripture writers generally, "*Holy men* of God, spake as they were moved by the Holy Ghost." 2 Pet. i. 21. Thus it appears from the *history* itself, as I think, that Solomon did not perish. But, if all this were blotted out, I would not believe he was lost, until—7. The ABSOLUTE PROMISES of God in regard to *every* saint are blotted out also.*

PETER did not *finally* fall, as all admit. That he did not

* Were there good reason to doubt of Solomon's salvation, we might put upon our opponents the burden of proof that he ever was a *real saint,* in the sense before defined. But we prefer to give our real sentiments and interpretation of the Bible.

totally fall, is evident to my mind from Luke xxii. 32, where our Lord says, "Simon, Satan hath desired to sift you as wheat; but I have prayed for thee that *thy faith may not fail;*" from which it is evident that his faith did not *entirely fail.*

OBJ. VI. "Some acknowledged apostates were once saints, as *Saul, Judas, Hymeneus,* and *Philetus.*"

As to *Saul,* it is said the Lord "turned him into *another man* and gave him *another heart,*" 1 Sam. x. 6, 9; (i. e. made him a *wiser* and *greater* man, to qualify him for the kingdom;) but it is nowhere said God gave him a *new* heart and made him a *holy* man, and there is no evidence that he ever had grace. "But he had the Spirit of the Lord and prophesied." True, and so had some in the New Testament, Matt. vii. 23, who "*prophesied* and cast out *devils* and did many *wonderful* works," and yet Christ says, "I *never* knew you." That is, they *never were* saints.

Of *Judas,* it is said that he was once a good man, because the Lord says, "Have not I *chosen* you twelve?" John vi. 70. We grant he was *chosen* to the *apostleship,* but not to *salvation!* Thus the Lord says, "I speak not of you all, I know whom I have *chosen.* Ye are clean, but not all." John xiii. 10, 18.

Obj. "But would Christ call 'a devil' to the apostleship, and send him forth to preach the gospel? What should we think of a church now that would send forth a wicked man to preach the gospel?" Ans. Which is the worse, to *call* a devil unto the apostleship, or to *continue* him in the apostleship *after* his character is discovered? And did not our Lord do this? David foretold, many centuries before, that one of the disciples would be a wicked man, and Christ knew this well and who it was that should betray him when he called him to the apostleship.

Obj. "But he cast out devils, and if he were a devil at this time, then did Satan cast out Satan, which our Lord says is absurd." Ans. This is a mere *quibble.* Suppose Judas did cast out devils, it was not *Satan,* but *our Lord* who gave him the power and the disposition to cast them out.

Obj. But it is said, "Judas, by transgression, *fell.*" True, and the same passage states what he fell from, to wit, "the *ministry* and *apostleship.*" Acts i. 25.

Obj. Jesus says, "Them which thou hast given me I have kept, and none of them is lost, *but* the son of perdition, that the Scriptures might be fulfilled." John xvii. 12. The objection turns on the word "*but*," as if it implied that the "son of perdition" was one of those "given to Christ." And in our English idiom, the inference would be natural. "But," in the Hebrew idiom, implies no such thing. The expression no more proves that Judas was one of those given to Christ, than the expressions (Luke iv. 24, 25) prove that the widow of *Sarepta* was one of the widows of *Israel;* or that Naaman, the *Syrian*, was one of the lepers of *Israel;* or that those whose "names are written in the Book of Life" were of the class that "maketh a lie." Rev. xxi. 27. See, also, Acts xxviii. 22, and 1 Cor. ii. 11. "There shall be no loss of any man's life; *but* of the ship." Quere: Was the *ship* a man's life? "Even so, the things of God knoweth no man, *but* the Spirit of God." Is the Spirit, therefore, a man?

Hymeneus and *Alexander* are also said to have fallen from grace, because they "put away a good conscience and made shipwreck of faith." 1 Tim. i. 19.

Ans. 1. A man may have a "*good conscience*" and not be a Christian, for Paul "lived in all good conscience" before his conversion. Acts xxiii. 1. And the "faith" of which shipwreck was made is the *doctrine* of the gospel. As it is said in 2 Tim. ii. 18, "Hymeneus and Philetus concerning the *truth* have erred, saying that the *resurrection* is past already, and thus overthrow the *faith* of some." 2. These apostates are expressly *distinguished from true saints* in the next verse. After mentioning their fall, the apostle says, "*nevertheless* the foundation of God standeth sure, having this seal, *the Lord knoweth them that are his*,"—plainly implying that Hymeneus and Philetus never were really "his."

Obj. VII. "The warning given concerning the righteous in Ezek. xviii. and xxxiii. proves that the righteous may fall away," &c.

Ans. 1. Look at the *object* of the sacred writer, which is to teach that *God will "deal with men according to their ways."* In the 18th chapter the object is to do away the parable of the "sour grapes," or the punishment of children for the sins of their parents. The Lord declares that the *righteousness* of a *parent* shall not save a *wicked son;* neither shall the wickedness of a *parent* prevent the salvation of a *righteous* son. And, in the 33d chapter, the object is to show that no *past* righteousness shall save a man *if* he falls away; and no *past* sins shall ruin a man *if* he repents. There is nothing in this contrary to our doctrine. 2. The "*righteousness*" here spoken of *may* be a mere *external*, ceremonial righteousness, such as Paul had before his conversion. Phil. iii. 6. And I do verily believe that *apparent* righteousness, rather than *real* sanctity, is here spoken of; and also that the *rewards* and *punishments* here more immediately alluded to, are of a *temporal* kind. The contrary, at any rate, never can be *proved.* We admit that from *such* a righteousness a man *may* fall away. 3. If we grant that the *righteousness* here mentioned be *real sanctification*, it does not follow that a righteous man ever *did* or ever *will actually* fall from grace. The text only makes a *supposition.* "*When* a righteous man turneth away from his righteousness—*If* he trust to his own righteousness," &c. Now, we grant *if* he does this, and *when* he does this, he will be lost.

But it is an old maxim in logic, "*suppositio non ponit in esse;*" i. e. supposition of a case does not prove its actual existence. *Suppose* "an angel from heaven should preach another gospel, he would be accursed." Gal. i. 8. Our Lord says, "*If* I should say I know him not, I should be a liar." John viii. 55. But these suppositions do not prove that an angel *ever will* preach another gospel; nor that our Lord ever *will* declare a falsehood.

OBJ. VIII. "*The breaking off the Jewish branches proves falling from grace.*" Rom. xi. 17.

Ans. 1. The *olive-tree* from which these branches were broken off and others grafted in is the *visible church.* From this the Jews were cast out, and the Gentiles introduced. If this is "falling from grace," we do not deny it. 2. That there was not a single *saint* lost by the rejection of the Jews, is evident from the first part of the chapter, "Hath God cast away *his people?* God forbid. *God hath not cast away his people whom he foreknew. The election hath obtained it,* and the rest were blinded." (Verses 1, 3, 7.) Hence it appears that every elect person or every Christian was saved. 3. At the conclusion of the account, the apostle makes this remark: "The gifts and calling of God are *without repentance;*" i. e. without any change of mind on his part—without any recalling of his saving grace.

OBJ. IX. "*Paul laboured lest he should be a castaway.*" 1 Cor. ix. 27.

ANS. So did *our Lord;* he was "straitened until his work was accomplished," but he had no *fear* of being finally cast away. The apostle, in all his epistles, as shown already, expresses his *full confidence* of the final salvation of every saint; and, if he ever *doubted* of his own *salvation*, it was because he doubted his *conversion*. But I do not believe that, after his being caught up to the third heaven, and the clear testimonials of a Saviour's love, he ever doubted either. In this text he simply intends to show *how he lived and laboured*, as an example for them to imitate. He exhorts them to run *as if* for a prize, as a racer would, who knew that *if* he did not run well he would be disgraced. Our Saviour compares himself to a *thief*, to express the *unexpectedness* of his coming, though he resembled him in nothing else. So the apostle compares himself to a *racer*, to show the intensity of his labours, though, unlike a racer, he was *perfectly sure of* victory. Hence he says, (26,) "So run I, *not as uncertainly;* so fight I, not as one that beateth the air." See, also, Gal. ii. 2, and 2 Tim. iv. 6–8, 18: "And the Lord will deliver me from every evil work, and preserve me unto his heavenly kingdom."

After all, it is not said he *was* cast away, or that any saint *will* be cast away. So that all such texts prove nothing against perseverance. That we *should all run and strive* in the same manner, every Calvinist grants.

OBJ. X. It is said of the Galatians, "*Ye are fallen from grace.*" Gal. v. 4. This is an objection drawn from the mere *words* of Scripture, without noticing the scope and *intention*. By the same rule I could prove "there is no God." Ps. xiv. Or that the apostle was a "robber of churches." 2 Cor. xi. 8. The *doctrine* of Scripture, and not the mere *words*, is the truth of God. Now, let any one glance at the preceding part of the epistle, and he will readily perceive what "*fall*" was referred to—even a fall from the *doctrines* of grace. They had "turned away to another gospel," and, forsaking the doctrine of salvation by *faith,* they sought justification by the works of the *law.* Therefore, he says, "Christ has become of no effect unto you, *whosoever of you are justified by the law;* ye are *fallen from grace;*" i. e. from the *doctrines* of grace. The text is hypothetical, and no more proves "falling from grace" than it does "justification by law." And, as none are *really* justified by law, how does it follow that any *really* fall from grace! Barnes's Notes, *in loco.*

Observe again, that, if it could be proved that the Galatians fell *totally* for a time, there is no proof they fell *finally,* and therefore here is no proof that any real saint will be *finally* lost. Of course, understand it as you will, it argues nothing against our doctrine.

OBJ. XI. "Salvation is everywhere offered on *condition* of perseverance, which shows that the *condition may fail to be complied with.*" Ans. It shows no such thing; but only that, *unless* the condition be complied with, the blessing will be lost. This we freely grant. But we contend that the *conditions* (if they must be so called) are *sure* to be complied with by every one of Christ's people. Thus when it is said, "*If* ye abide in me, ye shall ask what ye will." "*If* ye continue in my word, then are ye my disciples indeed." "We shall reap, *if* we faint not," &c. &c. It is all certainly true. But, unless our opponents prove that some real Christian *actually fails* to "*abide,*" "*continue,*" &c., these texts will not prove the loss of a single believer.

And I have shown already that these "conditions" are *sure* to be performed by *all* of Christ's people.

OBJ. XII. "*It is impossible for those who were once enlightened, if they shall fall away,*" &c. Heb. vi. 4, 6.

The objectors must prove two things:—first, that these were *real Christians;* and secondly, that they *really fell away.* But, in my opinion, neither of these things can be proved. I see no reason to believe them real saints. 1. Because these expressions may apply to those who had only those *miraculous external gifts* so common in that day. There is nothing said of these persons more extraordinary than of the false professors mentioned, (Matt. vii. 22, 23,) of whom Christ says, "I *never* knew you." The *stony ground* hearers "tasted of the good word of God,"—"they received the word with joy," and yet had "*no root* in themselves;" that is, were not truly converted. 2. They are manifestly compared to the *barren* ground in the 8th verse, which is a proof the soil of their hearts was never prepared by the Holy Spirit for a true reception of the seed. 3. The apostle had no idea real *Christians* would thus fall away. "But, beloved, we are *persuaded* better things of *you*, though we thus speak." (Verse 9.)

In fact, the whole is a *solemn warning* to persons who have been *enlightened* and *convicted*, not to stifle their convictions, lest they commit the unpardonable sin.

But, could it be proved these were *real Christians*, it is not said they *will certainly fall;* but "*if* they shall fall away," &c. And this I have before shown proves nothing as to the *actual event*. Besides, if it proves an actual "falling away," it proves the "impossibility" of recovery! Do our brethren believe this?

OBJ. XIII. "A sinner may tread under foot the Son of God, and count the blood of the covenant *wherewith he was sanctified* an unholy thing," &c. Heb. x. 29. From which it is argued that a man may fall from *sanctification* and from saving grace. It is taken for granted in the objection that "he who was *sanctified*" is the *apostate*. Whereas,

1. It is generally supposed by commentators that the "*Son of God*" is here referred to; and, according to the grammatical construction of the sentence, the "Son of God" is certainly the last antecedent. And it is equally true of Christ that he was *sanctified* and *fitted* to be the Mediator "by the blood of the covenant." John xvii. 19; Heb. xiii. 20. 2. But, admitting it to refer to the *apostate*, it remains to be proved that the *sanctification* was any thing more than *external* and *ceremonial* sanctification. That both persons and things are called *holy*, and said to be *sanctified*, which are only externally *dedicated* to God, we have abundant evidence in this same epistle. In the preceding chapter, 13th, 22d and 23d verses, we read of a *sanctification* which had nothing to do with the *heart*. "*The blood of bulls and of goats*, and the ashes of a heifer sprinkling the unclean, SANCTIFIETH to the *purifying* of the *flesh*," &c. What sanctification of *heart* could ever be accomplished by the

"blood of bulls and goats?" And yet if a person upon whom this blood had been *sprinkled* should despise the ordinance, he would be guilty of "trampling on the blood of the covenant," for this typified the blood of Christ. In like manner, if, after having been *baptized*, and making profession of religion, we break our covenant vows and apostatize, we "despise the blood of the covenant wherewith we were sanctified," or *separated* and *dedicated* to the service of God.

The whole, however, is merely a *caution* against apostasy from our profession, and does not teach that any *will* thus despise the blood of the covenant—much less that any will fall from real sanctification of heart. "*If* we sin wilfully after having received a knowledge of the truth, *there remaineth no more sacrifice for sin*." (26.) If this proves "falling from grace," it proves also that after such fall *there is no recovery!* for such persons "there remaineth *no more sacrifice for sin*, but a fearful looking for of judgment," &c. But these texts prove nothing as to the *actual event*, which is the thing to be proved.

OBJ. XIV. "*If any man draw back, my soul shall have no pleasure in him*." Heb. x. 38.

Ans. 1. This is perfectly true in its *literal* sense, and not at all opposed to our doctrine. An opposite doctrine would be horrible. 2. There may be a difference between "drawing back" and "drawing back to *perdition*." A saint may draw back *in part;* and, if he draws back at all, God will be *displeased* with him. 3. Here is the "*if*" again, by way of *caution*. 4. It is expressly said *immediately after*, that real Christians *do not* draw back to perdition. "We are not of them who draw back unto perdition, but of them that believe to the saving of the soul."

OBJ. XV. "A man may escape the pollutions of the present world, and afterward fall away," &c. 2 Pet. ii. 20.

Now, 1. All this may be said of those who are only *externally reformed* from the infidelity, vice, and immorality of the world, and have a *speculative head knowledge* of the ways of righteousness. That such persons may and do fall away, we do not doubt. 2. That these persons were not changed in *heart*,—that their *nature* never was renewed, is evident from the *comparison* used by the apostle on the subject. He compares them to "a *sow* that was *washed* returning to her wallowing in the mire." The *nature* of the animal was not changed; though externally washed, her appetites remained the same; she was a *sow* still. Had her *nature* been changed to that of a *sheep,* she would *never have returned!*

Thus I have noticed some of the strongest arguments I have ever heard or read against the "perseverance of the saints." There are others adduced of the same general nature, but no more difficult to answer than those I have mentioned. Some of them are drawn from *metaphysics*—some from *supposed facts*—and the rest from what is thought to be *implied* in several passages of Scripture. If I understand the controversy, the only *express* declaration of the *fact* of falling from grace, which they adduce, is Gal. v. 4. And that text, as I have shown, evidently speaks of a falling, not from *sanctification,* but from *orthodoxy.* There is not in all the Bible, that I have ever seen, a solitary declaration *that any real saint ever actually perished.*

That there are *cautions* and *warnings* of the most solemn kind against drawing back at all, we cheerfully admit. But, as I have brought *express declarations* of Scripture, and *absolute promises* of God that *every saint shall persevere,* all the cautions and warnings and apparent apostasies before mentioned must be understood as *not inconsistent* with our doctrine.

Let me now state in a summary way the arguments which have been advanced.

RECAPITULATION.

It has been shown that the infallible perseverance of the saints is clearly implied and proved, in their conversion by efficacious grace—in their election to salvation—in the predestination of all the called to glory—in the nature of the covenant of grace, and the faithfulness of their surety—in the absolute promises made to those who come to Christ, that they shall never be cast out, and to his sheep that they shall never perish. And again, because predestination, calling, justification, and glorification are so many links of an

Almighty chain; because neither things present nor things to come shall ever separate them from the love of God in Christ Jesus their Lord; because the promises were made immutable and absolute for the very purpose of affording STRONG CONSOLATION and an ANCHOR to their souls; because the saints are kept as in a garrison by the power of God, through faith unto salvation; because grace abides in believers as an incorruptible seed, so that they cannot live and die in sin; because all who are converted are sealed by the Holy Spirit unto the day of redemption, and the gift of the Spirit is *God's earnest of heaven;* because the very fact of believing is a proof of a foreordination to eternal life; because the life of Christians is hid with Christ, and is kept by him and not by themselves, and while he lives they shall live also; because, though God may chastise, he will "not utterly forsake" his children; because all apostates are spoken of as proving by their apostasy that they never had grace; and, finally, because many dangerous absurdities follow from the opposite doctrine—while it spreads darkness over the dying hours of God's best people, by resting their hopes of perseverance to the end on their own uncertain steadfastness, rather than on the UNCHANGING FAITHFULNESS AND GRACE OF GOD.

CONCLUSION.

Thus I have endeavoured to give my views of the "Perseverance of the Saints." I have sought to do it in perfect charity toward those who differ. Should similar charity be granted toward us, for *their* sakes I shall rejoice. For myself, no conduct of others, by the grace of God, shall ever alter mine. The law of God, the law of *love*, and not the conduct of others, is our rule.

The sum of what has been said is this:—There are *express declarations* and *unconditional promises* in Scripture that *every saint*, without exception, shall be saved. There is no express declaration that any saint ever *has been* or ever *will be* lost. There are many instances of saints *falling into sin*, but no proof that such persons *never rose again*. There are instances of *apostates* who fell from their profession and died in sin; but there is no proof they were ever real saints;

and many intimations to the contrary. There are many *cautions* and *warnings* against falling away; but these are stimulants to watchfulness, and means of grace as necessary on our plan as any other. And, finally, salvation is offered on certain *terms;* but these *terms* are *sure* to be complied with by all Christ's people.

And now, unto Him who hath loved us with an everlasting love, and therefore with loving-kindness hath drawn us to himself; unto Him who is able to keep us from falling, and to present us faultless before the presence of his glory, with exceeding joy; unto the only wise God our Saviour, be glory and dominion for ever and ever.

HYMN.

How firm a foundation, ye saints of the Lord,
Is laid for your faith in his excellent word!
What more can he say than to you he hath said,
You who unto Jesus for refuge have fled?

In every condition, in sickness, in health,
In poverty's vale, or abounding in wealth;
At home and abroad, on the land, on the sea,
"As thy days may demand shall thy strength ever be.

"Fear not, I am with thee, O be not dismay'd!
I, I am thy God, and will still give thee aid;
I'll strengthen thee, help thee, and cause thee to stand,
Upheld by my righteous, omnipotent hand.

"When through fiery trials thy pathway shall lie,
My grace all-sufficient shall be thy supply;
The flame shall not hurt thee; I only design
Thy dross to consume, and thy gold to refine.

"E'en down to old age all my people shall prove
My sovereign, eternal, unchangeable love;
And when hoary hairs shall their temples adorn,
Like lambs they shall still in my bosom be borne.

"The soul that on Jesus hath lean'd for repose,
I will not, I will not, desert to its foes;
That soul, though all hell should endeavour to shake,
I'll *never*—no, NEVER—no, NEVER forsake."

No. 3.

HOW SHALL MAN BE JUST WITH GOD?

BY

ALBERT BARNES.

The Presbyterian Publication Committee.

DEPOSITORIES:

PHILADELPHIA: PUBLICATION HOUSE, 386 CHESTNUT STREET
NEW YORK: IVISON & PHINNEY, 178 FULTON ST.

STEREOTYPED BY L. JOHNSON & CO.
PHILADELPHIA.
PRINTED BY I. ASHMEAD.

No. 3.

HOW SHALL MAN BE JUST WITH GOD?

I. *The importance and difficulty of the inquiry, How man can be justified.*

THE question "How shall man be justified with God," (Job xxv. 4.) proposed by an Eastern Sage, may be regarded as an inquiry by *man—by human nature.* It expresses the deep workings of the human soul in all ages, on one of the most important and difficult of all subjects. The question means, How shall man be regarded and treated as righteous by his Maker? What methods shall he take to secure such treatment? What can he do, if any thing, to commend himself to the favourable regards of a holy God? What can he do, if any thing, to make amends for the past? What can he do, if any thing, to turn away future wrath? Can he vindicate himself before the Eternal Throne, for what he has done? If not, can he see how it is consistent for God to treat him as righteous? These questions meet us everywhere, and enter into and mould all the forms of religion on earth. The inquiry, as illustrating and expressing the feelings of human nature, may be considered with reference to two points:—its importance, and its difficulty.

I. *The importance of the inquiry.*

(1.) Its importance will be seen by this consideration—*No one can be saved unless he is just, or righteous, in the sight of God.* Unless there is some way, by which God can consistently regard and treat us as just or righteous, it is impossible to believe that we can enter heaven when we die.

Unless man is personally so holy that he cannot be charged with guilt; or can justify himself by denying or disproving the charge of guilt; or can vindicate himself by showing that his conduct is right; or can appropriate to himself the merit of another as if it were his own, no one can believe,—no one does believe—that he can enter heaven. Probably there is no conviction of the human mind more deep and universal than this, and every man, whether conscious to himself of acting on it or not, makes it elementary in his practical belief. If any one is disposed to call this proposition in question, or if he is not conscious of acting on it, he will see that it must be true, by looking at it for a single moment. The proposition is, that no man can be saved unless he is just, or righteous, in the sight of God. Can God save a wicked man *as such* and on account of his wickedness? Can he hold him up to the universe as one who ought to be saved? Can he take the profane man, the scoffer, the adulterer and the murderer, to heaven, and proclaim himself as their patron and friend? Can he connect a life of open wickedness with the rewards of eternal glory? Nothing can be more clear than that if a man is made happy forever in heaven, there will be some good reason for it, and that reason cannot be that he was regarded as an unrighteous person. There will be a fitness and propriety in his being saved; there will be some reason why it will be proper for God to regard and treat him as righteous.

This view, which is perhaps sufficiently obvious, may be illustrated by a reference to a human government. No just government could become the patron and friend of the pirate and the murderer, or bestow its rewards on one who, in all respects, deserved to meet the penalty of the laws. On this belief also, every man acts in reference to his own salvation. Each one has a firm conviction that no man can be saved unless he is just in the sight of God. A man when he thinks of being saved, always either thinks that he has kept the law of God; or that he has a good excuse for not complying with it; or that he can make reparation by penances, pilgrimages, sacrifices, or fastings; or that he can appropriate to himself the merit of another. He never thinks of finding favour with God *as* a transgressor, or on account of his crimes; he never supposes that his iniquity can be the foundation of his salvation. God made the human soul, and he so made it, that it never *could* believe that he would save a man *because* he was wicked, or unless there was some way in which he could be regarded and treated as righteous.

(2.) Secondly, the importance of the inquiry is seen from the testimony of man everywhere. Man is *apparently* greatly indifferent to religion, and it often seems impossible to arouse his attention to the great and momentous questions connected with it. But, taking the race together, he is not so indifferent to the subject as he appears, and could we know all the secret thoughts and feelings of each individual, we should find that his indifference is often in appearance only. There are workings of the soul which are carefully excluded from public view. There are thoughts, which every man has, of which he would not wish others to know. There are deep, agitating, protracted questionings resulting in settled conviction, or tossing the soul upon a restless sea, which men would wish to hide from their best friends. There is often a deep interest in a man's mind on the subject of religion, when his whole soul seems to the world torpid and inactive, or when he would repel your inquiries, or when he would seem as "calm as a summer's morning."

A very slight acquaintance with the human mind, or with the history of opinions, is all that is needful to see the importance which the inquiry, on the subject of justification, has assumed in the view of man.

(*a*) It was seen in the investigations of ancient philosophers. "How shall man be just with God?" was the question which pressed itself on the minds and hearts of the speakers in the book of Job, and it was a question which was echoed and re-echoed in the whole heathen philosophic world. Many who are profound and patient students on other subjects, often regard investigations on the subject of religion as unworthy their attention. They think them appropriate themes for contending theologians; for disputatious and subtle schoolmen; for the feeble in intellect, or for the dying; but they regard them as having slight claims on a philosophic mind. But would they go and take lessons of the masters of science and of profound thought, they would think differently. Will such men tell us what points of inquiry have most occupied the attention of the intellects of other times? Will they refer to the volumes which contain the results of their investigations of past ages? Will they let Socrates once more speak, and Plato give utterance to his views, and Cicero and Seneca declare what most engrossed their attention? One thing they will find in all the past—one grand absorbing question they will meet with everywhere—one query to which all physical science was made subservient. It was the subject of religion; the question of man's acceptance with God; the grounds of his hope of future blessedness. The real inquiry among thinking men of all ages and lands has been, "How shall man be just with God?"

(*b*) The same earnest searching we find still in the heathen world. From the recorded views, and the religion of the heathen, we may learn much about man when he utters his sentiments without disguise; and what we find universally among them, we may regard as the language of human nature. Now there is no one thing expressed with more uniformity or more earnestness all over the Pagan world than this question, "How may we be just with God?" It was the foundation of all sacrifices, penances, pilgrimages, self-inflicted mortifications. All these things were intended so to make expiation for sin, or so to appease the anger of the gods, that they who thus performed the rights of religion, might be regarded and treated as righteous. Take this inquiry away, and their sacrifices and penances would be unmeaning. Take this away, and the earnestness of their religion would soon cease, and, degenerating into an empty form, would of itself soon expire.

(*c*) There is another method by which we may learn the views of the human soul about the importance of this inquiry. It is by contemplating the soul when under convictions of sin, and reflecting on its prospects about the future world. Then there is no thought so momentous in the view of the mind as this, "How shall a man be just with God?" There are many more persons in this state than is commonly imagined. There is probably no one who reaches the years of mature reflection, before whose mind this inquiry has not at some period assumed an engrossing importance. With almost no danger of error, you may assume of every man that you meet, that his mind either has been, or is now deeply interested on the subject of his salvation, and that in his life there are periods when no subject appears so momentous as this. In his moments of solitary musing, or in a time of bereavement, or under the preaching of the gospel, or when remembered truth seems to come with new-armed power to his soul, or when the recollection of guilt seems recalled to him by some invisible agency, or when lying on a bed of languishing, this great inquiry has come before him, "How may he be justified before his Maker?" How may the guilt of his sins be washed away? How may he be regarded and treated as a righteous man? To those who have been in this state—and who has not been?—it need not be said, that *then* no question seems more momentous than this. In time of revival of religion, the student in a college loses his relish for his ordinary studies, and almost the capacity to pursue them, absorbed in the more important study respecting salvation; the merchant loses his relish for his gains, engrossed in the greater inquiry how he may obtain everlasting life; the farmer, the mechanic, and the mariner feel that they can hardly pursue their wonted employments, for a more momentous subject has engrossed the soul. The eye may be on a passage in Horace or Livy, but the thought shall be elsewhere; and the hands may be employed in labour, but it shall be performed with a heavy heart, and when toil is pursued almost unconscious of what is done. The calm, fixed, steady, contemplative eye of the student, and the readiness of the man of business to leave his counting room and place himself under religious instruction, show with what intensity this inquiry has seized on the soul. The busy, the studious and the gay often become entirely absorbed in it, and then no honour of scholarship, no amplitude of gain, no brilliancy of pleasure or amusement, seem comparable in value to the solution of the question, "How shall man be just with God?" We need not pause here to consider whether this is a just estimate which the soul thus puts on the magnitude of this subject. We are concerned only in getting at the language of man himself when in his sober moments. It will at least be conceded that in those moments of profound absorbing thought; those moments when men of all classes are willing to turn aside from their usual pursuits; those times when the great inquiry can make the pleasures of the ball-room and the scenes of the splendid amusement, tasteless, and can loosen the hold of the votaries of gold on their gains, and cause the ardent student to turn aside from his books, that then the human mind is as likely as ever to judge correctly of the importance of what has come before it. Yet there is but one sentiment then—that this question absorbs and annihilates all others.

(3.) There is another consideration which shows the importance of this inquiry. It is, that the views that are entertained of justification, modify and shape all the other doctrines of religion. It is the central doctrine in the whole system, and spreads its influence over every other opinion which man holds, on the subject of salvation. The views entertained on this subject, distinguish respectively the Protestant and the Papal communities; divide Protestants themselves into two great parties, evangelical and non-evangelical; separate heathens from Christians; give form to all the systems of infidelity and Deism, and constitute the peculiarity of every man's individual faith. When it is known definitely what a man thinks on this one point, it may be known whether he is a Papist, or a Protestant; a Christian or an infidel; a heathen or a friend of the Saviour; a formalist or a devoted servant of God. Luther did not say too much when he said of this doctrine of justification, that it was the article on which depended the permanency or ruin of the church; and with a sagacity equal to that of Talleyrand, when from a very slight matter he predicted that the throne of France would be overturned, Luther saw that the doctrine of justification would meet every corruption of the Papacy and eventually overturn the system. The fabric of the Papacy is an ingenious attempt, originated and arranged under the auspices of a higher than a human intellect, though fallen, to delude man with the belief, that there is some other way by which he may be justified with God, than by faith in the Saviour. The whole system of heathenism is an attempt to answer the question, "How man may be justified with God?" The systems of infidels, and of men who are depending on their own morality, or relying on penances and pilgrimages, are another answer which is given to the question.

If the observations now made are correct, it will be conceded that this doctrine has an importance which cannot be over-estimated. If it be so, that no man can be saved who is not justified in the sight of God; that the race everywhere, in the anxious inquiry of sages, in the systems and sacrifices of the heathen, and in the deep working of the soul rendering every other pursuit tasteless and valueless, has shown its sense of its importance, and that it spreads its influence over every form of belief, the importance of the inquiry will be admitted.

II. The second point proposed to be noticed as preparatory to a consideration of the subject of justification is,—*The difficulty of the inquiry.*

What *is* the difficulty? Why has the human mind been so much perplexed in relation to it? Why may not God admit man to heaven, and regard and treat him as if he were righteous? These questions can be answered in a single remark, and the whole difficulty may then be seen at a glance. It is, *that man is in fact not righteous.* The difficulty is to see *how God can regard and treat him as if he were.* It is easy to see how *if* he were righteous, God could treat him so, or how he could treat him as a sinner, that is, according to his real character. But how shall he treat him differently from what he deserves, or as if he had a character which it is known he has not? Whatever theories may be embraced by men, or whatever opinions may be entertained on the subject of religion, it is true as a matter of fact that these perplexities have been felt by men, that they have given rise to grave and agitating questions, and that man has not felt that he could give a solution that was wholly satisfactory. There is no inquiry which has taken hold on man everywhere, under all forms of government and opinion, and in every climate and amidst every degree of progress, which has not had some real foundation in the nature of things. The race, in its soberest moments, does not busy itself with trifles, and especially will not allow itself to be troubled and tortured by questions that are of no importance. The difficulty which has been felt on this subject is therefore not imaginary, but from the fact that the inquiry has been so universal, and so beyond the human powers satisfactorily to explain, it is clear that God meant that it should be regarded by man as a point to be solved only by divine revelations. The real difficulties in the case, and the state of the human mind in regard to them, may be illustrated by the following observations:—

(1.) There was the impossibility of man's vindicating himself from the charges of guilt brought against him. If he could do this, all would be clear, for God will not condemn the innocent. But it could not be done. These charges were brought in such a way, and enforced in such a manner that man could not so meet them as to escape the conviction of their truth. They are brought, where there is a revelation by God himself in his word; and where there is not, as well as where there is, by conscience. Man is told in the word of God that he is a sinner; his recollection of what he has done, assures him that it is so; the dealings of God with him, convince him that there must be some cause of alienation between himself and his Maker; and every sick bed, and every grave, and every apprehension of future wrath, confirms the conviction. If man were to undertake to convince himself that he is not held to be guilty, the argument could not be derived from the dealings of God with him in this world. It is not easy for a man to satisfy himself that he is not a sinner, when the earth is strewed with the dying and the dead; when his best friends are cut down all around him; when he himself is to die, and when he is so made that he cannot but tremble at the apprehension of the judgment. If one wished to construct an argument to prove that he is not a sinful man, and that man can be just with God, he would desire to be removed to some world where he would not see so many things that seem to be mementoes of human depravity, and so many evidences that his Creator regards him and his fellow-men as guilty. Men have everywhere felt this difficulty. There is no one sentiment in which men more uniformly agree than in this. Every man regards every other man as a sinner, and puts himself on his defence against him, for his locks, and bolts, and notes, and bonds, and securities all demonstrate this; and every man knows that he himself also is a sinner. There is nothing of which he is better apprised, nothing he believes more firmly than this. There is not a living man that could bear the revelation of his thoughts to others for a single day, and that not merely because others have no right to know what is passing in his mind, but because he feels that they are wrong. Confusion, blushes, shame, and shrinking would diffuse themselves over every assembly, and through every crowded thoroughfare in the streets of a great city, and in every lonely path where strangers should meet strangers, if each one knew that another was surveying closely the thoughts of his heart, and saw what was passing there. If every man felt that his bosom were so transparent that all the workings of his soul could be observed by others, no one would venture out of his chamber; no one would move along the pathways where he might encounter a fellow man; the thronged places of business would be deserted, and our great and crowded cities would become like the cities of the dead. No man would venture, at midnight on the mountain top, or on the lonely prairie, to stretch out his hands to Heaven, and say, "I am pure as the stars that shine upon me, or as the God that made them." So universal is the consciousness of guilt, and so certain does every man feel, in his sober moments, that he cannot vindicate himself before God. *How then shall man be just with God?*

(2.) There is the difficulty which must have been early apparent to men, and which any one can see now, if the guilty were saved, or if they were regarded and treated as righteous. How could this be done? Man does not do it himself, in reference to those who are guilty, and how could God? No father feels that it would be proper to regard and treat an offending child as if he were obedient; no friend acts thus toward one who professes friendship; and no government acts thus toward its subjects. All order and happiness in a family would cease at once if this were to occur; and government on earth would be unknown. There is a great principle of eternal justice which seems engraved in the convictions of the soul, that every one ought to be treated according to character, and that there *ought* to be a difference in the divine dealings toward the good and the evil. But what if God treats all alike? What if he makes no distinction in regard to character? What if he admits all to favour; punishes no one, and rewards piety and impiety, fraud and honesty, vice and virtue, reverence and blasphemy, alike with the same immortal crown? What if the murder of the innocent, and the highest deed of benevolence were equally a passport to his favour? What if he met the licentious, and those of virgin purity of soul, when they came before him, with the same smile of approbation? Would not the universe feel that he was regardless of character? Would it be possible to correct the impression?

But it will be said, perhaps, might he not pardon the guilty, and the fact of pardon constitute a ground of distinction which the universe would understand? True, if it would be proper to pardon in this state of things. But are there no difficulties attending the subject of pardon? Can it always be done? Can it be done to an unlimited extent? Does a father feel that it is safe and best to adopt it as a universal rule, that he will forgive all his children as often as they may choose to offend him, and to do it without any condition? Any one may easily see the difficulty on this subject. There are thousands of men confined in penitentiaries; many of them are desperate men, regardless of all the laws of heaven and earth. Would it be felt to be safe or proper at once to open their prison doors? Who would wish to be in the neighbourhood when they should be turned impenitent and unreformed upon the world? If the community is scarcely safe now with all the precautions and guards of justice, what would it be if they were all withdrawn? These difficulties must occur to any one when he asks the question, How can the guilty be justified?

(3.) It is a matter of simple fact that men have felt this difficulty, and the methods to which they have resorted to devise some way of justification, show how perplexing the subject has been to the human mind. We may learn something of the embarrassments which men feel, by the devices to which they resort to overcome them. Look then for a moment at some of the methods to which men have been driven in order to answer the question satisfactorily, How can man be just with God?

(*a*) One class have denied the charge of guilt, and have endeavoured to convince themselves that they *are* righteous and that they may safely trust to their own works for salvation. If this could be done, all would be well. But the mass of men have felt that there are insuperable difficulties in the way of doing this. We shall hereafter inquire whether it is practicable.

(*b*) Many have endeavoured to excuse themselves for their conduct, and thus to be justified before God. They are sensible that all is not right, but if they can find a satisfactory excuse, that is, if they can show that they had a right to do what they have done, or could not help it, they feel that they would not be condemned. And they are right in this. To do it they lay the blame on Adam, or on ungovernable passions, or on a fallen nature, or on the power of temptation, or on the government of God. They attempt to show that they could do no otherwise than they have done; that is, they have a right to do it in the circumstances, and of course are not to blame. We shall inquire hereafter whether this position can be made out.

(*c*) Many have endeavoured to make expiation by blood,

and have sought to be justified in this way. Hence the sacrifices of the heathen—the flowing blood and burning bodies of lambs, and goats, and bullocks, and prisoners of war, and slaves, and of children—offered to appease the anger of the gods. Thousands of altars smoke in this attempt, and the whole heathen world pants and struggles under the difficulty of the inquiry, How may a guilty conscience be justified with God?

(*d*) Many have sought the same thing by pilgrimages and penances; by maceration and scourging; by unnatural and painful postures of the body; and by wounds which their own hands have inflicted on themselves. The victim of superstition in India lies down beneath the car of his idol, or fastens hooks in his flesh, or holds his arm in one posture till it is rigid. Simeon in Syria, on an elevated column, spent his years in misery. Antony in Egypt went and lived in a cave, and Benedict originated the monastic system in Italy. Mecca is crowded by pilgrims seeking for righteousness by a visit to the tomb of the prophet; and the shrines inclosing the bones of the saints are encompassed by throngs in Italy for a similar purpose; the garment of hair frets and tortures the body, and the sound of the lash is heard in the cells of the convent, and the whole system of penance and self-inflicted torture all over the world is just a commentary on the question, How shall man be justified with God?

(*e*) To crown all this, another device has been resorted to. It has been held that there were extraordinary merits of saints who lived in former times; that they performed services beyond what were required, that these merits were garnered up as a sacred treasure, and are placed at the disposal of the head of the papal community, to be distributed at his pleasure to those who are conscious of guilt; and this is one of the answers given to the question, How shall man be justified with God?

From these remarks it will be seen what men have thought of the difficulty of this question. In these various ways, human nature speaks out and reveals what is passing in the bosom. They are the methods to which men have resorted as the best answer which they can give to this inquiry. To see the real difficulty, however, we should be able to go down into the depths of the soul, to guage all the agonies of guilty consciences; to look at the woes and sorrows which men are willing to endure that they may be justified, and then to see how one and all of these plans utterly fail; how they leave the conscience just as defiled as it was before, the propensities to evil unchecked, the grave as terrific as ever, and the judgment-bar as full of horrors. When we stand and survey these things, we ask with deep concern whether any one of these is the way by which man can be justified with God? If not, is there any other way, or is there none?

2. *Man cannot justify himself by denying or disproving the charge of guilt.*

The term *justify* is a legal term, but it is also in common use, and is intelligible to all. An illustration or two will make it plain, and will lay the foundation for the train of thought which will be pursued in this section. A man is charged with murder. He may put his defence on one of two grounds. He may either deny the fact of killing; or admitting that, he may show that he had a right to do it, or is excusable for it. If the fact of killing is not made out against him, of course he is just in the sight of the law, and is acquitted. Or, if the fact be made out or admitted, he may take the ground either that he did it in self-defence, or that it was done under such a state of mental derangement as to destroy responsibility—and he is acquitted. He had no "malice prepense." He intended no murder; he committed none; and the law does not hold him guilty of the charge. A man is charged with trespass. He takes a similar ground of defence. He denies the fact, or maintains that he had a right to do what he has done. He sets up a claim to a "right of way" over a field which his neighbour owns, and having established that, he is acquitted, or is held to have done no more than he had a right to do in the case. He is a just man in the eye of the law, and may pursue his own business, enjoy the immunities of a good citizen, the honours of an unsullied name, and protection in his rights unmolested. It may be added here, that there is no other way by which a man can justify himself in the sight of the law. He could not do it by admitting the fact of the trespass, and by paying the fine, or making compensation for the injury done; for, though he might be discharged, yet this would be no justification of what was done, and would do nothing toward showing that he was right in doing it. It does not make a wrong right, either, to intend beforehand to pay for the mischief, or to make amends for it after the deed is done. This remark will be used hereafter in examining the attempts which men have made to justify themselves.

Now if man attempt to justify himself before his Maker, he must take one of the grounds referred to. He must either deny the charge brought against him; or, admitting the facts in the case, he must show that he had a right to do what he has done. If he can do either of these, he will be justified, for God does not condemn the innocent. We will suppose then the case of a man arraigned at the bar of his Maker, as we all soon shall be, on trial with reference to eternity. There are two things that occur to us at once. What is the charge against him? What is the defence which he sets up? If there is no charge, he is justified of course. If his defence is valid, he will be acquitted.

It is necessary then, first to look at the charge which is brought against man.

The charge is, that he has violated the law of his Maker,

or is a transgressor. It is that of apostacy or revolt from God; the entire failure to keep his laws; living constantly in the neglect of acknowledged duty; and the habitual commission of known sins. It may be assumed here that every reader of this Tract is sufficiently familiar with the Bible to know the nature of these charges, without their being specified in detail. No one trained in a Christian community can be ignorant of the account of our race which the Bible gives. These charges of guilt do not make the impression which they ought, for these reasons: because we are so familiar with them; because others are implicated with us; because we do not cordially believe them. Many a man reads the account of human nature in the Bible without supposing there is any thing serious in the matter, or much fitted to trouble him. There is many a one who would pass a sleepless night, if he knew there was a charge of petty larceny against him, which would bring him into court to-morrow, who has no trouble at the charge of total apostacy and utter revolt brought against him by God. There is many a one who would be in the deepest consternation if he knew that his name was before a grand jury in some such connection as his conscience could easily suggest, who has no alarm at the thought of the "Grand Assize;" and no dread of the formidable catalogue of crimes drawn up against him in the secrecy of the divine Councils. A few remarks will demonstrate that these charges against man in the Bible *ought* to make an impression and that men ought to be willing to look at them. A case or two may be supposed which will show how men ought to be affected in view of such charges brought by the Creator. The case of an officer in a bank may be referred to. He has been long there, or in other stations in public life, and has gained a character compared with which all the gold that the vaults of the bank could contain would be worthless as the sand. Suddenly, charges are brought against him of unfaithfulness to his trust. They come from quarters worthy of his attention; are of such a source as inevitably to gain the ear of the community; are such that his family must know of them; are sustained by such circumstances of actual losses in the bank as to render the charge credible, and are of such a character as to make it necessary for him to leave his post, disgraced perhaps forever. Now it is not necessary to suppose that these accusations are true. All that is designed is to show the effect which charges of guilt from a respectable quarter usually have on a man's mind. But suppose he secretly knew they were all true, how could his conduct be explained, if he was utterly indifferent and unconcerned?

In regard to the charges which are brought against man a few remarks may be made here, showing that they should be allowed to make an impression on the mind.

(1.) One respects the source from whence they come. They are professedly the charges of our Maker and final Judge. They are those on which we are to be tried at his bar, and in reference to which our destiny is to be determined.

(2.) They are the most fearful of all accusations which can be brought against a creature. No crime can be equal to that of being an enemy of God; and no offence against human society can equal in enormity and ill desert, the crimes of which man is charged against his Maker.

(3.) The charge extends to every human being. No exception is made in favour of youth, beauty, rank, or blood; none in favour of the amiable, the honest, or the moral; none in favour of those who have endeavoured to wipe away the accusation by their own good living. It is not indeed charged that one is as bad as another, or that any one is as bad as he can be, but it *is* that every one is guilty of violating the law of God, and is held to be such a sinner that he cannot save himself.

(4.) It is charged that each and every one is of such a character that the eternal pains of hell would be an adequate recompense for his crime. He is held to be under condemnation and to be justly exposed to punishment that shall be severe in the extremest degree, unmitigated and everlasting. Each one is held to be such an evil-doer that it would be wrong for God to admit him to heaven as he is, but not wrong to consign him to unending wo. It is important not to disguise any thing about this, or to seek to hide it by soft names. The robber is deemed worthy of the penitentiary; the murderer is regarded as deserving death on the gibbet; and in like manner it is held in the charges brought against man, and the threatenings appended to them, that every man deserves the pains of everlasting death, and that if he should receive what is properly due to him, he would be cast off from God, and punished forever. Such is the nature of the charges against man. On these he is held guilty; on these he will be arraigned. The Bible has two aspects. It reveals a way of pardon; but it is also the grand instrument of indictment against man. It is designed to reveal his character; to record his crimes; to overwhelm him with the conviction of guilt; and be the rule of judgment on the final day. The question then arises, now to be considered, whether if these are the charges against man, he can vindicate or justify himself. It has been already remarked that there are but two grounds to be taken in such a vindication. One is, to deny the facts charged on man; the other is, if the facts be admitted, for him to show that he had a right to do as he has done. There is nothing else that can be conceived of in the case, to be done by him, unless it were to attempt to make expiation or reparation by extraordinary merit; by penance or by sacrifice; though this would not *justify* him for what he had done, any more than a man's paying a fine made it right for him to put out his neighbour's eye, or burn his house. If neither of these things can be done, it will follow that man cannot be justified by his own righteousness. These points will now be considered in their order. The first is that man cannot deny the truth of the charges brought against him. In support of this the following considerations may be urged:—

(1.) The source whence these charges come. They are made by God himself. It is assumed here that the Bible is true, and the argument will be conducted on that assumption. In another part of this Tract it will be shown that it is equally impossible to deny the main facts, whether the Bible be true or false. The position now is that the sinner cannot take the ground that God has mistaken the facts about man, or that he has designedly brought a false accusation. It surely cannot be necessary to go into an argument to prove this, but an illustration or two may be allowed.

(*a*) One is that it is impossible for God to mistake on this subject. Men often do mistake in reference to character and conduct. Charges are often falsely brought and men are often condemned as guilty, on false accusations. This may be intentionally done; or judges and jurors may be mistaken; or witnesses may be suborned to sustain the accusation, or those needful for the defence may be absent, or a combination of circumstances which no human sagacity can control may seem to confirm the charge of guilt against the innocent. But obviously no such mistake can occur in relation to the charges brought in the Bible against man, nor can man set up a vindication of himself on the ground that his Maker has erred in reference to the facts alleged.

(*b*) As little can he urge that the accusation has been overdrawn; that a degree of guilt has been charged such as the facts would not justify; or that there has been an intermingling of prejudice or passion that has given a colouring to the charge, and that a calmer view may modify these accusations. We can easily admit that such things may occur among men. Judges and jurors are liable to the same passions as other men, and in a time of popular excitement it may happen that the contagion may reach the bench and the jury-room, and hence the laws are careful that the administration of justice shall proceed with as much calmness and coolness as possible. It may happen also that false charges are brought against men because they are obnoxious to those in power. Many a one who has stood in the way of the purposes of a tyrant, has been removed under the form of law to gratify the passions of such a man, and many a pure name has been covered with infamy by the malignity of those in authority. But it is not needful to show that none of these things can be alleged by man in regard to the charges brought against him by his Maker. It cannot be pretended that God has been hurried into these charges under the influence of passion; or that man is obnoxious to his purposes and that he would have him removed. The charges are made with the utmost deliberation. They are made by the most benevolent Being in the universe; by one who can have no pleasure in finding out proofs of guilt; by one who, from his nature, is disposed to make every possible allowance for weakness and infirmity; by one who sees better than man can state it, every thing that can be said in his defence; by one more disposed than any human being ever was to do justice to all that is amiable and pure. If man wishes to find a friend who will be kind to his infirmities, and do justice to him when the world does him wrong, he can find no such friend as God.

(c) It may be added here that the charge is one that no denial affects. It has been deliberately made, and is that on which we are to be tried. We may deny it, or disregard it, but it is not affected. Whatever we may choose to think of it, it does not change the estimate which our Maker affixes to our character any more than the private views of a prisoner at the bar modify the estimate of the judge and jury. God will pronounce sentence on us according to his own estimate of our character, and the only security which we can have that we shall not meet with condemnation, will be in the fact that our character will be such that he will regard it as not proper to condemn us. But that cannot be by attempting to deny the truth of the charge which he brings against us, or by holding him either to be malignant or mistaken.

(2.) To show that man cannot deny the truth of that which is alleged against him as a violator of the law, it may be observed, secondly, that so far from obeying the perfect law of God, he has failed of yielding perfect obedience to the very lowest rules of morality. The standard at which man aims is in general low enough, and one which it might be supposed was sufficiently accommodating to satisfy one who wished to save himself by his own righteousness. That standard is, at any rate, at an immeasurable distance from the holy law of God. Yet let a man take any standard of conduct which he pleased, and he would fail in all attempts to show that he had always been conformed to it. Who would undertake to prove, before any tribunal that could take any cognizance of the motives, the thoughts, the words as well as the outward conduct, that he had always been honest, true, kind, chaste, or courteous? Who would attempt to prove, that he had on no occasion failed in his duty in the tenderest relations of life? What child is there that would undertake to prove, that he has never failed in his duty to his father or his mother; that he has always been as respectful, obedient and grateful as he ought to have been? Is there no compunction when he sees a father die? Is there nothing which he would wish to recall when he stands by a mother's grave? What brother would undertake to vindicate all his conduct toward a sister? or what friend is there that has never had a feeling toward his friend which he ought not to have? Who is there that would undertake to say that he has never failed in the duty of perfect honesty and truth in the transactions of business? Nay, to come down to a lower standard, who, professing to be governed by the laws of honour, would venture, when he comes to die, to stake his eternal welfare on the fact that he has never failed of perfect conformity to that arbitrary code? Who that professes to be governed by the rules of etiquette would attempt to maintain that those laws have always been perfectly observed? Let a man choose his own standard of action; let him refer to any code by which he professes to regulate his conduct—would he be willing that every thought, and word, and feeling and action of his life should be brought out to noonday, and that his eternal welfare should be determined by the issue of the question whether he had or had not been perfectly conformed to that code? If not, how shall he vindicate himself from the charge of sin? And if he cannot vindicate himself in reference to these low and imperfect standards, how shall he stand acquitted of the charge of a violation of the high and holy law of God—that he has never made a standard or rule of life—that he has never attempted to obey? The love to his Maker which that requires he has never once attempted to exercise. The holy duties which that enjoins he has never endeavoured to perform; its sacred injunctions he has never thought of bearing with him to the relations of life, to the counting-room, to the circles of his friendship, or to the scenes of his amusement. How, then, will he proceed in attempting to show that the charges of guilt brought against him are not true?

(3.) The charges which are brought against man by his Maker are sustained by all the facts of history. What ground would that man take who should attempt to show that the accusations in the Bible against the race—that it is sinful and prone to evil—are unfounded and false? On what would he base his argument? To what part of the world—to what historic monument—to what recorded opinions would he turn? Men often feel that the account in the Bible of the character of man—of the human heart—of the tendency of our nature—is harsh and gloomy. They are inclined to think better of the race, and to suppose that the views in the Bible must have been derived from the observation of man in a peculiarly dark age of the world, or were the result of feelings bordering on misanthropy. They think that man is better than he is there represented, or at least that, by certain modifications in society, he reaches a state where that description does not apply to him. On this account it is felt that the charge is one that cannot be sustained, and that it is not true now that all hope of salvation, on the ground of an upright life, is cut off. But let a few indisputable facts be submitted to candid men.

(*a*) One is, that the historic account of human conduct in the Bible is no worse than in other records. The narration of crimes, of wars, of ambition, of carnage, of blood, of sensuality, of venality, of political profligacy or corruption of manners there, is no worse than is to be found in Livy or Suetonius; in Gibbon or Hume. Every crime recorded in the sacred narrative has more than one parallel in the records of profane history, and every sentiment there expressed about man can be confirmed by any number of testimonies that the most sceptical could demand. The world has been many a time in a state like that described by Moses as the cause of the deluge; and the earth now bears up many a city, where all the crimes on account of which Sodom was overthrown still have an existence. Herculaneum and Pompeii have been revealed, by the monuments exposed to human view from beneath the ashes that covered them, to have been as corrupt, and corrupt in the same sense, as the cities of the plain; and a single one of the capitals of Europe embosoms probably now more revolting sins than they all. There is not an instance of fraud, corruption, or villany, attributed to man in the Bible, which has not its parallel in the present age of the world. The instances of depravity, whose deeds are recorded in the Bible, find abundant parallels in profane history, and not one of the names of guilt there referred to surpasses in wickedness those of Nero, or Tiberius; of Alexander VI. or his wretched son; of Henry VIII. or Charles II.; or of the leaders of the French Revolution.

(*b*) The account contained in the Bible, of human depravity, is sustained by the opinion of the sober and reflecting in all ages. Those who have given themselves to the contemplation of the condition of the world, have seen it, (the sad tendency to depravity in human nature,) lamented it, and sought to correct it; and yet the current of iniquity has swept over every barrier which man could erect against it, and sweeps on unchecked from age to age.

(*c*) The same view of the human character has been taken by wicked men themselves. Byron had no confidence in human virtue; Walpole said that every man had his price; Chesterfield regarded all virtue as false and hollow; Robespierre and Danton acted under the belief that every man deserved the guillotine. And

(*d*) Every man acts on the presumption that every other man is a sinner, and that no confidence can be placed in him without securities, and expects that every other one will regard him in the same light. This security is not in human virtue, but in vaults, and bars, and locks and bonds, and he himself expects to be treated by every other man as if he had the same character. His head neither hangs down with shame, nor do his eyes flash with indignation when he is asked for security that he will pay an honest debt, or when he is told in a bank, or on exchange, that no individual or corporation will trust him, without having some other security besides himself that he is a safe and honest man. In these circumstances, how can man go before God and attempt to justify himself on the ground that the charges against him are not true? Can he take the ground that his Maker is mistaken, or that he has maliciously brought a false accusation?

(4) There is but one other observation which it is necessary to make on this part of the subject. It is that conscience sustains the truth of all the charges which are brought. Man exhibits this very strange and remarkable characteristic, that he often frames an argument to show that the race is not as guilty as is alleged, and, perhaps, succeeds in convincing others; but still his argument does nothing to affect the proof as it lies in his own soul. There is that within himself which is to him overpowering demonstration that his arguments are all false, and that the charges against him are true. God has so formed the soul that he has there at all times what may be summoned forth at his pleasure, as a living witness that all that he has charged on man is true, and that shall render nugatory in a moment all the reasonings of men about the uprightness of their own hearts. This proof is found in a man's own conscience. This is a device by which man himself is made to coincide with and confirm the views of the Almighty—to approve where He approves—to condemn where He condemns. It stands apart from the deductions of reason; is little affected by the arguments which men may employ; is susceptible of being called up to give judgment at any time; often pronounces sentence against the favourite opinions of the man himself; uniformly declares judgment in favour of right, and condemns what is wrong, and is always on the side of God and his claims. This mysterious and wonderful power is wholly under the divine control. No matter what may be the cherished opinions of man; no matter how he may call in question the correctness of the divine testimony against human conduct, and no matter how reluctant he may be to admit the impossibility of being saved by his own works; yet God has power, at any moment, to summon the mind itself to sustain His own account of the state of the heart, and to put it into such a condition as to leave not a shadow of doubt that all

that He has said respecting its depravity is true. It requires all the art of a sinner to keep the voice of conscience silent, and to save himself from its rebukes. Well he knows that, if suffered to speak out, it will be in tones of deep condemnation. It often does speak out. In solitude; in the silence of the night; under the preaching of the gospel, when the mind in its lonely musings runs back by some mysterious law of association to the past; in a revival of religion; on a bed of sickness; or in the prospect of death, conscience often utters its voice in tones that are so distinct that they can neither be misunderstood nor suppressed. These are circumstances when man is most likely to judge according to truth, and in such circumstances he is so made as to feel, without a doubt, that the judgment pronounced by conscience is in accordance with that of the Most High, and that the views pressed upon his conscience then, about his own character, are those which will be confirmed by the sentence of the final Judge. "In thoughts from the visions of the night," said an ancient sage, "when deep sleep falleth on man, fear came upon me, and trembling, which made all my bones to shake. Then a spirit passed before my face; the hair of my flesh stood up: It stood still, but I could not discern the form thereof: an image was before mine eyes; there was silence, and I heard a voice, saying, Shall mortal man be more just than God? shall a man be more pure than his Maker? Behold, he put no trust in his servants, and his angels he charged with folly: How much less in them that dwell in houses of clay, whose foundation is in the dust, who are crushed before the moth!" Job iv. 13—19.

The point that has been now considered is, that man cannot justify himself before God by taking the ground that the facts are not as charged upon him, or that he has not in fact violated the law of God. This has been shown by these considerations: that it is impossible to believe that

God would bring a false charge against man; that, as a matter of fact, man fails of perfect conformity to the very lowest standard of morals; that the account in the Bible of the human character is confirmed by all the records elsewhere existing of the character of man; and that, when man has denied the charge against him, conscience comes in to confirm the accusations and the decisions of the Almighty.

III. *Man cannot justify himself by showing that his conduct is right.*

In the previous section, it has been shown that man cannot justify himself before God by denying the truth of the charges brought against him. In other words, he cannot take the position that the facts, in regard to his character and conduct, are not such as they are stated to be, or that his conduct has been, in all respects and all times, perfectly conformable to the law of God. He cannot take the ground which could be taken with propriety by sinless angels, that, as they have never departed in fact or in form from the strict requirements of a holy law, therefore they can claim it as a *right* to be treated as holy beings. Man cannot take the position before his Maker which a good citizen can before his country, that he has violated none of its laws, and therefore is *entitled* to its favour and protection.

The only other ground of defence, or of justification, which man can set up, is, that it was right or proper for him to do as he has done: that, admitting the facts in the case to be as they are charged; that he does not love his Maker with a perfect heart; that he violates his laws; that he is under the influence of unholy passions, and that he neglects many things which are required of him, yet that such are the circumstances in which he is placed, that it is not wrong for him to do as he has done, or that he has a valid excuse, and ought not to be condemned. His condition, he might be ready to admit, is one that is to be pitied; but his conduct is not such as to deserve blame or punishment. If a man can make this out, he will not be condemned; for God will not condemn the innocent. If man has a good and sufficient excuse for what he has done, there is no being in the universe who will look more benignantly on it than the Almighty; for there is no one so ready to do justice to the innocent, or to allow its proper weight to all that ought to exculpate. It is necessary, therefore, to examine this ground of defence, or to inquire whether man can set up the plea that he has a right to do as he has done—to live as he is in fact living.

Man is soon to stand before his Maker on a high charge of guilt. If he cannot deny the facts charged on him, he must take the ground that he has a right to do as he has done; that he has a valid reason which excuses him; that he ought to be acquitted, and that his deliverance should be hailed everywhere with songs and rejoicing, and that he ought to be received to heaven in triumph. What is this ground of defence? What is its value? Will it avail on the final trial?

Here it may be observed that man will not set up the plea of insanity, though more insane on the subject charged on him than many who have been acquitted on that ground by human tribunals. Man has too much pride and too much confidence that he is right, and that God is wrong, to urge this plea. Nor would he maintain that God has no jurisdiction over the case; for nothing is plainer than that he owes allegiance to the laws of his Maker, and that he cannot go beyond the limits of his empire. The points on which the accused sinner must rely, if he would undertake to show that he is not to blame for what he has done, and to justify himself, must be such as the following:—Either that the constitution of things under which he is placed, is such as to make it inevitable that he should do as he does; or that he is but acting out the nature which God has given him, and that therefore it must be right; or that the law of God is unreasonably severe and stern, and he is excusable for not obeying it; or that the time of preparation for eternity is too short, and that too great interests are made to depend on this brief period of existence; or that the penalty is too severe, and that if a man acts as well as he knows how, though he does not conform to the holy law of God, he ought not to be recompensed with eternal torments. If these points can be made out, man ought to be acquitted. If they cannot, has he any other ground of defence on which he can rely?

1. The first of these grounds of defence is derived from the constitution of things under which we are placed. Our minds, when we set up this defence, go back to the arrangement with Adam, and the effect of his sin on his posterity. The form of this defence is, that his fall, by the divine arrangement, placed us in far more unfavourable circumstances for salvation than we would otherwise have been; that his apostacy made it certain that all his descendants would sin; that it made it certain that the first act of each moral agent on earth would be wrong; that there was a strong probability thus created that all his posterity would be lost, and that all our strong propensities to evil, and our exposure to ruin, are to be traced to this arrangement. If they who rely on this ground of defence were disposed to take shelter under the declarations of Scripture, the defence would be found in the following statements of the apostle Paul: "Through the offence of one, many are dead." "The judgment was by one to condemnation." "By one man's offence, death reigned by one." "By the offence of one, judgment came upon all men to condemnation." "By one man's disobedience, many were made sinners." The law entered that the offence might abound." Rom. v. If these things are

so, how can man be held to be guilty for conduct thus rendered certain and inevitable?

The question now is, whether this can be regarded as a vindication of the undisputed facts in the conduct of man. Will it be admitted as a sufficient reason for what we have done in violation of the holy law of God, when we stand at his bar? The fact is undeniable that man thus early goes astray, and that he continues to wander farther and farther, unless he is restrained or reclaimed. Is it a sufficient excuse for this that Adam fell, and that we live under such a constitution that his sinning made it certain that we would sin also?

Now, in examining this question, we may admit two things. One is, that our circumstances, in consequence of his fall, are in many respects less favourable than they would otherwise have been; or that incalculable evils have come upon us in consequence of his apostacy; and the other is, that there is much about it which neither Revelation nor human philosophy explains. But these are different points from the one before us, whether that act of our first father is a sufficient excuse or apology for our crimes; or whether we can take shelter under that constitution as a vindication from the charge of guilt. In reply to this, two or three remarks may be made.

The first is, that we are responsible not for his sin, but for our own. The sin which is charged upon us is not his, but ours. The question is, not whether his acting as he did will free us from accountability, or ill-desert, on account of *his* act, which is plain enough; but whether it will free us from ill-desert, on account of *our own* sins. We could not be held guilty, *i. e.* blameworthy, for his sin; and if this were the charge, the defence set up must be conclusive. No reasoning has yet shown that man either *is* or *can be* regarded as blameworthy on account of the crime of his first father.

Again, the fall of Adam, and the constitution under which we live, compel no one to sin. Whatever may be their theories about native depravity, yet clear thinkers universally hold that all which is properly sin, is voluntary, and there is nothing in which man more consults his own pleasure than in the course of life which he pursues. Every profane man means to be profane; every dishonest man prefers to be dishonest; every sensual man has pleasure in moral corruption. It is a great law of our being, that where freedom ends, responsibility ends, and there is nothing more universally true than that a wicked man does only what he prefers to do. Nay, the sins which are charged on him are very often the fruit of long and deliberate plan; and so attached is he to a course of iniquity, that no argument or entreaty is sufficient to induce him to attempt to change his method of life. So voluntary are men in their sins, that there is no argument or topic of persuasion which will induce those living in sin, of themselves to break off their transgressions and turn to God. A man must take the ground that he is compelled by the act of Adam to do what he would otherwise not do, before the apostacy of our first father can be a vindication from the charges alleged against him. Further, this plea would neither be urged nor admitted by man himself in any other case. In all the numerous charges brought against men before human tribunals in different lands and ages, it is probable that this has never once been alleged as a vindication. To no murderer, thief, pirate, or traitor, has it ever occurred to urge this in his own defence. The state of the world has never been such that it would be tolerated for a moment; nor has the consideration that Adam fell, and that we are under a constitution where all men sin, ever, probably, in a single instance, even modified the verdict of a jury. There have been men on the bench and in the jury-box who have held this as a theological dogma, or as an excuse for their own sins before

God; but in a court-room nature speaks out, and no man would venture to apply such a dogma of theology to a decision of the bench. What would it avail on a charge of murder before any court in the world?

One other remark: It remains yet to be shown that the facilities for obtaining the divine favour, by men in their fallen state, are less than they would have been had they entered the world in the condition of their first parents. Are any sent to hell for Adam's sin alone? That remains yet to be proved. Are any infants lost? Not a particle of evidence has ever yet been furnished of this. Is it beyond the capacity of children to please God? Let the remarks of the Saviour about the hosannahs in the temple answer. Is it less easy for *us* to obtain the divine approbation and to be saved, than it would have been if Adam had not fallen? That remains to be proved. If a choice were to be made, it would seem to be easier for a fallen being to believe on Christ and to trust to him for salvation, than for even a holy being, who was liable to change, to keep a holy law unbroken forever. And, in fact, both our first parents, who were holy, and a portion of the holy angels, failed to retain their uprightness, while God vouchsafes his powerful grace to enable us to believe. If these things are so, then man cannot put his defence on the ground that he is brought into the world under a constitution which made it certain that he would be a sinner.

11. A second ground of defence to which man resorts in self-vindication, akin to this, but more common and plausible, is, that he is but acting out the propensities of his nature. He did not make himself. He is as God made him. He is but indulging inclinations which his Creator has implanted in his bosom, and the indulgence of which, therefore, cannot be attended with blame, or followed by His displeasure. Can it be wrong for him to look upon the light of the sun? Can it be wrong for him to be charmed with

the beauty of a sweet landscape, or the pleasant music of a waterfall? Can it be wrong for him to allay the demands of hunger and thirst, to protect himself from cold, and to provide a shelter from the storm? The innocence of these things being admitted, as it must be, he applies the concession to *all* the propensities and inclinations within him; to all that has led him to do what is charged upon him as wrong, and says, I am as God made me, and for that I cannot be held to be guilty. I ought, therefore, to be acquitted of the charge of guilt. Let us inquire whether this will answer as a ground of defence before God.

The most obvious remark in regard to it is, that, if it is a valid excuse in reference to religion, it is in reference to human conduct generally. For why may not any man accused of crime urge the same thing in self-defence? Has he done any thing more than act out certain propensities which he found in his nature? When Cæsar crossed the Rubicon, Hannibal the Alps, Alexander the Granicus, and Napoleon poured his armies on Italy, Egypt, Austria or Russia, did either do any thing more than follow out the inclinations of his nature? Did they not find stirring within them a spirit of ambition which urged them on to trample down the liberties of mankind? Did Robespierre or Diderot, Alexander VI. or Cæsar Borgia, do any thing more than act out certain propensities in their souls? Did Torquemada in the inquisition, or Cortes in the butcheries of Mexico, do any thing but act out what they found within theirs? And the assassin, the duellist, the murderer, what does he do more? Is he not as God made him, as much as the sinner who urges this plea? And would not this plea be as good for the one as the other?

But, further, this plea is contrary to the convictions of common sense and the universal judgment of right among men. If it were well founded, then the true course for man, if he would please God, would be to give unrestrained indulgence to every inclination in his bosom. Nay, then it would be wrong for him to check *any* of his passions, and his duty would be to give them the rankest growth and the broadest indulgence possible; for should not man cultivate all that God has implanted in his bosom? Then all the restraints on the passions of children must be displeasing to God; all the lessons of order, morality, and religion, are a contravening of his wishes; all colleges, schools, and churches are a nuisance; all court-houses and prisons are a violation of human liberty. Then the great benefactors of the race, and those who have been especially the friends of God, and have obtained the highest seat in heaven, have been those who have proclaimed the innocence of universal licentiousness, or who have furnished the greatest facilities for the indulgence of passion. From the preachers of religion; from pious princes; from the dispensers of justice; from the patrons of order and of law; from Paul, Aurelius, and Hale, the crown is to be transferred to such moralists as Paine, such princes as Charles II., and such judges as Jeffries. But who is prepared to take this ground? This view goes against the common sense and the common judgment of men. There *are* things in man to be restrained, in order that he may be virtuous. It is not sufficient to secure the meed of virtue to say, I am as God made me, and am but acting out the propensities of my nature. What, then, is the mistake which is made in this plea? What fallacy is there in it, for it seems to have plausibility and truth? An answer may be readily given to these questions by making a distinction, which the young man may apply through life to the noblest purposes of self-improvement. In the pleas set up, two things are confounded which are wholly distinct, and to be dealt with on different principles—our constitutional propensities as God made them, and our corrupt propensities which have another origin. The former are to be cultivated and carried to the highest pitch of perfection possible; the latter are to be checked, restrained, subdued. The former are innocent, noble, and ennobling; the latter are debasing and degrading—"earthly, sensual, devilish." There *are* propensities of our nature, and laws of our being, which God has implanted, and which, if kept within proper limits, are harmless, or which may contribute to our highest elevation in the scale of existence. To eat, to drink, to sleep, are laws of our animal being—harmless if restrained, debasing if indulged in contrary to the just rules of temperance; to aspire after knowledge, to seek a "good name," to rise to the fellowship of higher intelligences, to bring out and cultivate the benevolent affections, is to follow nature as God has made us, and never betrays or debases us. But to follow out the inclinations of ambition, and pride, and vanity, and lust and revenge, is a different thing. These debase and sink to a lower level than that of brutes; for, in proportion as we may rise, so may we descend. The star that culminates highest may sink the lowest, and as woman, if vile, sinks lower than man can, so man, if debased, sinks beneath the brute.

Men mistake, then, in this. When they indulge in these things, they are *not*, in any proper sense, acting out their nature. They are not as God made them. They are sunken, debased, fallen. Let men act according to the great laws which He has impressed upon their being, and they will be noble, holy, godlike. Thus acting, man would have met the approbation of his Maker, and might have pleaded innocent to the charges of guilt. But let him not give indulgence to corruption, and then seek shelter in the plea, "I am as God made me."

III. A third ground of defence would be, that the law of God is stern and severe, and that his requirements are of such a nature, that man has no power to comply with them. The position which would be taken is, that there is no obligation where there is no ability, and that, as man now has no power to yield obedience, he cannot be held to be chargeable with guilt. The principle here stated seems to be one that is based on common sense, and that must ever command the assent of all men who are not blinded by theory or by prejudice. It is impossible for man to feel himself guilty or blameworthy for not doing what he had no power to do. He may count it a misfortune, or he may experience calamities and suffer losses, because he has no greater power; but it is not possible for him to feel on this account the compunctions of remorse. With the limited powers of man, it is impossible for him ever to feel himself guilty for not creating a world, or not guiding the stars, or not raising the dead, and he cannot conceive that, by any revelation whatever, or any course of reasoning, or any requirement laid on him, he should ever feel himself blameworthy for not doing those things. If, then, it were so that God has required of man more than he is in any sense able to perform, the nature which he has given us (and which, in that case, would be a very strange and unaccountable endowment) would teach us two things: one, that his government was a tyranny, and the other, that man could not be to blame. Such a creature, under such a government, might be made to suffer, but could not be punished; he might experience pain of body, but he never would know the pangs of remorse. But is this so? The law itself is the best exponent of the views of God on this subject, and that law is clear and explicit. "Thou shalt love the Lord thy God with all thy heart, and with all thy soul, and with all thy mind." This is the first and great commandment. And the second is like unto it: "Thou shalt love thy neighbour as thyself. On these two commandments hang all the law and the prophets." Matt. xxii. 37–40. Could any thing be more reasonable than this? God asks nothing which we have not; nothing which we have no power to render. He asks "*all*" the heart, the mind, the strength, and he asks no more. He does not require for himself the service claimed of angelic powers, but that adapted to our own; he asks no love for our neighbour which we do not feel that we are abundantly able to show to ourselves. To take shelter from the charges against us, under the plea that our Maker has required services beyond our power to render, is therefore directly in the face of his own requirements; is to charge him with tyranny where his requirements are as clear as noonday, and as equal as they can be, and where he has expressly told us that the plea cannot and will not be sustained:—"O house of Israel, are not my ways equal? Are not your ways unequal? Therefore will I judge you, O house of Israel, according to your ways, saith the Lord God. Repent and turn yourselves from all your transgressions, so iniquity shall not be your ruin." Ezek. xviii. 29, 30.

IV. A fourth ground of defence, on which man charged with guilt is secretly relying in self-justification, is, that the penalty of the law of God is unreasonably severe, and that no consideration can make it right to recompense the errors and crimes of this short life with eternal punishment. The ground here taken is, that it would be *wrong* for God to punish man in this manner, and therefore that man has a claim to eternal life. The inference drawn by the sinner charged with guilt is, that if the penalty is unreasonably severe, he cannot be held to be guilty, and has a right to disregard the law of his Maker. Now it is not designed here to attempt a defence of the doctrine of eternal puishment, or to show that the impenitent sinner will suffer for ever. It must be admitted that there are mysteries on that subject which the human powers at present cannot explain. All that the subject demands is to examine this reasoning which the sinner sets up in his defence. Is the severity of a penalty then, even supposing it to be wholly unreasonable, a valid excuse for violating law or for doing wrong? It is possible to conceive, for such things have been, that the penalty for the crime of treason may be entirely too severe; that its execution may be attended with barbarous cruelty; and that it may be followed by a taint of blood, and by inflictions on the family of the traitor wholly unjustifiable by any principles of equity; but would this be any justification of the act of treason? Does it make the betrayal of the state a matter of duty or of innocence? Is it such a meritorious act that he who performs it has a claim on the offices and emoluments which a sovereign has to bestow on deserving subjects? So in the matter before us. If there are things which we cannot explain about future punishment; if it has a degree of severity which we have no means of vindicating; is it fair to infer that it is *right* to violate the law of heaven, and has he who does it a *claim* on the crown of glory? Yet this seems to be what is involved in this ground of defence which a man charged with sin sets up. Would it be reasonable or proper for him to suppose that God would *admit* a plea, drawn from his own alleged injustice and cruelty, as a reason for the habitual violation of his law? But the plea has no force in another respect. Our relations to the administration of justice are not only concerned with the question what the penalty *is*, but with the question whether it is practicable to avoid it? There may be reasons operating in the appointment of a penalty which we do not understand. It is only necessary for us to know what the penalty *is*, and to have such freedom that we can avoid it by a correct life. They who live in England now, or they who lived under the administration of the laws in times of greater severity, can have no reason to complain, so far as appears, of the punishment affixed there to treason. It can be readily seen, indeed, that there would be much that would be painful and disgraceful in being drawn on a hurdle to the place of execution; in being quartered and publicly exposed; in the confiscation of property; the degradation of a family, and the taint of blood. Why should a good citizen, who did not design to commit treason, complain of it? It would be easy to avoid it, and his knowing the severity of the punishment should only make him the more cautious to do his duty to his country. Least of all, knowing what the penalty was, could he set up a plea of innocence when he had betrayed his country, on the ground that the penalty was severe. Without pursuing this reasoning any farther, may it not be asked whether it is not just as applicable to the government of God as to a human administration?

V. There is but one other ground of defence or self-justification which the accused sinner can be supposed to set up. It is that too great results are made to depend on the present life; that life is too short, that our days are too few and fleeting, that our continuance here is too uncertain, that we are liable to be too suddenly called away, to make it proper to suspend so great interests on any thing that we can do here. The accused sinner would take the ground that eternal consequences demand a longer probation, and that the longevity of the antediluvian patriarchs was a period quite circumscribed enough to make it proper to suspend so great interests upon life. Much might be said in reply to this; but the subject may be made, perhaps, sufficiently plain by a few remarks. Reference might be made to the instances which occur in the life of an individual, or in a state, where the most momentous and far-reaching results are made to depend on the action of a moment; but, without dwelling on the numerous illustrations which occur on that point, two remarks may be made in reply to this ground of defence: One is, that, as experience has, in millions of cases, shown, the time allotted to man is ample for a preparation for eternity. Countless hosts before the throne have found it so, and millions are on their way to join them who find the period of probation abundant to enable them to prepare for heaven. That all others are not with them in the same blissful path, is not because life is too short to enter it, but is to be traced to other causes. Men require length of days to amass wealth, or to perfect their schemes of earthly aggrandizement; but the purposes of salvation do not need it. The giving of the heart to God in sincerity through Jesus Christ—an act which may be performed in the briefest period which a moral agent lives—is enough to secure salvation. Wealth or honour could not be secured in that way in so brief a period; but the salvation of the soul may be. The other remark is, that this vindication is set up in circumstances which painfully demonstrate that it cannot be sincere. Not time enough to secure salvation! Too great interests suspended on this brief period of existence! Unreasonable to make eternal results depend on the fleeting hours of this short life. And from whom do these objections come? From those on whom the hours of life hang heavily, and "who are often wishing its different periods at an end;" from those who are impatient for some season of festivity or enjoyment to arrive, and who elude the slow-revolving wheels of time; from those whose days are weariness and sadness, for they have nothing to interest them, nothing to do; from those whose principal study is the art of killing time, and all whose plans have no other end; from those who waste the hours that might be consecrated to prayer in needless slumber, and from whose lips each morning, while they are now locked in repose, there *might* proceed the earnest breathing of a penitent heart that would insure salvation; from those who, over worthless, or corrupting verse, or in the perusal of romances, or in day-dreams, or at the toilet, waste, each day, time enough to secure the redemption of the soul. From such lips and hearts; from those who live thus, and to whom life puts on these forms, assuredly the objection should not be heard, that too great results are made to depend on this short life, and that therefore they are blameless in neglecting God.

If these are correct views, then the sinner cannot justify himself. It has been shown that he cannot deny the reality of the facts charged on him, and the grounds of defence which the human heart is disposed to set up in self-vindication have been considered. It is not improper, at this stage of the argument, to make a personal appeal to the reader, and to ask him to consider the views which have been suggested as a personal matter. The conclusion which we have reached is, that the unpardoned sinner is a lost and ruined being; that he is under condemnation; that he is held to be guilty in the sight of God; that he is soon to be arraigned on charges involving the question of his eternal welfare, and that, unless he is in some way acquitted of those charges, they will sink him to ruin. The views which have been thus expressed, lie at the foundation of the system of salvation by grace. They are such as, when felt, lead to the conviction of sin, and to that sense of helplessness which is preparatory to the reception of pardon and salvation by the grace of the gospel. If these views produced their fitting effect, they would leave the impression of guilt, helplessness, and danger on the mind of every one who is not converted and pardoned. Sooner or later every one will feel this. The sinner may be unwilling to admit the force of these arguments now; for no one, if he can help it, will be overwhelmed with the conviction of guilt, or have his mind unsettled and harassed by apprehensions of danger. But not always can he put this subject far from him. He will lie down and die, and those are sad feelings which the dying sinner has, when he reflects that his life has been spent in sin, and that he is dying under condemnation. He will, from the bed of death, look out tremblingly on the eternal world—on that shoreless and bottomless ocean on which he is about to be launched, and it will be sad to feel that he is about to enter that vast and fearful world, an unpardoned sinner. He will tread his way up to the bar of a holy God; and, little as he may be concerned about that now, it will be sad to tread that gloomy way alone, and to feel, as he goes, that he is under condemnation. He will stand and look on the burning throne of Deity, and on his final Judge; he will await, and with what an agony of emotion! the sentence that shall fall from his lips sealing his eternal doom. Oh, how can he then be just with God? How vindicate his ways before him? How stand there and justify his neglect of his commands, his neglect of prayer, his neglect of the offers of mercy, his neglect of his own soul? How, then, can he show his Maker that it was *right* not to love him, not to pray to him, not to thank him, not to embrace his offer of mercy? How can he show that it was right for him to live without hope and without God in the world? How *can* he be saved?

IV. *Man cannot merit salvation.*

In the previous section it has been shown that man cannot justify himself either by denying the facts charged on him, or by showing that he had a right to do as he has done. The inquiry at once presents itself, How then can he be saved? There are but two ways conceivable: one by his own merits—that is, that he somehow deserves to be saved; the other, by the merits of another, or of others. If it be in the latter way, it must either be by the merits of Christ, or it must be because certain eminent saints have done more than was demanded of them, and that their merits, garnered up and deposited in certain hands, can be made over to others. It is not proposed to inquire now whether this latter method be in accordance with truth, but whether men can merit salvation for themselves. They can do it if their lives are such that they deserve to go to heaven, or if it would be wrong for God to punish them forever, for "God will not do wickedly, neither will the Almighty pervert judgment." Job xxxv. 12. The importance of this inquiry will be at once perceived, for the great mass of mankind are depending on their own righteousness for salvation, and the grand issue between Christianity and the world lies just in this point. There are two subjects of inquiry, which, if they can be made clear, will conduct to the truth in the case.

I. What is meant by merit?

II. Can man merit heaven?

I. What is meant by merit? The word is in common use, and the common use is the correct one. We speak of merit when a man deserves a reward for something which he has done, or when it would be wrong to withhold it. He renders to him who employs him an equivalent, or what is of as much value as is paid him for his services. Two or three simple illustrations will make the common use of the word plain, and show its bearing on the question before us.

You hire a day-labourer. You make a bargain with him at the outset; he complies with the terms on his part, and at night you pay him. He has earned, deserved, or merited that which you pay him; he has been faithful to his part of the agreement, and the service which he has rendered is *worth* as much to you as the wages which you pay him. You *could* have done the work, perhaps, yourself; but you preferred to hire him, for you might yourself be more profitably or pleasantly employed. At all events, what he has done is worth to you all which you pay him, and it would be wrong, on every consideration, for you to withhold it. If you choose to give him, any thing more than was specified in the agreement, it would be a gratuity; but that which you agreed to give him he has a right to demand, and you are not at liberty to withhold it. He has deserved or earned it, for he has rendered you a full equivalent, according to the terms of the contract.

A man enlists to defend his country as a soldier. It is supposed, in the contract which is made with him, that his service will be of equal value to his country with the pay which he receives. By fighting its battles; by guarding its seacoasts, villages, towns, and hamlets; by keeping its fields from being trod down by an enemy; by protecting the lives of aged men, helpless women and children; and by defending the flag of the nation from insult, it is supposed that his services are worth full as much to the country as he receives in his pay. The pay is graduated, in part, by the best estimate which can be made of the value of the service which a man can render in this calling, and the nation would be no *gainer* by dismissing him from its service. He complies with the contract, and when he comes and shows his scars, and tells of his perils and privations, his weary marches and his risk of life, and his separation from home and friends in the cause of his country, his country will not grudge him the pittance that he receives; for he has earned it and merited it, and it would not be right to withhold it from him.

You employ a physician. The service which he renders you is regarded as a full equivalent for what you pay him. What you receive from him in his care, attention, skill, and sympathy, you consider to be fully equal in value to the compensation which you give him. Your relief from pain, your recovery of the use of your bodily powers, or the restoration to your affectionate embrace, in sound health, of a wife or child, you consider as an ample equivalent for all which he asks you for his services, and, were an election to be made, you would much prefer to pay the amount of the physician's fees, to going through those sorrows again. What he receives, you feel that on every account he deserves or has earned, and it would be wrong for you to withhold it.

In each of these cases, that is true which the apostle

Paul affirms: "To him that worketh, the reward is not reckoned of grace, but of debt." These illustrations will explain the proper sense of the word "merit." In each instance, there is an equivalent for what is paid; in each instance, what is demanded could be enforced as a claim of right. There is no other sense in which the words *merit or desert* can be used. All besides this is *favour* or *grace*. If you choose to give the day-labourer, the soldier, or the professional man, more than you agreed, or more than his services are worth to you, you have an undoubted right to do so; but you would not put it on the ground of his merit or desert. You would feel that it was a gratuity which could not be enforced by justice, and where no blame would be attached to you if it were withheld. If his perils, or services, or self-denials and sacrifices, were greater than you anticipated when the contract was made, or if the service rendered was really of more value to you than the amount which you are pledged to give him, you may consider yourself bound by equity to give him more; for you feel that he has earned or merited it. Thus you would be glad to compensate, if you could, the wounded soldier who has perilled all in your defence; and on the same principle, if you could do it, you would wish to recompense the man who, at the risk of his life, should save your child from the devouring flame, or from a watery grave.

II. We come now to apply these principles to the case before us. Keeping this explanation of the nature of merit in view, we approach the inquiry, whether man can merit heaven. Can he be saved because he deserves it? Can he be so profitable to God that he can advance a just claim to an admission to the world of glory? If he can, he will be saved; if he cannot, he should lose no time in endeavouring to ascertain whether there is any other way by which he may be saved? In reference to this inquiry, the following considerations may be submitted:

(1.) Man can render no service to his Maker for which the reward of heaven would be a proper equivalent. Or, in other words, the amount of service which he can render is not such as can be properly measured by the reward of everlasting life. His service to his Maker and to the universe is not of so much value that he can claim eternal life as an equivalent. We have seen that this does exist in the case of the day-labourer, the soldier, and the physician. We can see a correspondence between the service rendered and the compensation, in these cases, which makes us feel that there is a propriety and equity in the reward. But, in reference to any connection or correspondence between the service which man can render his Maker and the rewards of heaven, we can see no such propriety and equity. The one does not measure the other. The universe is not so much benefitted by the service of man, that everlasting life and infinite happiness would be only a fair equivalent, or that wrong would be done if that reward should be withheld. Yet is it not a fair principle that this must be the case if man deserves or merits salvation? Must there not have been such an amount or value of service rendered that it would be injustice to withhold the reward—injustice such as would occur in the case of the faithful day-labourer, the soldier, the physician, if their pay was withheld? That must be extraordinary service rendered to the universe, or to God, which deserves the glories of an eternal heaven as its reward. That is extraordinary service rendered to you, if a stranger rescues a child from impending death and restores him to your transported bosom, and you feel that no compensation which you can make would be more than an equivalent. That was extraordinary service which was rendered to their country by the heroes of the American Revolution; and, as the results of their patriotism and perils are seen in the unexampled prosperity of the land which they rescued, we feel that the pension of the old soldier is a very inadequate recompense. That was extraordinary virtue which led the father of his country through the trials, perplexities, and perils of that time, and which he evinced when, having laid the foundation of our liberty, he voluntarily retired to private life, leaving the people in the enjoyment of freedom, and we feel that no wealth which the nation had to offer, no monument of marble or of brass which art could rear, would equal the measure of his praise. But has man any such extraordinary service to render to his Maker and to the universe? Has he done any thing, can he do any thing for God and for the empire which He rules, which would make the wealth of heaven and its everlasting glories only an equitable recompense? Obviously, there is no congruity, no fitness, no correspondence between the one and the other, and when men talk about *meriting* heaven, or when they feel that they *deserve* to be saved, they have not well considered the import of language. They use it correctly in common life. Is it not right to ask that it may be used with the same exactness in religion?

(2.) This general principle, which appears so obvious, may be illustrated with particular reference to the *religious* service which men render to their Maker. If man merits heaven and is to be saved on account of his own deservings, it will be conceded that the service must be in some way connected with religion, or of such a nature that it can be regarded as the service of God. You would not feel yourself bound to pay a day-labourer if, instead of working for you, he worked all day for your neighbour, or was idle; you would not think of recompensing a soldier if he slept on his post, or fought under the standard of the enemy.

There *are* religious men upon the earth, men who are honestly engaged in the service of God, and who, in connection with their religious services, are looking for the rewards of heaven. Our subject, in its progress, demands that we inquire just here, whether the service which they render is of such a nature that they merit eternal life? Is it because they are so profitable to God and his cause that the rewards of heaven would be only an equivalent for the service which they render? Let us look a moment at this matter.

A man who is truly religious renders a real and valuable service to the cause of virtue and of God. His existence is a blessing and not a curse. The universe is made better and happier because he lives. It would be a loss to society and to the universe, if his example, his conversation, his plans of wisdom, his experience, and his generous deeds, were annihilated, or had not been. When the "rewards" of heaven are bestowed upon him, it will not be without some reference to a fitness or propriety that they should be so bestowed. There will be a sense in which every man will be "rewarded according to his works." But, in reference to the bearing of this indisputable fact on the case before us, there are two or three things that deserve to be considered.

(*a*) One is, that your individual existence is not necessary to secure the service which is now actually rendered. God is not so dependent on you that he could not accomplish his purposes without you, or that, if you should be removed, service of equal value might not be secured in some other way. By the great law of his kingdom, the agency of man is to be employed in the accomplishment of his purposes; but your individual agency is not indispensable. The services of a minister of the Gospel who is eminently useful, and who is at a time of life, and has a measure of experience and learning, that seems to fit him for an important station, can be supplied by some one that God can place in his stead. When he is taken away, a mighty chasm, indeed, seems to be made; but his withdrawal soon ceases to be felt, for others rush in to fill his place; as the surface of the ocean soon becomes smooth, and it seems to be as full as it was before, though the waterspout has lifted up and carried away a portion of the mighty deep, or the sun causes it to ascend in vapours; for streams and rivers all the while pour into that ocean and it is always kept full. The man that was so learned and wise that it seemed that no one else could supply his place at the head of a college, or so sagacious and prudent that it seemed that some vast plan of benevolence depended on him, is removed—but the chasm is soon filled up; just as in storming a city, when the leader falls, some subaltern steps into his place, and leads on the conquest with the freshness of youth, and with wisdom and valour that had been in training for just this breach which God foresaw would occur. Let us not then suppose that *our* services are indispensable to God. Let us not imagine, that he is dependent on us or is under obligation to us. In the bosom of society there are undeveloped powers which will more than fill our places; in the church there is piety maturing which can do more than we can do—and the very purposes of human advancement cherished in the divine mind, may demand our removal.

(*b*) The religious man will reflect further that his best services do not *deserve* heaven. A man who is truly pious, and who has any proper sense of his own imperfections, and of the glory to which he is looking forward, never feels that there is any proportion between the services which he renders to God here, and the immortal blessedness to which he hopes to be elevated hereafter. He renders no service to the cause of truth and virtue, which, in his own estimation, is an equivalent for the rewards which he trusts are in reserve for him, and after all his toils he feels that those rewards will be not of "debt" but of grace, and that he is an "unprofitable servant." God has taken effectual care of this in his plan of salvation; and whoever he may be that expects heaven on the ground of his own merit, it will not be he who gives evidence that he is truly a devoted and faithful servant of God.

(*c*) If, however, at any time this feeling of *merit* or claim should arise in the mind of a truly pious man, it is effectually checked by a moment's reflection on the way in which he has been disposed to engage in the service of God at all. It is not by any native inclination or tendency of mind; it has been solely by grace. Whatever service he may render, the origin of it is to be traced back to that distinguishing mercy which led him to seek after God, when he was disposed to pursue his own ways; which recalled him when he was a wretched wanderer from the paths of truth and salvation. The case is like this. You go into a "market place" and find a man "idle," and inclined to be idle. You reason and remonstrate with him, and by persevering entreaty and the offer of reward, arouse him from his indolence and induce him to spend his time in your service. Now, however faithful he may be, or however valuable may be the services which he may render you, he will never feel that any merit is to be attributed to himself. He owes to you his industrious habits, and all which he can ever secure by his labour. Or to take a case more in point. You go into a miserable hovel, and find a wretch in the lowest stages of vice and misery. He was once a man in heart as well as in form, but now he has wholly lost the manhood of the one and almost of the other. He is loathsome by vice and disease, and is a wretched outcast. He has no wish *to be* a man again; he has no energy to arouse him from his condition; he has no friend to take him by the hand, or even to pity him in his vices and woes. You take compassion on him. You clothe him in decent apparel. You remonstrate with him on his evil course. You remind him of what he was, and tell him of what he may be still. You rekindle the dying spark of self-respect; show him that he may yet forsake the paths of vice and be respectable again; gradually breathe into him the wish to be virtuous and pure and happy; give him a comfortable home to dwell in, and a piece of land to cultivate as his own; speak kindly to him when he is discouraged; shield him when he is tempted by his old companions; offer him ample reward for any services which he may render you; and he returns to the ways of industry, and rises to a condition of competency and respectability. Perchance in doing this, you have lighted on a "gem of purest ray serene" in that rubbish, and the unhappy wretch whom you have rescued, had a genius which takes its place among the brightest constellations of talent, and its light beams afar on the nations. Yet how will he feel in these circumstances? Will he feel that this is to be traced to his own merit, or that the wealth or honour which may gather around him are the measure of his desert? But for you he will feel that he would even now have been occupying that wretched hovel, or more likely would have been in the drunkard's grave. Whatever he has of moral worth, influence, or reputation is to be traced to you. Thus it is with the Christian; and feeling this, he cannot regard himself as so profitable to God as to merit the rewards of heaven.

(3.) If it were conceded that the rewards of heaven were a proper recompense for the religious services which man can render to God, yet they would not be the suitable reward of those who are commonly expecting heaven on the ground of their own merits. The truly religious man, as we have seen, expects heaven, not on the ground of his own deserts, but through the grace of God. We may, therefore, lay the case of such out of the question in the inquiry whether men can deserve salvation by their own merits. The other class, embracing the mass of mankind, expect to be saved because they deserve to be saved; or, which amounts to the same thing, because they do not deserve to be damned. The ground of their claim is not that they are religious,—for they do not profess to be, and not that they render such service to the cause of God that the rewards of heaven would be an *equivalent* for their services—for they do not profess to be engaged in his service at all. What then is it? It is that they are honest, true, faithful to their contracts, honourable in their dealings, disposed to aid others in their distress, and courteous in their treatment of their fellow-men. One who leads such a life they suppose does not *deserve* to be cast off and made miserable forever; or, what is the same thing, they suppose that in all justice and equity, he *ought* to be made happy in a future state; that is, that he may be saved on the ground of his own merits. What is now the value of this claim? With the principles before us which have been laid down, let us endeavour to answer this question. This is the inquiry, Is heaven the appropriate reward of such a life? An illustration or two will make this plainer than abstract reasoning would do. You hire a man as a day-labourer. He comes to you at night for his pay. If he has been industrious according to the contract, and faithful to your interests, the case is a plain one, and you do not hesitate. But you put the interrogatory to him, "Did you go into my vineyard, and spend the day in cultivating it for me, and in a careful regard to my interests?" "No," is the honest reply, "but I *have* spent the day diligently; I have not been an idle man. I have attended to the cultivation of my own vineyard, and been faithful to my family, and I may appeal to all my neighbours for my general courtesy and honesty of life." If you now say that this is a case which is so palpably absurd that it never could occur, it may be replied that it has been made absurd on purpose. Such a man would be only speaking out, in the honesty of his heart, what is the secret claim of every one who is not engaged in the service of God, and who yet feels that he ought to be saved. He does not even profess to be attending to the interests of his Creator or engaged in his service. You send a clerk into the Western States to collect your debts. He returns. "Have you been diligent and successful in the duty assigned you?" "I *was* diligent. I travelled much. In all my journey I injured no one; I treated no one roughly; I addressed no one in any other manner than in the language required in refined life. I also entered valuable lands for myself, and have a prospect of rising to affluence and respectability." "But what has this to do with the reward which would be appropriate for one employed in *my* service?" "Nothing," a child would reply. But has it not just as much to do with it as the claim of a man who does not profess to serve his Maker, and who lives only to regard his own interests, has to the rewards of heaven? You have a servant or an apprentice whom you have a right to punish if he does wrong. You enjoin on him a specific duty, a duty of much importance to yourself, and one that is clearly reasonable in its nature. At the proper time you call him to an account. The duty is not discharged; the service is not rendered. He pleads, however, that he does not deserve punishment. He has been steadily engaged all the while; he has been entirely honest and upright in his dealings with his fellow-servants; he has treated them with perfect courtesy, and has even acquired an enviable reputation for amiableness of manners; nay, he has more than once relieved a fellow-servant that was poor, and sick, and dying. All this is very well, it would be said in reply; but how can this constitute a claim for the specific reward which was offered? How can it show that he who has wholly omitted a known and specific duty does not deserve the punishment which was threatened? With what face could such a servant claim the reward due to faithful service in the cause of his master? These plain and obvious principles are as applicable to religion as they are to the common transactions of life. God requires of us a specific service. It is not general and indefinite, or left to our choice as to what it shall be. It is that we shall serve *him;* that we shall obey his commands; that we shall seek his glory; that we shall love him, honour him, and treat him as our God; that we shall be penitent for our past sins, and be willing to accept his favour on his own terms; that we shall be serious, religious, prayerful, believing, holy. If this is done, he promises heaven. But it is *not* done. Those now referred to do not even lay claim to *any* of these things. One of the last things that they would claim, or that their friends would think of claiming for them, is that they are religious, or that they act habitually from reference to the will of their Creator. They claim to be moral, honest, true, urbane, kind, but how can this lay the foundation of a claim to the appropriate reward of piety? How, in these things, can they render *any* service to God, when they do not even intend it, which would be the proper basis of his rewarding them in heaven? No more than the day labourer, the clerk, and the servant carefully attentive to their *own* interests, but wholly regardless of the interests of their employers, can expect a reward.

Having thus stated these arguments, to show that man cannot by any services which he can render, make himself so profitable to God as to merit salvation, or be of so much advantage to his cause as to be an equivalent for the reward of heaven, it remains only to remark,

(4.) Fourthly, that, if he cannot do this by a life of obedient holiness, he cannot by any offering which he has it in his power to make. The reasons for this are so obvious as to make it needless to dwell on them. One is, that no offering which man can make, can be of any advantage or profit to God. He is made no richer by any oblation of silver and gold which we can bring him; he has no unsatisfied wants which can be supplied by our ministrations. "If I were hungry," says he, "I would not tell thee; for the world is mine and the fullness thereof. Will I eat the flesh of bulls or drink the blood of goats?" Ps. iv. 12, 13. Another reason is, that all that we possess is his, and we can give to him nothing to which he has not already a prior and supreme right. "Every beast of the forest," says he, "is mine, and the cattle upon a thousand hills. I know all the fowls of the mountains, and the wild beasts of the forest are mine." Ps. l. 10, 11. Another reason is, that nothing that we could offer would be a compensation for our past offences, or repair the evils which we have done by our neglect of duty and by our open sins. "Wherewith shall I come before the Lord, and bow myself before the High God? Shall I come before him with burnt-offerings, with calves of a year old? Will the Lord be pleased with thousands of rams, or with ten thousands of rivers of oil? Shall I give my first-born for my transgression, the fruit of my body for the sin of my soul?" Micah vi. 6, 7. And how shall a man profit God; how lay him under obligation to save him; how render such service as to be an equivalent for heaven? Shall he flagellate his own body? Yet how will that profit God? Shall he gird sackcloth on his loins, or wear an irritating haircloth garment to torment himself? Yet how will that benefit his Maker? Will he go on a pilgrimage to some distant shrine? How will his Maker be advantaged by that? Will he shut himself up in a gloomy cell, and withdraw from the light of the sun, and the moon, and the stars, and from the society of living men, and doom himself to wretchedness and wo? But will his God be made more rich, or happy by such austerities? Will he seize upon the objects dearest to his heart, and destroy before bloody altars the lives which his Creator has given? But will it profit God if we kill his own creatures, and pour out their blood before him? If none of these things will do, with what plea of merit can we come before him? How can we render such service as to have a claim on heaven?

In view of this train of thought, two additional observations may be made.

1. First, we see the falsehood of that system of religion which speaks of human merit; of the treasured and garnered merits of the saints of former times. If the principles now suggested are correct, how can there have been any such extraordinary and superabounding merit in past times that it may be available now for men? If there were such treasured merit left by the saints of other days, it might still be a question what claim of right any man has now to distribute it to others; but any such claim of superabounding merit is alike at variance with the Bible, and with every just principle of reason. Yet this doctrine is one of the principal supports of the papacy, and is one of the dogmas that come to our shores and demand credence in our land, and of this generation. It will be shown hereafter, that there *is* ample merit in him who died to atone for our sins, to supply all our deficiencies, and the results of which may be ours. The claim that superabounding merit has been wrought out by the saints, derogates and almost annihilates this; and the claim that his merits and theirs are lodged in human hands to be dispensed or withheld at pleasure by a priesthood, is one of the principal supports of the most appalling and terrific system of spiritual despotism that has ever tyrannized over man. Thanks to him who has bought us our portion, the disposal of the merits of his sacrifice is committed to no human hands, and can be interrupted by no human power!

2. This subject is one of direct practical interest to all. If we are ever saved, there will be a good reason for it—for nothing is merely arbitrary in the matter of salvation. There are but two ways possible of being saved—the one by our own merits, the other by the merits of another. If in regard to the latter there are no merits of the "saints" on which we can rely; no merits of parents or pious friends of which we can avail ourselves, then the merits of the Lord Jesus constitute the only foreign dependence which we can

have. The whole question is then just this. Do we rely on our own merits for salvation, or the merits of Jesus? Here the world is divided—the Christian on the one side; the pagan, the Mohammedan, the infidel, the moralist on the other. This single question separates the inhabitants of the globe into two great parties never to be united. But if the principles above suggested are correct, it may be put to every man—to his reason, his conscience, his heart, whether he *has* any merit on which he can rely as a ground of salvation? Has he done any thing for which the equivalent is to be found in the rewards of an eternal heaven? Has he so deserved the rewards of life, has he rendered such services to his Maker that he can stand at the final bar, where we all must soon stand, and claim an admission to heaven? Can he demand it as a right that heaven's portal should be thrown open to him, and he be welcomed there? If so, on what ground? What is the basis of the claim? Religion? The unconverted sinner makes no pretension to it. Repentance? He has never shed a tear over his sins. The love of God? He has no spark of love to that glorious Being in his heart. Sacrifices in his service? He has made none. An honest endeavour to do his will? He has never made this the rule of life. What *is* the service which he has rendered? What has been the life which he has led? What is the state of his account with God? What is the condition of his heart? O, let him look at the broken law of God, his violated Sabbaths, his rejected gospel, his grieved Spirit, his neglected word; let him look at his own life of thoughtlessness, selfishness, and vanity; his neglect of prayer, his pride and opposition to God; let him look at the sins of childhood and the worldliness and wickedness of riper years; let him look at the times when God has called and he has refused, when the Saviour has stretched out his hands and he would not regard it; let him look at his broken vows and promises, the times when he promised that he would be a Christian if he reached a certain period of life, the solemn covenant which he made when he was sick, that if God would spare him he would be his; let him look at these things and then see whether he has a claim to an admission to heaven, and whether he can be received there because he has been profitable to God.

V. *What is meant by the merits of Christ?*

There are few phrases in more common use than the merits of Christ; few declarations that are repeated more frequently by ministers of the gospel and others, than that man can be saved only by His merits; and few things that are more frequently uttered in prayer than that we plead His merits only for our salvation. The frequency with which this expression occurs, and the bearing which it has on the general subject now under consideration, make it proper that we should attempt an explanation of it. Common as the use of it is, a formal attempt to explain it is not often made, and it is to be feared that it is often used without an intelligent apprehension of its meaning.

The phrase does not occur in the Bible; but the idea which is intended to be conveyed by it exists there as a vital and central thought in the whole plan of justification by faith. In the prosecution of this subject it will be proper,

1. To explain what is meant when we speak of the merits of Christ; and

2. To show in what his merits consisted.

1. What is meant by the merits of Christ?

The general idea is expressed in the passage—John i. 16: "and of his fulness have we all received, and grace for for grace." There was an "*abundance*" or "*fulness*" in him of which we might partake; that is, there was a completeness—*πλήρωμα*—which, in our conscious want or deficiency, could meet all our necessities, so that we could receive "grace" corresponding with that which was in him. When we speak of the merits of Christ in connection with our salvation, it is meant that there was an amount of merit in his services which he did not need for any personal advantage or for himself; which had been secured with a special purpose to supply the great and undisputed deficiency of man, and which can be made available to us on certain conditions, and in the way which God has revealed as the ground of our acceptance. The main object is not now to prove that there *are* such merits treasured up in Christ, but to explain the language. Whether the doctrine be true, and if there be such merit in him, how it may be available to us, will be the subject of future inquiry. In the explanation of the subject we may then advert to,

(1.) The doctrine respecting *merit* laid down in the last section. A man merits a reward when he has earned or deserved it; when he has fully complied with the terms of the bargain; when his services are worth as much to you as you pay him. We may recall the illustrations from the day-labourer, the soldier, the physician, in each of which cases it was said that the service rendered was fully equal in value to the pay which was given. The service measures the pay; the one is equal, or is supposed to be, to the other. To withhold the compensation is injustice, or is palpably wrong. This is the ordinary and proper sense in which the word *merit* is used among men, and it was in this sense that we endeavoured to show that man cannot merit salvation. We observe,

(2.) That cases may arise where much more may be done for you than one who is in your employ is strictly bound to perform. A reference to some of these cases will enable us to explain the subject before us.

(*a*) You have a man in your employ engaged under the ordinary condition of service as a labourer or clerk. Without any special agreement with him, or without any thing being said about it in your contract, he is to do what is commonly understood to be required in that condition of life; what is usually done by those in the same employment. He is to be at his post at a certain hour in the morning, and to remain until a certain hour in the evening, and is to be faithful to his employer's interest, and diligent in the prosecution of the business entrusted to him. On these conditions, without any thing more specific, the contract is usually made with clerks, and book-keepers, and day-labourers, and journeymen-mechanics, and lawyers and ministers of the gospel. It is not deemed necessary to be any more specific than that they shall be faithful to the interests of their employers, and render the amount of service which is usually expected in that occupation. But it is very possible to conceive that one may go much beyond that. He may be engaged at a much earlier hour than is usual, and may prolong his toils far into the shades of night. He may evince uncommon tact and sagacity in the management of affairs entrusted to him, and such may be his skill and success that his services may have a value far beyond any thing which you had anticipated in the contract. You would not feel yourself at liberty to turn him off, or to complain if he had *not* done this; will not feel that he has a legal claim on you for any thing *more* than you promised to pay him, for you did not contract with him for this special service; but you will be likely to feel that he has a claim of honour on you; and if, when he leaves your service, you know of any situation of special advantage that can be obtained, you would feel yourself under a sort of moral obligation to endeavour to secure it for him. Here is something *merited* beyond what he was *bound* to do.

(*b*) A second case. A man in your employ may be placed in circumstances where he may have an opportunity of doing something for your *special advantage*, though of a nature which was not distinctly specified in your contract with him. He may have great sagacity, and may watch the changes and chances in the market, and enable you to make important and advantageous purchases; he may be in possession of intelligence respecting coming changes in the markets which may be of great service to you; or he may, by uncommon tact in business, be enabled to save you from inextricable bankruptcy. Now, if he is a mere book-keeper, or salesman, you could hardly *claim*, as a matter of right, that he should bring his sagacity in these things into your service; perhaps you would hardly blame him if he took advantage of it to advance his own interests, provided he did not injure you. His specific business is to keep your books correctly, or to sell your goods in the manner in which you shall direct him, and his sagacity and tact in *these* departments you have a right to require to be employed in your service. But your contract and your claim extend no farther. Yet, if he *chooses* to go beyond this, and actually, while he incurs no possible risks, is the means of great advantage to you, an honourable man would feel that he *deserved* an appropriate acknowledgment. Many instances of this kind might be referred to; but these will illustrate the point under consideration.

(3.) It is necessary to make but one other remark, in order to see the bearing of these illustrations on the case before us. Reference has been made to *abounding merit;* to cases in which service is rendered *beyond* what was in the contract; to that which was wholly voluntary, and yet where there would be a claim *in honour*, at least, for a suitable acknowledgment, or where an honourable man would feel himself under obligation to bestow a reward. The remark which is now to be made, is that he who has this extra claim on you may do what he pleases with the reward which you may feel willing to give. It may not be needful for him, or he may not choose to make use of it for himself, but he may be disposed to make another use of it, which will develop some trait of mind that will by no means diminish your respect for his character. Suppose some such cases as the following in the application of the instances referred to: that he should ask you to aid a younger brother of his that was just beginning business, and who was greatly in need of credit; or that, on the supposition that he should die, you would show kindness to an aged father or mother; or that you should appropriate the gratuity which you designed for him to some young man who was struggling to obtain an education. Or, suppose that the faithful servant should ask you to release from bondage his wife or child, in consideration of the extra and quite equivalent services which he had rendered to you. Or, to take another case, suppose a friend of his had, in an unhappy moment, defrauded you, might he not ask you to "set that to his account?" In either case, would you not feel that what he asked he had a right to ask? And would you not be the more deeply affected with respect for his character by this request? He did not perform the extra service for reward. He did not expect it. He did not mention it to you. He did not claim *any* reward. But when *you* felt that he had a claim to it, and pressed it upon him, and would not be refused, he looked not for gorgeous or gay apparel for himself, or for a purse of gold, or a splendid house; nor did he ask you to trumpet his fame; but he looked round on those struggling with poverty, crushed and enfeebled by age, bound in affliction and iron, or burdened with debts, which they could never discharge, and asked you to forget him and to remember them. The developments of such a character would fill your mind with new conceptions of its beauty, and your heart would be insensibly knit with his.

It will be perceived that these illustrations bear on the explanation of what is meant by the merits of Christ. His merit was of this extraordinary or superabundant kind. It was beyond what could have been demanded of him, and was such that if he chose to ask it, or so designed it, it could be made available to others. This leads us to

2. The inquiry, in what his merits consisted. Keeping the remarks already made in view, it will be necessary to show that all that he did when on earth was of this extraordinary character; that he rendered real service to the universe for which the rewards given him will be no more than equivalent; and that his merits were of such a nature that they may be made available to others.

(1.) All that he did was of an extraordinary character, or was service which could not have been demanded of him. This remark is based on the fact that he was divine, and has no pertinency except on that supposition. When it is said that his service, or work, was such as could not be demanded, it is meant that there was no law or obligation which could bind the Divinity to become incarnate, to be an humble teacher of mankind, to minister to their wants with his own hands, or to make an atonement for their transgressions. The entire transaction was of a kind which could be enforced by no law. If He be equal to the Father and one with him, he was under no law but the infinite and eternal law of his own divine nature. There was no obligation on him to become a man, a priest, a sacrifice; to toil, to weep, to die.

Another illustration may be introduced here. There is an heir apparent to a crown. Every consideration of propriety, and perhaps a statute law of the realm, require him to perform the duties of a son in the palace, and to appear and act on all occasions as becomes the first man in the realm next to the throne. But there is no law which requires him to become a day-labourer, or a menial, or that makes it his duty to go into some peasant's cottage and watch the long night by the cradle of a dying child. There may be, perhaps, no law against it if he chooses to do it; but it *cannot* be demanded of him. The Son of God in heaven would appear there always in a manner appropriate to his unequalled relation to the Father; but what law was there requiring him to come down to earth, to be a man of sorrows, to take part in our sadnesses and woes and to die? If he did this, the service was altogether of an extraordinary character, and was entirely a work of merit. This remark is obvious. Its bearings, if conceded to be true, are of great importance. The force and pertinence of this illustration, as has been already remarked, proceeds on the supposition that he is divine. If he is not, however exalted as a created being he may be, it does not appear how he could have *any* extra merit, and consequently how the doctrine of justification by his righteousness could be held. If he is a mere man, or an angel, or an archangel, or creature of any rank, no such extraordinary service could be rendered—none could be made available to us.

We have seen that man may acquire extra merit from his fellow-man, merit which may be made available to others. The question is, why a creature may not do this in reference to the service of God; and why, if the Saviour were less than divine, he might not do the same thing for us? The answer to this question is obvious. When you employ a man, you contract for a certain amount of service or of time. You do not contract for *all* that he has. You contract for what is usual, or what you specify. All beyond the limits of that contract remains his. But there is no such contract, understanding or stipulation, express or understood, between a creature and God. *All* his powers, his time, his talents, his service, his skill, his learning, his influence, belong to his Maker. Of every creature, he demands "all the heart, the mind, the might, the strength." There is not a moment of time in which a creature can feel that he is released from the claim of his Maker; there is not a power or faculty of mind or body which he possesses, that is beyond the range of the demand of His law; there is not a service of prayer, or praise, or sacrifice, which he could render which is beyond the limits of his duty; there is not an act of benevolence to the poor, the needy, the sinful, or the dying, he can perform, which he can feel is beyond the all-comprehensive grasp of the divine command to do good. Can a creature of the Almighty put himself into the midst of a service acceptable to God which he will feel was not required of him? Can he love with an ardour beyond what God requires? Can he maintain a degree of fidelity in temptation beyond what is demanded? Can he stoop to some scene of wo, and do good to a sufferer in a way which the law which binds him to God did not make his duty? Can he evince compassion for the sinful and the sad beyond what the law of his nature and the commandment of his Maker demands? If he cannot, how can there be such extra merit that it can be made available to others? And if the Lord Jesus were a mere man, as one class of Socinians tells us; or an angel of exalted rank, as another class assures us; or the highest created intelligence, as the Arian affirms, how could he have wrought out any merit which could be available to us? How could he have done any thing beyond what he was bound as a creature to do? How could he so step beyond the limits of the divine law, as by abounding merit, to save a world. It is difficult to see, therefore, how he who denies the divinity of the Lord Jesus can hold to the doctrine of a meritorious sacrifice on his part, or to the doctrine of justification through his merits at all; and there is a melancholy consistency in the philosophy and practical faith of those who deny his divinity, in yielding up the doctrine of the atonement, and then the whole doctrine of justification by faith. But admit that he is God, equal with the Father, and all is clear. Then, being under no obligations to become incarnate, being bound by no law to leave the throne of heaven and seek a home in a manger, a lodging place without a pillow, a death on a cross, and a burial in the grave destined for another, all this is the work of extra merit, and may all be available for others. We see him in our world, not as a mere man, and thus bound by law to render every service to the cause of God, but as Immanuel—God with us—the voluntary messenger from heaven—the equal with God, performing a service to which no law bound him, and to which no other powers were adequate, and which therefore may constitute a fulness of merit which may be available for those who have none.

(2.) The second remark is, that he rendered real service to the universe by his work. His coming, his teaching, his death, his resurrection, were an advantage to the cause of God and of virtue, to the full extent of the reward which he will receive. The universe has been so much profited by his voluntary and wonderful service in the cause of virtue and salvation, that there is a propriety that he should be rewarded for it, and the reward which he will receive is no more than an equivalent for the value of the service rendered. It will be asked, What has been the advantage of his work to the universe? In what way is it to be measured or estimated? It may be replied, We do not know fully yet, nor are our minds in a condition now, if they will ever be, to estimate what is appropriate to "satisfy" him for the "travail of his soul." But the general answer, whoever can appreciate its meaning, will be that the value or worth of his voluntary services is to be estimated by *all the evils which his coming has arrested or prevented, and by all the happiness in this world and in heaven of which it has been the cause.* If we could ascertain this, we could estimate the extent of his services to the universe, and of course the reward which is due him, or the amount of his merit. No attempt can be made by us to gauge the amount of this merit. All that can be done is to submit a few hints to illustrate the real nature of the service which he rendered.

(*a*) He did voluntary good through his life. He healed the sick; gave sight to the blind; hearing to the deaf, and vigour to the lame; he restored the maniac to his right mind, and brought back the poor outcast who "dwelt among the tombs" to the comforts of home. All this was doing good to the world, which if he had not come would not have been done.

(*b*) He set a most holy example of virtue to mankind. He showed what true virtue is; how man should live, and how he should meet the temptations of the great enemy of the soul. All this is so much gained to the cause of virtue, above what would have been if he had not come—and the value of having one perfect example in a world where there had been no such standard, and amidst the conflicting opinions of men on the subject of morals, cannot be estimated.

(*c*) He taught man by his example how to bear trials. He himself went through all the usual forms of wo and grief, and showed in each one of them, how man ought to endure calamities, and how in them consolation might be found. But who in a suffering and dying world can estimate the value of such an example?

(*d*) He taught man the true character of God; the nature of his law; the kind of worship that would be acceptable to him, and the way in which the throne of mercy may be approached. But who can estimate the value to a sinful world of the knowledge of the way of pardon?

(*e*) He introduced a religion which has contributed everywhere to the promotion of industry, purity, chastity, truth, honesty, intelligence, and liberty; which has raised one sex from the deepest degradation, and softened the asperities, and removed the tyranny of the other; which has led to the founding of hospitals and asylums, and which will ultimately put an end to all the forms of evil and vice which tyrannize over man; and who can gauge the amount of service which he has thus rendered to man and to the universe?

(*f*) He made an atonement for sin—his greatest, noblest work. He vindicated by his death the honour and the law of God; and solved the question which has everywhere confounded the human intellect, how justice and mercy can meet together, and how righteousness can be maintained and yet the sinner go free. He secured to the universe by his death, all the advantages which could have been secured by the everlasting punishment of the sinner himself, and all the advantages which now result from admitting to heaven countless millions, who, but for his sacrifice, would have been eternally wretched: and what finite mind can estimate the value of this service rendered to the universe?

(*g*) He checks evil by his gospel and his grace, and turns the disobedient to the paths of virtue. Take one single example as an illustration of the amount of service which he rendered—the case of Saul of Tarsus. Think of what he would have been with his extraordinary talents, his uncommon learning, his vast energy of character, his restless ambition, and his proud and self-confident heart, if there had been no atonement, and then of what he *was* after he was converted to the cause of virtue and of truth. Think of his influence while he lived, in meeting the evils and corruptions of idolatry, in closing temples of polluted worship, in purifying the fountains of morals, and in diffusing abroad the principles of pure religion. Think of the good which has been done since his time, by his incomparable writings in maintaining the truth, and imparting consolation in a world of sorrow, and see in the conversion of that man an instance of the kind of service which the Lord Jesus rendered to the universe. Then reflect that the case of Saul of Tarsus is but one of many hundreds of millions—individually less bright, but in the aggregate outshining his, as the mingled light of the galaxy is of greater glory than the twinkling of a single star: and then ask who can estimate the amount of service which the Son of God has rendered to the universe? All that has been done by his holy life and example; all that has been accomplished on earth by the influence of his religion; all that his death did to honour the divine law; all that has been or will be done by arresting evil and staying the desolations of sin; all the additions which have been or will be made by redemption, to the numbers of the heavenly host, and all the immortal songs and joys of the redeemed in heaven; all these things are to be taken into this estimate, and will be the measure of the voluntary service rendered to the universe by the Son of God. It remains only, in order to a complete explanation of the subject, to add,

(3.) That all the merit of his work—all the reward which he deserved, is available to others. It is that superabounding service which has been before referred to, which can be appropriated in any way that he shall ask. Not needing it for himself, for he dwells in "the glory which he had with the Father before the world was," it can be appropriated to those who are poor and needy, and destitute of any claim of merit. The reward for all his extraordinary service may be such as he shall wish, and his heart will not ask augmented glory for himself in heaven as divine, but will seek it in the elevation and immortal felicity of the poor and lost upon the earth for whom he died. By such a reward the universe will *lose* nothing, but will on every account be a gainer, and the benevolent heart which rendered these extraordinary services, may be abundantly satisfied by asking that the "lost may be saved." It was on grounds like these that it was said in the promise, "Ask of me, and I shall give thee the heathen for thine inheritance, and the uttermost parts of the earth for thy possession." Ps. ii. 8. Thus too the promise was, "he shall see of the travail of his soul;" the fruit of his wearisome sorrow, "and shall be satisfied." Isa. liii. 11. Thus too, in asking in his parting prayer, that his work on earth might be remembered, he could use with propriety the strong language when he said, "Father, I *will* that they also whom thou hast given me, be with me where I am, that they may behold my glory which thou hast given me." John xvii. 24. To secure their salvation and the universal spread of his gospel, he can urge the extraordinary claim of the service which he has rendered by his life of spotless virtue, his pure example, his relief of human woes, and the sorrows which he voluntarily endured, in order that the law of God might be maintained, and eternal justice asserted even when salvation was offered to men.

If these views are correct, then it follows

1. That we are to look nowhere else than to Christ as the meritorious cause of salvation. Had it been possible for any mere created being to have wrought out sufficient merit to save the soul, the incarnation of the Son of God, and his death on Calvary would never have occurred. The moment it is maintained that man may merit salvation for himself or for others, the doctrine of the atonement is denied, and the work of Christ dishonoured; and the doctrine that there are anywhere or in any hands garnered up the merits of holy men, of which we can avail ourselves, derogates to just the extent in which it is held, from the great sacrifice, and is an attack on the fundamental doctrines of the gospel. In our hopes of salvation we have but one place to which to look. It is not what our own hands have done, or what has been done by holy men of other times, it is the infinite merit of the Son of God.

2. The merits of the Saviour are sufficient for the salvation of all mankind. If the view which has been taken is correct, it is clear that the benefit which he has rendered to the universe by his holy obedience and death, are commensurate with any rewards which he may receive in connection

with the salvation of men. "It pleased the Father that in him" in every respect, "should all fulness dwell," and alike in his power, his benevolence, his willingness to save, and the merits of his work, there is an ample sufficiency for the wants of all mankind. Needing none of the results of his great work on earth, for the promotion of his own happiness, all that he did may be made available to others, and all men may come with equal freeness and confidence. He had the promise of an ample and satisfactory reward when it was said that he "should see of the travail of his soul and should be satisfied," and on the basis of that promise he himself uses such language as this, "If any man thirst, let him come unto me and drink;" "Come unto me all ye that are weary and heavy laden, and I will give you rest;" and "whosoever will, let him come and take the waters of life freely." There was no original deficiency in the merits of the Saviour for human salvation, nor has his merit been exhausted by the numbers that have already been saved. Salvation in him is like a copious fountain breaking out in a desert. Such a fountain is free for all who may come. It stands in the pathway where the multitude move—where the caravans pass along, and no one has a right to appropriate it to himself. No tribe of men may inclose it or may obstruct its waters. One company of weary travellers has as much right there as another, and to no one particularly appertains the office of dispensing it to the fainting pilgrim. Any one who will come and kneel down there may drink freely. And it will never be exhausted. The fountain will pour out its waters from age to age. The present company of thirsty travellers will soon pass on. They will pursue their journey and go off to die, but then the stream will flow on unexhausted and inexhaustible to the end of time. So it is with the fountain of salvation. As many of the present generation as choose may come and partake, and then as many of the next, and the next, and still the fountain will flow on unexhausted and inexhaustible. It will flow just as fresh and just as full in the last generation that lives, as it did in the days of the Saviour's personal residence on earth; as it does now; and the last sinner that is to be saved, will find it as pure and as life-giving to his soul as it is to ours.

VI. *In what sense we are justified by the merits of Christ.*

In the previous sections, it has been shown that man cannot justify himself, and that he has no claim of merit before God, but that there is in the Lord Jesus infinite merit of such a nature, that it may be made available to us. In the prosecution of this general subject, it is proposed now to illustrate two points:—

1. What is meant by justification in the gospel; and
2. In what way we are justified by the merits of Christ.

1. What is meant by justification in the gospel?

The object here is to state what is the exact condition of a man who is justified. In what respect does he differ from what he was before? What change has taken place in reference to him? How is he regarded by his Maker differently from what he was before? What new relation does he sustain to God, to his law, and to his plan of providential dealings? These, it will be seen, are important questions which probably every one is disposed to ask who attentively considers this subject. They are questions, also, on which serious mistakes are sometimes made as well by those who attempt to explain the subject, as by individual Christians in reflecting on this new relation. A few remarks, showing what is *not* meant, and what *is*, will make the subject clear.

(1.) It is not meant that a man who is justified on the gospel plan, is justified in a *legal* sense. What it is to be so justified has been before explained. It is when a man is accused of a crime, and is able to vindicate himself either by showing that he did not do the act charged on him, or that he has a right to do it. If he can do either of these things, or, which is the same thing, if the charge is not proved against him, he is acquitted by the law, or is held to be righteous in regard to the offence charged. In the previous sections it has been shown that, in this sense, man cannot be justified before God, and whatever may be thought of the argument in the case, it is certain that this is not the kind of justification described in the gospel. It is needful here to remark, only, that Christ did not come to aid man in justifying himself in this sense. He did not come to take the part of the sinner against God, and to enable him to make out his cause. He did not come to be his advocate in the sense of assisting him in rebutting the charges made against him; in showing that the charges had been falsely laid; in explaining his conduct so that it might not appear to be wrong; or in offering palliations for admitted criminality. Whatever be the nature of the work which the Lord Jesus came to perform, and however he may aid us in our salvation, it is all done with the concession on his part, that we are guilty to the full extent which the law charges on us.

(2.) It is not, in any proper sense, a *legal* transaction. Justification by the law is known only in one way—by perfect and uniform obedience. The law of God, in conformity with the general principles of law, knows no other mode. It makes no provision for the pardon or justification of those who violate it, any more than a human law does. The plan of justification in the gospel is a departure from the regular process of law; and whatever inferences may follow from this, either against the system or in favour of it, the fact is not to be denied. "But now," says the apostle Paul, "the righteousness of God without the law is manifested;" that is, the method of justification in a way different from that known in the law. Rom. iii. 21. All attempts to show that the plan of justification in the gospel is a legal transaction, or is in accordance with legal principles, have been signal failures, and if there can be no other justification than that which is properly legal, the whole effort to be saved must be given up in despair. Nor does it mean,

(3.) That the man who is justified ceases to be ill-deserving or guilty in the proper sense of the word. When a man is justified by law, he is declared to be *not* guilty or ill-deserving. But it is not so when a man is justified by the gospel. It is expressly said, respecting this plan, that God "justifies the ungodly," (Rom. iv. 5,) meaning that it is admitted they *are* ungodly at the time, or that they are personally guilty. The act of justification does not change the nature of the offence, or prove that to be right which is in itself wrong. Crime is what it is in its own nature, and is not modified by the manner in which he who commits it is treated. To pardon a man out of the penitentiary does not prove that the act of burglary or theft for which he was committed was innocent; to forgive a man under the gallows does not prove that he is not ill-deserving for the act of murder. To be led from any consideration to treat a man who has injured us as if he had not done it, does not prove that the act was not wrong; or that he should not regard himself as blameworthy for having done it. Our kind treatment of him will not be likely, in any degree, to diminish his sense of his criminality, and the act of pardon with which an offender against God is met when penitent, will not lessen his sense of his own guilt. God never comes in the act of justification to convince him that he has not done wrong, but to save him, though it is admitted that he *is* a great sinner, and the consciousness that he is a sinner will attend him and humble him through life. He will lift up his eyes and his heart with thankfulness that he is a pardoned man; not with pride and self-complacency, that he is an innocent man. He will have the spirit of the publican, not of the Pharisee. The publican that went down to his house justified would not go feeling that he was innocent; he would be filled with gratitude that so great a sinner might be forgiven.

(4.) Justification in the gospel does not mean mere pardon. It has been supposed by many that this is all that is denoted by it. But there are insuperable objections to this opinion. One is, that it is a departure from the common use of language. When a man who has been sentenced to the penitentiary is pardoned before the term of his sentence is expired, we never think of saying that he is justified. The offence is forgiven, and the penalty is remitted; but the use of the word *justify* in his case would convey a very different idea from the word *pardon*. Another objection is, that the sacred writers have so carefully and so constantly used the word *justify*. If mere pardon or forgiveness were all that is intended, it is difficult to see why another word has been constantly employed, and a word so different in its signification. And another objection is, that mere forgiveness is *not* all which the case seems to demand. There was required a reinstating in the favour of God; a restoration to forfeited immunities and privileges, and a purpose in regard to future treatment which is not necessarily involved in the word pardon. It may be conceived that, in cases of pardon for high offences, there would be required, in order to meet all the circumstances of the case, not only a remission of the penalty, but a distinct act restoring to the offender or his family his title, his hereditary honours, and his place in civil relations. The pardon of Lord Bacon would not have restored him at once to the bench, nor the forgiveness of Raleigh to his station in the court of Elizabeth. In the case of a sinner against God, pardon respects mainly the *past;* justification the purpose of God in reference *to the future.* Forgiveness remits past crimes; justification respects the purpose of God to treat the offender *as if* he had not sinned,—and though these may be simultaneous, yet they may be separated in conception as distinct things. The one forgives the past; the other reinstates the offender in the lost favour of God.

(5.) It is not meant that, in the act of justification, the merits of the Lord Jesus become so transferred to us that they can be regarded as *literally ours*, or that his righteousness is in any proper sense our own. This is not true, and cannot be made to be true. Moral character is not capable of being transferred from one individual to another; and however the benefits of what one does may be conveyed to another, it will always be true that the character of an individual is what it is in itself. It will always be true that Christ, and not we, obeyed perfectly the law of God; that Christ, and not his people, died on the cross; and that the merit of his life and death is strictly his, and not theirs. It will always be true, also, that they violated the law of God; that their characters were sinful, and that they deserved not the mercy of God. No man can really believe that the moral character of one individual can be transferred to another, and no one should charge the Bible with inculcating any such doctrine either with respect to the effect of Adam's transgression on his posterity, or the righteousness of the Redeemer in the salvation of his people. We are prepared now to remark positively,

(6.) That justification on the gospel plan denotes a purpose on the part of God to treat a sinner *as if he were righteous*. It implies an intention not to punish him for his sins; not to regard him as any longer under condemnation; not to treat him as an alien, an apostate, and an outcast; but to regard and treat him in the future, in all his important relations, as if he had never sinned. It involves the purpose to shield him from the condemning sentence of the law and the wrath that shall come upon the guilty; to admit him to the fellowship of unfallen beings; to regard him as entitled to all the privileges of a child of God, *as if* he had not fallen; to throw around him the ægis of the divine protection and favour to the end of the present life, and then to admit him to immortal life in heaven. These things would have been his if he had not fallen; and these things are now made his in virtue of the merits of the Redeemer. In all his great relations, in all the most permanent and important things that affect him, he *is*, and is to be, *as if* he had not sinned. The main evils of the apostacy in his care are arrested, and it is the purpose to regard and to treat him as a child of God.

It is important to remark that, in these statements, it is not designed to affirm that, in *all* respects, the act of justification places a man in precisely the same situation in which he would have been if he had not sinned. It is, indeed, designed to teach that, in the direct divine dealings with him, he will be regarded and treated as if he were personally righteous. But why, then, it will be asked, does he suffer and die? Why is he not removed to heaven, as Enoch and Elijah were, without seeing death? Why does the justified man ever pass through severe bodily trials, like Job or Hezekiah; or experience the evils of poverty and want, like Lazarus; or why is he called to part with beloved children; or to be thrown into prison, or to lie down in the sorrow of the most painful form of death, as thousands have already done, and as the children of God now often do?

It is necessary to make such exceptions or qualifications as these in explaining the nature of justification. Though justified, man is not, in *fact*, treated in this world, in all respects, as he would have been if he had not sinned. In the life to come he will be. But nothing is plainer than that, in the present life, things occur, in reference to the treatment of those who are justified, which would not have occurred if man had not sinned, and which will not occur in heaven. Poverty, sickness, bereavement, death, and kindred evils, come upon the righteous and the wicked, the saint and the sinner, the man who is justfied and the man who is not. These evils are, indeed, softened and mitigated by religion, and may be among the means by which the justified man is better prepared for heaven, but still they exist *as* evils; and are to be regarded as among the fruits of sin not removed by the act of justification, and as furnishing the exceptions or qualifications alluded to when it is said that, in this life, the justified man is not treated in *all* respects as if he had not sinned. The *reasons* why the evils of sin are not entirely arrested by the act of justification, and why the believer is not treated in this life, in all respects, as if he had not sinned, seem to be principally two:—

(*a*) One is, that it is not the nature of religion to arrest or change the operation of physical laws. It will have an indirect and gradual effect in checking some of those laws; but to have made that effect direct and immediate, would have required a constant miracle. It is not the design of religion to restore health or property which have been wasted by dissipation; to check the results of vice in those who have been led astray by evil example, or to stay the effects of a life of guilt on our physical frame. A life of virtue will ultimately do much to accomplish this; but to do it at once would require the physical power of a miracle. For the same reason, to be justified does not save from temporal death, and death in accordance with the laws of our physical being. No one can doubt that God *could* have saved us from this, but it would be easy to suggest reasons why it has not been done.

(*b*) Another reason why the act of justification does not secure the same treatment in all respects here as if man had never sinned, is that he who is justified, and who is at heart a true believer, is often in circumstances where he needs the discipline of the hand of God. He is not at once made perfect; and his imperfections, his wanderings, his neglect of duty, his worldliness, often demand the interposition of God for his own good in a way which would neither be necessary nor proper in the case of one who had never sinned. Hence if the Christian sins, he may be recalled even by stripes. Hence he comes under the regular physical laws of the divine administration in the world. Hence he is sick or bereaved. Hence, like other men, he may be cut off by the pestilence, may be swallowed up in the promiscuous ruin of an earthquake, or lie down on a bed of long and lingering disease, and die. Here, he is subject to the physical laws of our being, and to the administration of a wise discipline; in the world to come he will be treated altogether as if he had never sinned. No distinction will be made between him and unfallen beings, nor will there be any such remembrance of his own former guilt that he will occupy a less elevated position, or have less ready access to the throne than if he had never been a transgressor.

It was proposed

2. To show how justification is accomplished through the merits of Christ, or how his merits become available to us for this purpose. It is not uncommon to say, in explaining this, that his righteousness is imputed to us, or that it becomes ours. But, as this language to many minds does not convey a very definite conception, and as on other minds it often conveys erroneous impressions, and seems to be irreconcilable with the common notions of men about moral character, it is necessary to explain in what sense we become justified by the merits of Christ. Perhaps in doing this, also, it may be shown that, so far from being contrary to the common notions of men about what is right and proper, it is, in fact, but carrying out, on the most elevated scale possible, what is practically occurring every

day in the common relations and transactions of life. It is to be observed then,

(1.) That we are often benefitted by what others have done. The meaning is, that what they have done is of the same advantage to us, for certain ends, as if we had done it ourselves. A case or two, taken from familiar transactions, will illustrate what is meant, and help to a proper explanation of the subject. Take the case of a father and a son. The reputation of the one is often a passport or recommendation to the other of very great value as he enters on life. The son has, as yet, no known character, no acquaintance with the world, no credit. The father has all these. He is widely known as a man of virtue; he has an extensive and honoured circle of acquaintance; he has ample credit in the business in which he is engaged. Now, while it is true that this character and credit belong to the father as his own, and cannot be literally transferred to the son, it is also true that, for certain purposes, it may be made to answer the same ends for him as if it were his own. Unless by his own misconduct he shall forfeit the advantage which he might derive from it, it will be a passport to him as he enters on life; it will go before him preparing many hearts to greet him with kindness; it will obtain for him the confidence of others; it may be the means of securing for him many a friend and helper when calamities come, even when his father lies in the grave. While it will always be true that all the merit and the credit appertain to his father, and while whatever may be his own subsequent worth, he will cherish a deep and abiding impression of that, it is also true that, for certain purposes, he could have derived no higher advantages in the case, if the character and the credit had been his own. It would not, indeed, to *all* intents and purposes be the same; but there are great and valuable ends in his passage through the world, which could be no better secured if all this had been his own.

The influence of his father's name and character, unless he forfeits the advantage, will attend him far on, perhaps entirely through, the journey of life.

Take another common case. A young man embarks in business without capital. He has acquired already, it may be, a character for industry, talent and honesty; but he has no means by which he can commence the business of his life. What he wants now is *credit.* If he had that he would be sure of success. But he has none, as yet, of his own. He has had no opportunity to make himself known to secure the extensive confidence of his fellow-men. You have had such an opportunity and have done it. To a certain extent and for certain purposes, you allow him to make use of your name. You endorse his paper, and agree to be responsible for him. Now this, to him, in the case referred to, is of just as much value as though the credit attached to your name were his. It will be worth as much to him in the particular matter referred to as though he himself earned all the influence attached to that name, and secured, by a long and upright life, the credit which it conveys. There will be, indeed, in other respects, important points of difference, but not in the immediate use which he designs to make of the name. He will have a very lively sense of the truth that he himself has *not* this credit; that he is unknown, and that he is under the deepest obligations to you. He will never so far mistake the matter as to suppose that your moral character and worth are transferred to him, or that he can regard either as, in any proper sense, his own; but he *will* consider that this is available for just the purposes for which he wants it. It is all he needs to secure the grand object of his life, and is as good to him *as if* it were his own.

Further: if we would look over society, we should find that this arrangement prevails everywhere, and that we are indebted to it every day. It may be doubtful whether we live a single hour, or execute a single plan of life, without being more or less indebted to it. It is an influence diffused around us like the air we breathe, or the sun which shines on our way; or it is like the tissues of the human frame where each part derives benefits in its functions from the numerous other parts with which it is more or less closely interwoven. It enters into the very texture of society that we avail ourselves of the toils, the sacrifices, the virtues, and the honoured names of those with whom we are connected. No man acquires a name for virtue who does not do much to benefit his children and friends in this way, and one of the chief stimulants to effort in parents is, that they may place their children on as high vantage ground as possible when they embark on life. That youth enters on life under great disadvantages who cannot encircle himself with this influence, and who is constrained to "cut his way" to respectability or to wealth alone. As a matter of fact, however, there are few that do this. The name and influence of a father or a friend; a letter of commendation from those who are known and loved, will be a passport to us in distant climes, and among strangers; will meet us with its benign influence on the Rhine or the Ganges; will help us where we should otherwise fall into the hands of freebooters in a foreign land, or when we should otherwise sink under poverty and want; or on a distant shore will raise up for us a friend on the bed of death. He enters life under the best auspices who can avail himself most of this without sacrificing his independence or being a sycophant or parasite; and he is the most foolish and ungrateful of mankind who would willingly renounce all this advantage, and choose to weather the storms of life and make his way through the world friendless and alone.

(2.) The second remark in explaining the way in which we are justified by the merits of Christ, is, that there are two methods by which we avail ourselves of the benefit of the character and virtues of others. The one is, by natural relationship. This occurs in the case of a child, who, as a matter of course, derives advantage from the industry, the character and the credit of a parent. The other is, by an arrangement made for that end. Instances of this latter kind occur everywhere. The case of an adopted child is one—a case where there is no natural relation, and no natural claim, but where one chooses for any reasons, that the child of another should be received into his family and treated *as if* he were his own. It occurs not unfrequently in the case of a matrimonial alliance, where the one party avails itself of the name and influence and rank of the other, and on that account has a degree of respect to which, otherwise, there would be no claim. It occurs in the cases already referred to, where the use of a name is conceded. The name of the missionary Schwartz was thus the means of saving from starvation the whole of a British garrison, and many a man owes his subsequent elevation in life, to assistance furnished him at the outset. Cases have arisen where the signet or the ring of a prince has been placed in the hands of another, conveying to him, if danger should befal him, all the influence and security which they would to the owner himself; nor is it very uncommon to give a *carte blanche* to a friend to be filled up at pleasure. It remains now only, in view of these illustrations,

(3.) To remark in explanation of the way in which we are justified through the merits of Christ. It is, that we are permitted to avail ourselves of his abounding merits, so that we may be treated as if they were our own. It is not that his merits are transferred to us, or that his moral character or righteousness becomes properly ours, or that we cease to deserve punishment, or that an apology is made for our sins, or that Christ takes our part against justice; but that *his* merits are so ample, his life and death have accomplished so much, and his work has been so meritorious, that we may, by a suitable connection with him, be regarded and treated *as if* we were truly righteous before God; so that "God can be just and the justifier of him that believeth in Jesus;" just and true while he "justifies the ungodly."

This connection between the Saviour and those who are benefitted by his merits is not a natural connection, for no such relation by nature subsists as would entitle any one to be regarded and treated as righteous on his account, but it is a relation which is constituted entirely by faith. The influence of faith in forming it, and in making it proper that they who are united to him should be treated as righteous, will be explained hereafter. It is sufficient now to remark, that the relation which is sustained is one that is *formed*, not one that exists by nature.

It is formed by a personal union of the soul to Christ, and by the gracious concession on his part in accordance with the divine arrangement, that we may avail ourselves of his infinite and inexhaustible merits, so that we may be treated *as if* they were our own. There are two additional thoughts which may be suggested to illustrate this:

(*a*) The one is, that his merit is inexhaustible. There is no diminution or exhaustion of the merit of his work, by the numbers that avail themselves of it. This makes the plan of redemption wholly different from any thing which occurs among men. A man of the widest credit and highest standing may be conceived to allow his name to be so often used by those who have no claim to it, or who turn out to be worthless, and abuse his claim, as to *exhaust* his credit, and make his name good for nothing. Not so the Saviour. No numbers that apply exhaust his credit, or diminish at all the merit of that blood by which they are saved. That blood is as efficacious now, and that holy name of our advocate is as much honoured in heaven now, as when the first sinner was justified, and when the gates of glory were first thrown open to receive a ransomed soul.

(*b*) The other remark is, that the Lord Jesus becomes the surety that the universe shall suffer no wrong by our being admitted to heaven. So far as we are concerned, he pledges himself to meet all the claims of the law and of justice upon us. That is, he becomes the surety, that, under this arrangement, as great good shall result to the universe by our being saved, as would be by our punishment forever. By such punishment, nothing would have been gained in regard to the honour of the law, the truth of God, and the interests of justice, which are not secured under the present arrangement by the substituted sorrows of the Son of God in making the atonement. Thus he becomes the "surety of a better covenant," (Heb. vii. 22;) and stands before the universe as the public pledge that no harm is done to any interest of truth and justice by the admission of one, who is an acknowledged sinner, into heaven. Thus the publican was justified; thus Paul, the persecutor and blasphemer, won Christ and was found in him, not having his own righteousness which was of the law, but that which was through the faith of Christ," (Phil. iii. 8, 9;) and thus multitudes of the profane and the sensual by believing on Christ, have entered heaven and been blessed. There stands the great Advocate, not for their *sins* but for *them;* and there stands the security, that no injury shall be done by treating even *such* sinners forever *as if* they were righteous, and that all that law or justice could ask—all that could be secured either by their own personal perfect obedience, or by their enduring the eternal penalty of the law, has been secured by *his* holy life and meritorious death. When, therefore, they enter heaven, it is not over prostrated law; over a humbled government; over disregarded threatenings; by a changeful policy, or by partiality in the administration; it is because their great Surety has himself secured the honour of the law, and that in their conscious destitution of merit he has enough for them all. His name is the guarantee to justice and to God; his inexhaustible merits the reason why they may be treated *as if* his righteousness were their own.

This is what is properly meant by *imputation*. The true doctrine implies no transfer of moral character; no infusion of righteousness into the soul; no physical identity between the Redeemer and his people; no charging of their sins to him, so that he became in any proper sense a sinner or deserved to be put to death,—nothing but the purpose on the part of God, in virtue of what he has done, to treat those who are themselves guilty, as if they were righteous. "By that righteousness being *imputed* to us," says President Edwards, "is meant no other than this, that the righteousness of Christ is accepted for us and admitted instead of that perfect inherent righteousness which ought to be in ourselves. Christ's perfect obedience shall be reckoned to our account, so that we shall have the benefit of it, as though we had performed it ourselves." Vol. v. 394.

These views have reference to the most important subject of religion. They pertain to that great doctrine which separates Christianity from every other system of religion; and to the answer which Christianity furnishes to the question asked with so much solicitude in every age, "How shall man be justified with God?" The answer is, "That we are justified freely by his grace through the redemption that is in Christ Jesus." Romans iii. 24. It is this doctrine which divides the religion of the gospel from all other systems; which makes it what it is; which gives it whatever influence or power it has in speaking peace to the troubled conscience, and bidding the spirit that is captive under sin go free. It is this which will enable man to appear before his final Judge justified, not by any miserable attempt to deny the fact that he is a sinner; to apologise for his errors and follies, and found a claim to favour on such apology; to substitute an external morality for that holiness of heart which the law of God requires, or to present as a ground of acceptance the vain oblation of outward forms.

But it should be observed also, that though this method of justification is entirely peculiar to Christianity, and separates it from all other religious systems, yet that it accords with principles prevailing everywhere in society, and on which men act every day and in every land. It is the embodiment and concentration of these principles, and shows their operation on the highest scale possible. Thus, as already remarked, in matters pertaining to this life, we owe to the name and standing and credit of others, an introduction to the world, facilities for doing business, valued friends who may succour us in trouble: and on substantially the same principles, though on an infinitely higher scale, we owe to the merits of another—the Son of God—an introduction to the divine favour; a passport to heaven; the friendship of angelic beings; the peace of pardon; the calmness of the Christian's death; and the crown incorruptible beyond the grave. Whatever we shall have in the long ages of eternity, of joy or peace, of honour or favour, is to be traced to the operation of this principle on the highest scale possible; that we may be benefitted by the sacrifices and toils; the name and merit; the righteousness and sufferings of another.

In common affairs we do not disregard or undervalue this. Those who enter on life regard it as a felicitous circumstance in their condition, if they may go forth with such passports and commendations to the esteem of the world. That young man would regard himself justly as destitute of every manly and generous feeling, as well as every principle of self-respect, who should discard and spurn this advantage, and prefer to go forth to the world without the commendation or the patronage of a single friend. *We* are going to a more important theatre of being than is this narrow world. We shall soon pass beyond its outer bounds and move through other regions. We are to go up and meet our Maker; to enter on a mode of existence that shall have no end; to be associated with now unknown orders of beings; and there are great interests at stake, compared with which all the interests of earth are trifles. We go to a royal court—the court of heaven—where we have no claim to a right to appear. We go up to obtain, if we are happy there, the favour of a Being whose law we have violated, and whose displeasure we have incurred. We go where we can take no wealth with us, and where if we could, it would avail nothing; where we shall be disrobed of all in a graceful exterior, or in fascinating manners that may commend us to others here, and where, if it should accompany us, it would be valueless; where the name of a father, or the powerful influence of a friend, that might commend us to the favour of men, would be of no avail; where nothing on which we here rely as a passport to others, can be a commendation. But there *is* one in human flesh that dwells there. He once lived among men. He was most holy, and lowly, and pure, but he died. He rose from the tomb, and the everlasting gates were opened, and he entered his native skies. To the very interior of the court of heaven; to the sacred seat of Deity; to the throne itself, he has been admitted, and is seated there. With all that heaven he is familiar, for he is there at home. With all its streets of gold, with all its far distant mansions, with all its many departments fitted up for the abodes of the blessed, he is familiar. His powerful aid he proffers us in our sin and ignorance and helplessness, and assures us that he is willing that we should plead *his* name, and make mention of his merits *as if* they were our own, as a reason why we should be welcome there. In heaven his plea has never been denied; the claim of his merits has never been dishonoured. Shall we refuse his offer? Shall we spurn his name? Shall we turn away from that friend, and advocate, and patron, and go there friendless and alone? Shall we seek to commend ourselves to a holy God by our own doings, and to stand there in our own attempts to vindicate our ways? Shall we spurn the robes of salvation which he proffers—so white, so pure, so full and flowing, and gird ourselves with the rags of our own righteousness?

VII. *The influence of faith in justification.*

In the last section, in showing how we are saved through the merits of Christ, it was remarked that the means by which we become interested in his merits, or by which they are made availiable to us, is *faith.* It was then proposed to go into a fuller explanation in the subsequent parts of this tract. That duty it remains now to perform.

The substance of the Christian doctrine on this subject is expressed in the following passages of Scripture:—"For I am not ashamed of the Gospel of Christ; for it is the power of God unto salvation, to every one that believeth, to the Jew first, and also to the Greek. For therein is revealed the righteousness of God from faith to faith; as it is written, "The just shall live by faith." Rom. i. 16, 17. The doctrine of this passage is, that a man is considered just before God, and treated as such, not in virtue of his own works, but in virtue of his exercising faith in Christ. "For therein," that is, in the gospel, "the righteousness of God," or God's plan of regarding and treating men as righteous, "is revealed from faith to faith;" that is, by faith unto those who have faith, or who believe, as it is written, "The just shall live by faith," or those justified by faith shall have everlasting life. It is needless to prove at length that this is the settled doctrine of the New Testament. "Therefore we conclude," says the apostle in the third chapter of this epistle, (ver. 28,) "that a man is justified by faith without the deeds of the law." Again, "By the deeds of the law, there shall no flesh be justified in his sight. But now the righteousness of God without the law is manifested, being witnessed by the law and the prophets; even the righteousness of God, which is by faith of Jesus Christ, unto all and upon all them that believe; for there is no difference." Rom. iii. 20–22. So the apostle Paul says again, "A man is not justified by the works of the law, but by the faith of Jesus Christ." Gal. ii. 16. In accordance with this, is the great doctrine which the Saviour taught his disciples to promulgate as comprising *all* that he designed them to teach: "Go ye into all the world and preach the gospel to every creature. He that believeth and is baptized shall be saved; but he that believeth not shall be damned." Mark xvi. 15, 16. That is, there is no other method of being saved but by believing, or by faith, and if a man has not this, he must be lost.

Probably every one who has ever read these passages has been disposed to ask, Why is so much stress laid on *faith* in the plan of redemption? Why is it made so central, and so indispensable in the salvation of the soul? What inherent virtue is there in this act that has given it such a preeminence over all other virtues? What is there in this that should make it a substitute for all the good works that men can perform? Perhaps some will be disposed to add, that the system of Christianity is thus removed from all other systems, and is different from all the laws and principles on which men act in other things. Merit, in other cases, is not in accordance with a man's *belief*, but according to his virtues—his moral worth—and why should *faith* have such special eminence in the eye of God? The rewards of this life are not distributed according to a man's faith or credulity, and why should the rewards of heaven be? We judge of the excellency of a man's character not according to the readiness with which he embraces what is proposed to him for his credence, but usually somewhat in proportion to his caution and the slowness of his belief, and why does religion require a man to hasten to believe that which is proposed to him, as if this were the chiefest of the virtues? When, also, a man is put on trial, he is acquitted, not because he exhibits an example of trusting in his judge or his advocate, but because he is able to vindicate his conduct; and why shall we not look for something analogous in religion? Why are pardon and hope; life and joy; heaven and glory; peace here and bliss hereafter; all made to depend on faith—" the centre and the circumference; the beginning, the middle, and the end, according to the gospel, of every virtue? These are questions which it is natural to ask; they are questions which the friend of Christianity should feel it to be a part of his vocation to answer. The relation or connection which these questions bear to the subject before us is this:—Supposing that man has no merit of his own, as has been shown, and that there are infinite merits in the Redeemer through which we may be saved, why is it proper that we should avail ourselves of those merits only through faith? Why should faith be the instrument by which we may be treated *as if* those merits were ours?

The answer to these questions is, that, in the circumstances of the case, faith constitutes a union with the Redeemer, of such a nature as to make it proper to treat us substantially as he himself is treated; that is, as righteous; to make it proper that we should share his happiness, his favour, his protection on earth, and his glory in heaven; that the union formed by faith between the soul and the Redeemer is so tender, so close, and so strong as to imply an identity of interest, and to make it certain and proper that the blessings descending on him should, according to their capacity and wants, descend on those who believe. It is meant that the particular *reason* why faith has been selected as the means of this is, that it constitutes a union more close, firm, and enduring than any other virtue, and that it meets and overcomes more evils in the world than any other act of the mind would do. On this account, it is singled out from all other acts of the mind in the plan of justifying men. To many these remarks may appear abstract and obscure now. It is proposed, therefore, in a series of observations to show *why* faith is so important; why it is the very *cardo rerum*—the hinge of salvation.

One other preliminary remark should be made. It is that there is a great and essential difference between *faith* and *credulity*. We distinguish them accurately in common life; we fear that they are sometimes confounded when men think of religion.

The inquiry proposed embraces essentially the two following points:—Why *faith* is of so much importance in a work of salvation; and why faith *in Christ* is made so prominent and essential. The first point of inquiry is, why *faith* is of so much importance in a work of salvation. In reply to this inquiry let it be observed,

(1.) That faith acts an important part in the affairs of the world. Using the word in the sense of *confidence*, there is nothing else on which the welfare of society more depends, or which is more indispensable to its prosperous and harmonious relations. It enters into every thing, and we are every day and every hour acting under its influence, and depending on it as essential to all that we hold dear. It is the cement of families, of neighbourhoods, of governments, of nations. The faith of treaties, of compacts, of promises, of friendships, of affection, is that which holds the world together, and without which society would go to pieces. To loosen it at once, would be like loosening every rope in a ship, or unscrewing every fastening and bolt in a machine. It is by faith, or mutual confidence, that the relations of domestic life are maintained; that the harmony of a family is secured; that business, in a mercantile community, is carried on; that a banking institution effects the purpose for which it was chartered; or that a government can secure the ends for which it was instituted. It is by faith only that we derive lessons of valuable instruction from history, or act with reference to what is yet to come. If we had no more confidence in any of the testimonies of history than we have in the fabulous details of the dynasties of India, the mythological periods of Grecian history, or the legends of the saints, all past history would be utterly useless, for it would convey no certain lessons; if we had no faith in the stability of the course of events—the rising of the sun, the moon and the stars; the return of the seasons; the continuance of the laws of magnetism, of gravitation, or of vegetation, we should form no plan for the future; we should neither plant a field, nor build a ship, nor venture out on the ocean where we might soon be without sun, or star, or compass. We confide in our teachers, in a physician, a counsellor, a clergyman, and it would be impossible that the cause of education, jurisprudence or religion, could be maintained if there were no such confidence. The farmer of the Eastern States believes in the vast fertility of the West, of which he has heard, but which he has never seen, and, with his wife and children, leaves the graves of his fathers to seek that land on the strength of his faith; and the merchant believes that there is such a place as Canton or Calcutta, though he has seen neither; and on the strength of that faith would embark all his property in the same vessel, and stake the whole question about making a fortune in this world on his strong confidence that such places, of which he has heard, have an existence. In like manner we are exercising confidence in every thing. We believe the testimony of the historians, though we never saw Xenophon, or Thucydides, or witnessed the events of which they wrote; we vote for the man whom we have never seen; we confide in the bankers across the waters whom we never expect to behold. Were it not for this unceasing confidence in the varied operations of faith, we could not get along for a single day or hour. The affairs of the world would at once stand still. The bands of society would at once become loosened, and every thing would fall into irretrievable confusion.

It is true, there may be much credulity in the world, and multitudes in all professions and relations in life are imposed on. But so, also, there is much counterfeit money, and many may be injured or ruined by it. But the existence of a circulating medium is indispensable, and there is by far more genuine than false coin at any time in the world, and any quantity of spurious coin does not render that valueless which is genuine. So any amount of credulity does not prove that it is improper that men should ever repose confidence in one another, or that all faith is valueless.

(2.) The second observation illustrating the importance of faith with reference to the subject before us is, that faith is the strongest conceivable bond of union between minds and hearts. It is, in fact, the cement of *all* unions, and without which all else is valueless. In friendships, in treaties, in national compacts, in social intercourse, in the tender domestic relations, it is *the* very bond of union, and there is nothing else that can be a substitute for it. The seal which is affixed to a letter that is sent to a friend does not make it secure because no one has power to break it, but because there is confidence in each postmaster through whose hands it may pass, and in each stranger or friend into whose hands it may happen to fall, that he will respect the seal, and will not break it. The seal which is appended to a will does not render it secure because no one has *power* to break it, but because the testator has confidence that his friends and that the courts of his country will respect his wishes when his mouth is forever closed against the possibility of his declaring his desires, and his hand powerless to assert his rights.

Look into the relations of life. What is it that forms and preserves those numerous unions on which the very existence of society depends? What is the basis of the union of husband and wife, of parent and child, of brother and sister, of friend and friend? What is there but mutual confidence? And is it asked what is the strength of that? In answer to these questions an illustration may be employed, taken from the most tender relation in life. This illustration is used, because it is the very one more than once referred to on this subject in the Bible, and because it enters so vitally into the welfare of society. Here is a young man just entering on life. His character is fair; his profession is honourable; his person and standing are liable to no objection, and no suspicion—but what he *may* be yet no one earthly can tell, for no one can certainly predict about what a man will be, till he is tried. Here is a youthful female—the joy of her mother and the pride of her father's heart. She has been delicately trained; has a home that has every attraction; is secure there of unfailing friends as long as her father and mother shall live, and has ample means of support. She breaks all these ties; leaves the home of her childhood; bids adieu to father, mother, brothers, and sisters, and commits herself into the hands of this comparative stranger. A father's, and a mother's, and a brother's love she exchanges for his. Her hand, her heart, her property she gives to him. She pledges herself to go where he goes; to suffer what he suffers; to make his friends hers; to love him with an ardour with which she loves no other human being; to break away from every tie of country and home if he shall will it; and in a sense more absolute than exists in any other case, to commit her happiness into his hands. Every day and every hour that they will live, she is dependent on his prosperity, his virtue, and his smiles for her happiness, and the moment his affections are withdrawn, or he ceases to be a virtuous man, her happiness is dead. If he is virtuous, faithful, and kind, she regrets not the act of confidence with which she gave him her heart and hand. But what if he trifles with her happiness? What if he always meets her with a frown? What if he proves false to his vows? What if he becomes a wretched drunkard? Now what is the foundation and the source of its strength? Confidence; and when that is gone domestic peace dies. She has made a sacrifice of her happiness, and her earthly felicity is a wreck.

Let another thought be suggested here. It is, that this union of confidence secures an *identity* in their destiny. They are one—one flesh, said the Saviour—and the same events will now affect both. Before this union the storm might have beat on one of them, and sunshine gladdened the path of the other. Now the storm and the sunshine come on both alike. The light that gladdens the eyes of the one is also a pleasant thing to the other; the star that rises propitiously on one, rises propitiously also on the path of the other. The blessings of peace and joy that greet the one, greet also the other. There is one heart, one pulsation, one breathing, one soul made up of the two. And so if calamity comes; if, under the roof where they are to abide, the pale destroyer shall come with stealthy foot-tread, and change the rose on the cheek of a smiling babe to the lily of death, it will be a scene in which both their hearts will bleed alike, and they will weep together over the open grave. If one is sad, both are sad; if one is poor, both are poor. Their union, one pre-eminently of mutual faith plighted before the altar, constitutes an identity in all the great events of life, and secures to both substantially the same treatment from the Great Disposer of all things. They share the same fortune; the same honour or disgrace; the same sorrows and the same joys; they are wafted on to a port of bliss or are wrecked in the same vessel; they are greeted with the same welcome in life, they are buried in the same grave. It is easy to apply this illustration to the matter in hand.

(3.) The third illustration is, that faith is of such a nature that it is adapted to meet all the evils of the world. The idea is, that it has been made the hinge or turning point of salvation, because the want of it has been the source of all the calamities which man has suffered, and because, if this is restored, the evil of the world would be at an end.

The grand evil on earth, and the source of all subordinate evils, is *a want of confidence in God.* This was the evil at the start, that man reposed more confidence in the teachings of the tempter, than in the law of the Creator, and this has been the source of all our woe. Man has no confidence in his God. He does not believe that the Most High is qualified for universal empire; that he manages the affairs of the universe well; that his law is equal and just; that his dispensations are in accordance with equity; that his plan of salvation is wise. He does not show his confidence in him by yielding implicit obedience to his laws, or by submitting to his dispensations. He does not go to him and ask counsel of him in the darknesses and perplexities of life; he does not seek support in his arms in times of calamity. He does not commit his great interests to him, believing that he will be his guide through life, and that he will yet make "all things work together for good." He confides in other things. He confides in his own strength, till his strength fails; in his philosophy till it deludes and deceives him; in his fellow-men till they all betray him; in friends and kindred, till they drop into the grave; in his skill and sagacity, till he comes to a place in life where "the right hand loses its cunning." He confides in stocks and stones, in graven images, and fourfooted beasts and creeping things, but by nature he has no confidence in God.

This is the grand evil of the world; this the source of all our woes; for a want of confidence here produces the same kind of evils, though on a larger scale, as the same want everywhere. We have seen that the welfare of society depends on mutual confidence. Now, to see how wretched any society can possibly be, we have only to suppose the existence there of the same want of confidence which subsists between man and his Maker. If a perfectly malignant being wished to diffuse as much misery as possible through the world, all that he could desire would be to break up universal faith. He would go into a community, and with the touch of a magic wand would in a moment destroy all confidence in each merchant, bank and insurance office, and lawyer, and physician, and clergyman. He would go into each school, and destroy all confidence in the instructor. He would go into each family, and destroy everywhere the mutual confidence of husband and wife, and introduce universal distrust and jealousy. He would unsettle the faith of every child in his father, of every brother in his sister. What would be the result? He would at once arrest the wheels of commerce; put an end to business; make every professional man useless and wretched; take away sleep from the pillow of every husband and wife, and fill every family, and the whole community with heart-burnings, jealousies, contentions, and strifes. No man would know in whom to trust; no one could form a plan dependent in any manner on the fidelity of others; no one could be certain that any of his purposes of life could be effected. The scene at Babel would be rëacted again all over the world, and worse disorder than that which followed from confounding the language of the people there, would pervade all classes and conditions of mankind. The remedy for such a state of things would be the restoration of mutual confidence. In such a condition of ill, nothing would have so far-reaching an effect. It would in fact *meet all* those ills and make society harmonious and happy. The wheels of commerce, of government, of domestic peace, of public improvement, of education, would again roll on harmoniously, and happiness would again bless the world. The want of faith or confidence in God has produced all the ills on earth, of which those just supposed are but an emblem; the restoration of confidence in God would strike at the root of all those ills, and make this a happy world. It is this which makes heaven happy, where every being has faith in God and in all that dwell there; and with all our wants and sadnesses this too would be a happy world, if there were universal confidence in God. In our sorrows we should then have peace, for we should believe that all is well ordered; under our heavy burdens of life we should find support, for we would go and roll all on his arm; in all the dark and perplexing questions that now agitate us about the introduction of moral evil and the prevalence of iniquity, our minds would be calm, for we should feel that there was a reason for it all, and in the prospect of death—that which now makes us so sad—our hearts would find more than peace—we should utter the language of joy and triumph, for it would be only the coming of a messenger to bear us to a much loved Father's arms. The grand thing that needs to be done on earth to make this a happy world, is to restore universal confidence in God, and this is the whole aim of religion, this the object of the scheme of redemption. Hence the necessity of faith is laid at the foundation of the whole scheme; it is the cardinal thing in the plan of salvation. This restored, what a happy world, after all, would this be! For it is a beautiful world. It is full of the proofs of God's goodness and love. There are a thousand comforts that meet us every day and every night; and a thousand tender chords that should bind us to our Creator. If we confided in him as qualified for universal empire; if we felt that he was *fit* to manage the affairs of his own world; if we believed that he will yet bring order out of confusion and light out of darkness; if we trusted that his law is good and his commandments holy, and if we would go to him with the confiding spirit with which a little child goes and tells all his troubles to his father, this would be still a happy world. For that grand undertaking of the almighty Father of us all, to restore unwavering confidence in himself, manifested in the Gospel, the world should be unfeignedly thankful, and one of the principal topics of praise on earth should be, that he has required faith as the very elementary principle of his religion.

(4.) A fourth remark, in explanation of the subject, is that faith is required, or is made the condition of justification, for this reason :—There is an obvious propriety that, where salvation is provided and offered, there should be some act on our part signifying our *acceptance* of it. If we are to be saved through the merits of Christ, there should be some reason on our part why we should be. There should be some act indicating our wish or our will; some expression of our desire in the case; something that shall serve to distinguish us from those who are not saved. It evidently would not be proper, it would not be consulting the nature which God has given us, to receive the race indiscriminately into heaven without any intimation of a wish to be saved, or to save one part and leave the other, unless there were something that would indicate in the one a desire to be saved, which did not exist in the case of the other. What would better show this than faith? What would be a better expression of a desire to be saved? What act would be more appropriate in *accepting* salvation; in the intimating of a wish that the benefits of the death of Christ might be ours? What would constitute a stronger bond between the soul and him than this; what would come nearer toward constituting that identity on which it is proper that those who are united should be treated alike? You are a father; you have two sons. They both become disobedient. They leave your house at their pleasure; go where they choose; are out at such hours as suit their convenience; keep such company as they desire, and are wholly regardless of your laws. They heed neither your promises nor your threats, and they have gone so far that they have now no confidence in you. You have favours which you are willing to bestow on them. You would be willing to receive them to your house, and to treat them as sons, alike in your lifetime and in your will. But would you think it unreasonable that, as a condition of their being received and treated *as* sons, they should evince returning *confidence* in you? And if one of them *should* return, and should ever onward manifest the confidence due from a son to a father, and the other should not, would you think it improper to make a distinction between them in your lifetime and in your will? And would they and the world be at a loss for a *reason* why it was done? The remark here is, that faith in Christ is the appropriate *act* by which we *accept* of the benefits of his work, and that this constitutes a difference between him who accepts of his salvation and him who does not; and that this is a *reason* why the one should be treated *as if* he were interested in those benefits and the other not; that is a reason why the one is justified and the other not.

Bearing in mind the remarks now made, that a restoration to confidence would meet innumerable evils in a family, in a commercial community, between neighbours and between nations, and that the restoration of confidence in God would meet all the evils under which this world labours now, I proceed to show why *faith in Christ* particularly is made so important as a condition of salvation. With reference to this, three remarks may be made:—

(1.) The first is, that we are to repose faith or confidence in Christ as authorized to negotiate the terms of reconciliation between God and man. The whole system of revealed religion proceeds on the fact—a fact which is apparent without any revelation—that an alienation exists between God and man, or that man is in a state of revolt. It was with reference to this alienation that the Son of God came into the world to accomplish the most difficult of all undertakings, that of reconciling opposing minds, and of bringing them into harmony. On the one hand, there was the infinite mind of God, whose law had been violated, and whose government had been rejected and outraged, and whose threatenings had been disregarded; and on the other, there were countless millions of minds wholly alienated from the Creator. To bring the holy Creator and the millions of rebellious minds into harmony; to propose the terms on which God was willing to forgive sin; to make such arrangements as that he could consistently pardon; and to bring the minds of revolted men to a willingness to be reconciled, was the work undertaken by this great peacemaker.

But it is evident that this work could not be accomplished, unless *confidence* was reposed in him by both the parties of the unhappy controversy. In infinitely smaller matters, when nations are alienated, if a mediator proposes arrangements of peace, or if ambassadors are appointed to negotiate a peace, it is clear that the matter could not proceed a step unless there were confidence on both sides in in the mediator or ambassadors.

Christ is a great mediator; a peace-maker between God and man. On the part of God, there was every reason to repose entire confidence in him in so great an undertaking, for he was his only begotten Son; eternally in his bosom, and loved, with an infinite love, before the foundation of the world. John xvii. 24. By him the worlds had been made; (John i. 3; Heb. i. 21;) and under him, with reference to the work of redemption, their affairs had been administered up to the time when he appeared in the flesh.

God the Father reposed unlimited confidence in him when he appointed him to be the mediator, and intrusted to him the execution of the great purpose of reconciling the world again to the divine government. This confidence reposed in Christ in the work of mediation, is often referred to in the New Testament, by the Saviour himself, and by the sacred penmen: "This is my beloved Son," was declared from heaven at his baptism, "in whom I am well pleased." Matt. iii. 17. "Father," said the Saviour, just before his death, "glorify thy name. Then came there a voice from heaven, saying, I have both glorified it, and will glorify it again." John xii. 28. "Thou hast given him power," said he again, "over all flesh, that he should give eternal life to as many as thou hast given him." John xvii. 2. "All power is given unto me in heaven and in earth; go ye therefore and teach all nations." Matt. xxviii. 18, 19. "I am the way," said he, "and the truth, and the life; no man cometh unto the Father but by me." John xiv. 6. So we are told, that "there is one God, and one Mediator between God and man, the man Christ Jesus." 1 Tim. xi. 5.

These things show the degree of confidence which the Father reposed in him in the work of mediation—intrusting to him the message of mercy; appointing him to convey it to men; and endowing him *as* Mediator, with all the power and authority which were requisite to accomplish so great a work.

But confidence in him is not less required in regard to the other party than by him who had appointed him. It is clear that, unless we have confidence in him as the messenger and ambassador of God; unless we regard him as sent from heaven, and as authorized to propose terms of reconciliation; unless we feel that he can make a *definite arrangement,* and that what he proposes will be sanctioned by God; unless we feel that he is *authorized* to propose terms of pardon, and to declare our sins forgiven, and to pronounce us accepted and justified, it would be impossible for us to avail ourselves of any arrangement for salvation through him. We should feel that we were trifling with a great subject; and in our serious moments, when we thought of the great interests at stake, we should be in no humour to trifle. None of *us* would seriously think of embracing *any* terms of reconciliation with God proposed by Mohammed, or Zoroaster, or Confucius; by Lord Herbert or Mr. Hume; for we do not suppose that any of these men were *authorized* to propose terms of salvation. We have no confidence in them as ambassadors of God, whatever we may think of them in other respects. The primary ground of *faith*, therefore, in Christ, is, that we have confidence in him as a mediator, an ambassador, a peace-maker; as authorized to propose to us the *terms* on which peace may be obtained with our offended Creator. "If ye believe not that I am he, ye shall die in your sins." John viii. 24.

(2.) The second remark to which we referred, showing specifically why faith in Christ is demanded, is, that it is by his agency and merits only that we can be received into the favour of God. He came not only to *bring* the message of reconciliation, and to *propose* the terms, but to *do* and to *suffer* whatever was necessary to be done, in order that we might be accepted of the Father, or in order that we might be saved consistently with the interests of justice. The case somewhat resembles what it would be in the instance of an ambassador coming to negotiate a peace who should not only come to propose the *terms*, but should actually have in his possession that which alone could be regarded as a reparation for wrong done by one of the parties to the other, and who should come not only to persuade the party which had done the wrong to be willing to be reconciled, but also to avail itself of what he was ready to *furnish* to repair all the evil done, and to satisfy the other party. In such a case, it would not be unreasonable to ask *confidence* in himself, or to make this one of the conditions by which the favour might be available. In fact, it could not be consistently made available in any other way, or on any other conditions, and, unless there were faith in him, the negotiation could proceed no further.

Thus we are required to exercise faith in the Lord Jesus. We are destitute of merit. We have violated the law of God, and can do nothing to repair the wrong. We are debtors, to an incalculable amount, to justice; and we have nothing with which to pay the debt. We can do absolutely nothing to vindicate our own conduct; to undo the evils that we have done; to make up for the dishonour which we have put on the law of God; to atone for our thousands of faults and follies. At this point the Son of God appears, and he comes with the assurance that he has himself perfectly obeyed the law, and has honoured it as fully as it can be honoured by obedience; that he has suffered a most bitter death—a death aggravated by every form of cruelty—as an expiation for our sins; that he will become the guarantee or surety that the law shall suffer no dishonour if we are saved; that no injury shall result from our pardon, and that, in fact, all the good effects have been secured by his death which *could be* by our being doomed to bear the penalty of the law ourselves; and that all that is needful for us now is to become united to him by an indissoluble bond to put ourselves under his protection; and to be so identified with him that it will be proper to treat us *as if* we had personally obeyed the law, or borne its penalty. That which will constitute the *closest* union in the case, and which will do most to render this identity of treatment proper, is confidence in him as our Saviour, and reliance on his merits, or *faith.*

(3.) The third remark necessary to explain the subject, or to show why faith in Christ is made the turning point of justification and salvation is, that the act of believing on

Christ is made in circumstances and in a manner indicating *confidence* of the highest kind that ever exists in the human bosom, constituting a union of the closest conceivable nature. It is an act so identifying the soul and the Saviour as to make it proper that the same treatment which the Redeemer receives should in this measure be received by his people, or that in the divine treatment they should be practically regarded as *one.* The circumstances are these :—

(*a*) The sinner feels that he is lost and ruined. He is made sensible that he is guilty before God, and that he has no claim to his mercy. His heart is evil; his life has been evil; his whole soul is evil. If justice were done him, he feels that he would be forever banished from God and heaven. Yet he feels that he has a soul of infinite value. It is to endure forever. It is capable, in the long eternity before it, of suffering more than the aggregate of all the sorrows that have yet been endured on earth, and in hell. It is capable, also, in that infinite duration, of enjoying more than the aggregate of bliss of all that has been experienced on earth united with all that has been known in heaven. A boundless eternity is before the trembling sinner, and infinite interests are at stake.

(*b*) He despairs of salvation in himself. He feels now that he has no power to rescue his soul from death. He cannot confide in his own arm, or in the arm of any mortal. He has tried every method of salvation; every way of obtaining peace of conscience; every plan that proposed security to his soul, but in vain. He stands now a lost and ruined being trembling on the shores of eternity. The boundless ocean spreads out before him. Clouds and darkness rest upon it. He has deserved no mercy; he has no claim on God to be his guide and protector; he can urge no reason why he should be admitted to a world of peace.

(*c*) In these sad and perilous circumstances, he commits his soul with all its infinite and eternal interests, into the hands of the Lord Jesus. By a simple act of faith he embraces him as his Saviour, his friend, his sacrifice, his advocate. Renouncing all confidence in his own merit, he resolves to rely on the merit of Christ; abandoning every plea on the ground of what he has himself done, he resolves to urge the merits of the Saviour as his plea, and forsaking forever all reliance for salvation on birth or blood; on moral virtues or intellectual attainments; on rank in life or the commendation of friends; on the goodness of his own heart or on forms in religion, he stakes his own everlasting interest and the question of his final salvation on the belief that there *is* a Saviour, and that Jesus is the Son of God, and that he is able and willing to save him. He is willing to risk the issue on this belief, and he who was a moment before trembling on the verge of hell *as if* there were no hope, now calmly turns the eye to heaven, and smiles through his tears and says, "I know whom I have believed, and am persuaded that he is able to keep that which I have committed unto him against that day."

(*d*) This is a wonderful act of confidence. That is great confidence which is evinced when a drowning man seizes a rope that is thrown to him, and suspends the question of his safety on the belief that you can draw him to the shore. That would be great confidence which the man who was shipwrecked, and who had clambered up a projecting rock above the reach of the waves, should evince if he would fasten a rope let down from above around his body, and swing off over the raging billows, trusting to the rope and the strength of those above to draw him up. And that is great confidence in a case already referred to where a delicately framed youthful female leaves her mother and father and commits herself, for weal or wo, into the hands of a comparative stranger. But such acts are not equal to that by which the dying soul commits itself to the Saviour. They will hardly do for an illustration. For what are the raging waves of the ocean compared with the rolling fires of the world of despair? What is the perilled death of the body compared with the death of the soul? What are all the temporal interests which youth, or beauty, or virtue can commit to another here, compared with those eternal interests which are intrusted to the Son of God? It remains then only to add:

(*e*) That in virtue of such a union there *should be* identity of treatment. So we saw in the illustration of the husband and wife, where the union between them led on common sorrows and common joys; common successes and common reverses; common sunshine and common shade. Much more should it be so in the more tender and close union of the soul to the Saviour by the act of faith. They become one. He is the "vine," they are the "branches;" he the "head," they the "members;" he lives in them and dwells in them. He is "Christ in us the hope of glory." "We are members of his body, his flesh, and his bones." "I live," says the apostle, "yet not I, but Christ liveth in me." "Because I live," said the Saviour, "ye shall live also." Through all life's future scenes his people will be treated as he was; and the union with him is so close that it introduces them to common joys and triumphs with him forever. They will be made happy because the same blessings that descend on the "head" will flow to all the "members."

In view of these remarks, the following thoughts may be suggested:—

(1.) The simplicity and ease of the way of salvation in the Gospel are remarkable. The leading thing required of him who would be saved is faith or confidence in the Redeemer. Thus Paul said to the trembling jailer at Philippi, "Believe on the Lord Jesus Christ and thou shalt be saved." Acts xvi. 31. So again in the Epistle to the Romans, "If thou shalt confess with thy mouth the Lord Jesus, and shalt believe in thine heart that God hath raised him from the dead, thou shalt be saved. For with the heart man believeth unto righteousness, and with the mouth confession is made unto salvation." Rom. x. 9, 10. Here, as everywhere in the New Testament, salvation is represented as easy. The terms are as simple as possible. There is no requisition of our attempting to obey the whole law of God as a condition of salvation; no demand on us to offer costly sacrifices, or to make pilgrimages to a distant shrine, or to practise penances and fastings, or to lacerate the body, or to attempt to work out a righteousness by conformity to external forms, or by union to a particular church. The simple, the single thing demanded is faith on the Son of God. If man has this, he is safe. No matter what his past life has been; no matter what his complexion, rank, or apparel; no matter where he lives or dies; no matter whether he worships in a splendid temple or under the open vault of heaven, and no matter whether his body rests in consecrated ground or amid the corals of the ocean, he is a child of God and an heir of the kingdom. Whatever may be said of this plan of salvation, it cannot be said that it is not sufficiently simple, and that it does not breathe a spirit of benignity toward the lost and ruined children of men. The infidel cannot object that God has not adapted it to the condition of human nature at it is—made up, for the most part, of the ignorant, the down-trodden, and of children; nor that it has required more of any man than the human powers can render. Yet,

(2.) While thus simple and easy, it is on the great principles which we see everywhere prevail. There is required in salvation that which keeps the social world together, and causes human things to move on in harmony—that without which all the interests of man would be a wreck. There is required that which would arrest all human ills, and make this still a happy world—*confidence in our God.* Man wants but this to make him a happy being here; he will want but this to make him happy forever. As confidence is the great principle which cements society, so it was indispensable in religion that confidence in God should be restored. We cannot conceive that a human being could be saved without faith. Even if it had not been distinctly and formally *required in the plan,* it is impossible to conceive that there could have been salvation without it. The very process of returning to God from our wanderings implies returning confidence in him—for how or why should the sinner return to him if he has no confidence in him? And how could he be happy in heaven if he had no confidence in God? What would heaven be if there were the same distrust of the Deity, and the same jarring opinions, and the same alienation from him, and the same doubt of his being, his justice, and his goodness there which exist on earth? The plan of salvation by faith is laid in the deepest philosophy—and is based on the irreversible nature of things.

(3.) The subject suggests a remark on the nature and aims of infidelity. Men often think that unbelief is a harmless thing. They sometimes regard it as a special proof of meritorious independence to be an infidel. They pride themselves on their philosophy, and their freedom from vulgar prejudices and priestcraft—perhaps on their freedom from the prejudices instilled by a pious parent, a pastor, or a Sunday-school teacher. They consider the denunciations of unbelief in the gospel as singularly harsh, and use no measured terms in expressing their abhorrence of a system which denounces the eternal pains of hell on a man because he will not believe. The want of faith, say they, is a harmless or a meritorious thing. But are you connected with a bank? Would you think that a harmless effort in a daily paper which should attempt to unsettle the confidence of the community in your institution? Have you a character for virtue, which you have secured by years of toil, and of upright deportment? Is that a harmless report in the community which tends to destroy all confidence in that character? Are you a father? Is it a harmless effort of your neighbour when he attempts to unsettle the confidence of your own children in your virtue? Are you a husband? Is he a harmless man who shall aim to unsettle your faith in the wife of your bosom, and produce between you and her an utter want of confidence? And is there no evil in that state of mind where there is no confidence in God that rules on high—the God that made us, and that holds our destiny in his hands? Is it nothing to unsettle the faith of man in his God, and to introduce universal distrust in his government? Is it nothing to inculcate or cherish the thought that the governor of the world is a dark, malignant, harsh, and severe being, and to alienate the affections of creation from its God? Let the history of the earth answer. All our evils began in that unhappy moment when our first parents lost their confidence in their God. "Loss of Eden," toil, sweat, despair, perplexity and death, tell what the evil was. Calamities have rolled along in black and angry surges, and the dark flood still swells and heaves upon the earth. Peace will be restored and paradise regained only when man is restored to confidence in his God—and this is the grand and glorious work of the gospel. This done in any heart, and its "peace becomes as a river and its righteousness as the waves of the sea." This done all over the earth, and millennial joy will visit the nations. This done, as successive individuals or generations leave the world, death is disarmed of his sting, for the departing soul leaves with full assurance of faith on the Saviour.

VIII. *The bearing and importance of the doctrine of justification by faith.*

The points which have been illustrated in the previous sections are the following:—The importance of the inquiry how man can be justified with God; the fact that man cannot justify or vindicate himself by denying the truth of the charges against him; the fact that he cannot do it by showing that he had a right to do as he has done; the fact that he cannot merit salvation; what is to be understood by the merits of Christ; in what sense we are justified by the merits of Christ; and the agency of faith in our justification. It is proposed now, in the conclusion of the subject, to refer to some historical illustrations of the value and influence of the doctrine of justification by faith, and to show why it has the place which history has assigned it.

In illustrating the value and influence of the doctrine as shown by history, three periods of the world may be briefly referred to.

(1.) The first is the age of the apostles, when, perhaps, the effect of the doctrine of justification by faith was more vividly seen than it has ever been since. That this was the doctrine which Paul preached; which he made prominent in his writings; and which he everywhere defended, no one acquainted with his history can for a moment doubt. It would be needless here to transcribe the passages of his writings which declare his views on this point; or which show how earnestly he expressed his convictions of its truth and importance. Everywhere he maintained that a man is not justified by the deeds of the law, but by the righteousness of faith; that we are saved not by works of righteousness which we have done; that they that are under the law are under the curse; and that they who are justified by faith have peace with God through the Lord Jesus Christ. In the most earnest and emphatic manner he abjured all dependence on his own merits for salvation; disclaimed all reliance on the extraordinary zeal for religion which he had manifested in early life, and on his own blameless outward deportment, and declared it now to be the grand purpose of his soul to "know Christ, and to be found in him, not having his own righteousness which was of the law, but the righteousness which is of God by faith." Phil. iii. 9. In this he coincided with all the other apostles, who taught, as he did, that no reliance was to be placed on outward forms of religion, on good works, on an amiable character, or on alms, as the ground of salvation. It was then that the doctrine of simple dependence on Christ for salvation went forth with freshness and with power. It was unencumbered by any attending doctrine of a different character to fetter its movements; or to hinder its progress through the world. There was no necessity proclaimed of depending on rites or forms of religion; no reverence for sacred places inculcated as necessary to salvation; no connection with a particular church organized under a peculiar ministry, was declared to be essential; no saving efficacy was attributed to sacraments and to alms; no merits of the holy men of other ages could be depended upon to make up the deficiency of those who sought to be saved; no promise was held out that the dead might be saved through the extraordinary sacrifices and benevolence of the living. The naked doctrine of justification by faith in Christ stood out before the world; fresh in its youthful vigour; with no trappings or ornaments to hide and obscure it; a simple, solemn, sublime truth that all might appreciate and that might be available to all. This was then the sword of the spirit—slaying human pride; cutting down the self-righteousness of men; prostrating the great and the mean, the learned and the unlearned, the patrician and the plebeian, the master and the slave, the man in purple and the man in rags, alike—a sword whose keenness was not rendered useless then by being hid in a gorgeous scabbard.

The doctrine thus promulgated by the apostle stood opposed to the prevailing views of all the world. It was opposed to all the aims of the Pharisees—the essential tenet of whose religion was expressed graphically and honestly by one of their own number, "God, I thank thee that I am not as other men are." It stood opposed to all the views of the Sadducees, who held to the necessity of *no* kind of religion, denying the whole doctrine of the future state. It stood opposed to the Essenes, the remaining Jewish sect, who sought to work out their salvation by extraordinary fastings and privations, and by exclusion from contact with the world. It stood opposed to the whole system of sacrifices among the heathen, seeking to propitiate the gods, and to render themselves accepted by dependence on the forms of religion; and it was at variance with all the views of philosophy—the pride of the Stoic, confident in his own righteousness; the licentiousness of the Epicurean, justifying his own voluptuousness; and the self-complacency of the sage, who relied on his own wisdom. An apostle could go nowhere where the doctrine would not come in conflict with all the prevailing views in regard to the way in which men might be saved. Yet no one now can be ignorant of the effect of this doctrine as promulgated by the apostles. It changed the religion of the world, for Christianity made no other advances than as it taught men to renounce every other ground of dependence and to rely for salvation solely on the merits of the Lord Jesus Christ. It had no martial power by which to make its way; it had no influence derived from name and rank to enforce its claim; it had no authority derived from a venerable antiquity on which to rely; it had no gorgeous and imposing forms to enable it to command the respect of those who had worshipped in the Parthenon or the Pantheon; it had no claims to any new discoveries in philosophy. It had but *one* thing that was new, great, improving, commanding, and that was the announcement of Christ crucified, and the fact that men everywhere might now be justified by the merits of his atoning blood. Never has any truth on any subject stood more by itself, to make its own way without adventitious aid, than this did in the hands of the Christian apostles, and never before had any single truth on any subject produced such changes in the world.

(2.) The second fact, to which reference will be made, is the state of the world when the doctrine of justification by faith was obscured and almost extinguished in the Church. It soon began to be obscured. Very early the professed friends of religion began to lose sight of it. So strong in the human mind is the love of pomp and ceremony and form; so attached is man to splendour and show in religion as in every thing else; so prone is the heart to rely on its own doings; and so reluctant is the sinner everywhere to depend for salvation on the righteousness of another, that this doctrine gradually died away and almost ceased to be remembered in the church. Then arose the system which spread night all over the Christian world—the night of ignorance, error, superstition, and crime—a night deepening for ages till it terminated in the consummate depravity of the Papacy under Alexander VI. Under this forgetfulness of the doctrine of justification by faith, or of salvation by simple dependence on Christ crucified, arose the universal respect for sacred places and orders of men; zeal for splendid temples of worship and for gorgeous ceremonies; extraordinary veneration for the sepulchres of saints, and for their holy remains; pilgrimages to the holy land; the doctrine of baptismal regeneration and of absolution of sins by the imposition of holy hands; the belief that grace was imparted by sacraments administered by a priesthood; the doctrine that the merits of the saints of other days were garnered up for the benefit of future ages and placed at the disposal of the Church; the multiplication of sacraments with saving efficacy attributed to them all, and the belief of a peculiar sacredness attached to ground consecrated to the burial of the dead. All these were features of one great system. They had *some* relation to Christianity, and had grown in part out of the abuse of its doctrines. But though various, they were arranged evidently under the auspices of one master mind and with the same end in view. That was to render nugatory the doctrine of justification by faith, and to substitute in its place the doctrine of salvation by works. It was, indeed, salvation by works connected with the religion of Christ, and was a different system from that of the Pharisee who expected to be saved by conformity to the law of Moses; or the Grecian philosopher who hoped to reach heaven by the purity of his doctrine and his morals; or the degraded pagan who relied on the blood of his sacrifices; or the man now who relies on his own honesty and fidelity in the various relations of life; but it was essentially the same system. It excluded the simple dependence of the soul on the Lord Jesus for salvation, and substituted in its stead a reliance on human merit.

The effect was seen in the darkness, sin, and corruption of Europe before the Reformation. Every feature of the state of things in the "dark ages" can be traced to an obscuring of the great doctrine of justification by faith. Every advance of society into that deep and deepening gloom was connected with some loosening of its hold on that doctrine, and the substitution of something else in its place, until the hold was entirely gone, and Europe was plunged in total night.

(3.) The third historical fact, therefore, to be referred to, is the effect which the recovery and restoration of this doctrine had on the Church and the world at the period of the Reformation. To those who have studied the history of that period, as all Protestants should do, it is unnecessary to say that this was the elementary doctrine—the central view—the starting point—in the whole of that glorious revolution. This was the great truth that dawned on the mind of Luther, and which led to all that he attempted and accomplished for the restoration of the Church to its primitive purity, and it occupied an equally central position in the view of all his fellow-labourers. Three times was the doctrine of justification by faith brought before the mind of Luther, with the same sort of power which it had when promulgated by the apostles, and with such energy as to rouse all that was great in his soul into life. The first was when he was a monk in his cell. He had found a copy of the Bible, and he began to study it and to lecture on it. He commenced with the Psalms, but soon passed to the Epistle to the Romans. One day having proceeded as far as the seventeenth verse of the first chapter, the words quoted from Habakkuk—"The just shall live by faith"—arrested his attention. A new thought struck him. A new way of salvation opened before his mind. A new light shone upon his heart, and the words "the just shall live by faith" seemed never to leave him. The second instance was when he first visited Rome. These words followed him and lingered on his ear. One of his first impressions was that he was now in the very place to which Paul had addressed these words in his epistle. Yet in that city how were they obscured and unknown! On every hand were arrangements for being justified by works—by forms and ceremonies; by pomp and pageantry; by the merits of the saints, and by penance. What a total obscuration of the great doctrine which Paul had taught in the letter to the Church there, and which he had himself doubtless taught when he had dwelt in that city! The third instance in which these words were brought to the heart of Luther was more impressive still. "One day wishing to obtain an indulgence promised by the pope to any one who should ascend on his knees what is called

'*Pilate's stair-case,*' the poor Saxon monk was slowly climbing those steps which they told him had been miraculously transported from Jerusalem to Rome. But while he was going through this meritorious work he thought he heard a voice, like thunder, speaking from the depths of his heart, '*The just shall live by faith.*' He started up in terror on the steps up which he had been crawling; he was horrified at himself; and, struck with shame for the degradation to which superstition had debased him, he fled from the scene of his folly. This powerful text had a mysterious influence on the life of Luther. It was a creative word for the Reformer and for the Reformation."—*D'Aubigné.* It was this truth that wrought out the Reformation: and whatever there was in that work that is valuable and precious; whatever there was to shed a benign influence on literature, liberty and morals; whatever there was to spread pure religion over Switzerland, or Germany, or England, or ultimately over our own land, and then by a reflex influence on Asia Minor, on Palestine, on the palmy East, on dark Africa, and on the islands of the sea, is to be traced to those moments when this text broke with so much living power on the soul of Luther:—"The just shall live by faith." It became with him an elementary truth, that the doctrine of justification by faith was the "article of the standing or the falling church"—the very *joint* or *hinge* (*articulus*) on which the whole depended.* To that doctrine we owe, in its various developments, all that we value in this Protestant land, and all that distinguishes us in religion from what Europe was in the days of Alexander VI. and Leo X.; and there is not an interest of religion, liberty, or learning, which has not been moulded by it more than by any other single cause. Our modes of worship; our readiness to spread the Bible; our freedom of discussion;

---

* "*Articulus stantis vel cadentis ecclesiæ.*"

our general diffusion of intelligence; our untrammelled press; our separation of religion from the state; our societies for the spread of the gospel; our blessed and glorious revivals; our deliverance from superstition, and from the tyranny of a priesthood, and from the corruptions and abominations of the monastic system, and from the debasement of penance and pilgrimages, are all to be traced to the power of this single truth that blazed with such an intensity on the soul of the poor Saxon monk. Such being some of the facts in the case, let us,

I. Inquire why this doctrine has this importance and power. This will be seen if we can trace its connection with what it has been undeniably everywhere united with—a religion of deep spirituality; of simplicity of worship; of deadness to the world; of freedom of opinion; of liberal views, and of great and cheerful sacrifices for the good of mankind. There are but two systems of religion on the earth: the one is that of self-righteousness; the other that of salvation by the merits of Christ; the one that of men who attempt, in various ways, to justify themselves before God; the other, that of those who seek to be justified through the righteousness of the Redeemer. The bearing and importance of the latter, in contrast with the former, is the point now before us.

(1.) This doctrine of justification by faith has a power of reaching the soul and of calling forth every active energy of our nature which the other system never can have. It leaves the impresion that the soul is of vast value; that religion is of inestimable importance; that the grand purpose of living should be religion. The reason of this, which may not at once be apparent, is, that it finds the soul in such a state, wherever it is embraced, that it arouses all that is thrilling, and vast, and momentous in the soul itself, and in its hopes and relations. The language which the doctrine of justification by faith addresses to each individual is this:

"You are a lost sinner. You have no righteousness of your own. You never will have any. Your heart is by nature depraved, and your whole past life has been evil. In all that you have done, you have done nothing to merit the favour of God, or even to commend yourself to his approbation. All your righteousness is as filthy rags. All your outward forms of religion; your fastings, penance, and vows; your amiableness of character, your honesty, your integrity, your pride of birth and station, are all to pass for nothing before God in the matter of justification. Nor can you hope of yourself to do any thing more in the future that will commend you to God than you have done in the past. No form of religion; no flood of tears; no framing of the life by an outward law; no acts of self-denial; no fastings, prayers, or almsgivings can wipe away the deep stains of past guilt on the soul, or constitute an expiation for what you have done. In this state you are near the grave, and just over the world of wo. A moment might cut you off from the land of the living, and from the possibility of being saved. In this state you are wholly dependent on the sovereign mercy of God. You *may* be saved, but not by works of righteousness of your own. You *may* be saved, but it must be by renouncing all dependence on your own righteousness forever. You *may* be saved, but it must be wholly by the merits of another. Kings, sages, philosophers, priests, poets, warriors, knights, senators, judges; the gay, the accomplished, the rich, the poor, the vile, the bond, the free; all lie on a level before God. You *may be* saved; but it will only be by your making up the mind to a willingness to be saved in the same way as the vilest of the species, and to stand before the throne clothed in the same robes of salvation that shall adorn the most debased and down-trodden of the human race. Now it is easy to conceive, even for those who have not experienced this, that such a religion must have the elements of great *power* of some kind. It can make its way only by sufficient power to crush the pride of man; to bring down his lofty thoughts; to humble him in the dust, and then by imparting life where there was none. There is nothing negative and tame about it. It has living energy through all this process. No man reaches the position of self-abasement and self-renunciation where this doctrine finds him, without a struggle with his own pride. To come down there and to lie thus low before God, is the result of mighty power on a proud man's soul, and is no neutral or unmeaning thing. It is not the work of ease and of effeminacy, and the business of a holiday, for a man to renounce all his own righteousness, and to be willing to acknowledge, before heaven, and earth, and hell, that he is so great a sinner that he ought to be excluded from heaven, and banished from the earth and be doomed to unspeakable torments forever in hell. And it is not an unmeaning thing when in this state a voice from heaven bids him rise from the dust, and go forth a pardoned man, a renovated being, a child of God, an heir of heaven.

Accordingly this *is* the doctrine which arouses the world. It was this which produced the commotions in the apostolic times, when it was said, "These that have turned the world upside down are come hither also." It was this which produced so much excitement at Jerusalem, at Antioch, at Philippi. It was this which aroused Europe in the Reformation. It is this whose power is seen in every revival of religion. It is this whose energy is felt in the efforts made to carry religion around the globe.

To illustrate what has been now said, reference may be made to the case of two individuals who have stated the effect of this doctrine on their own minds. The first is that of the apostle Paul. It is found in the epistle to the Philippians. "If any other man thinketh that he hath whereof he might trust in the flesh, I more: circumcised the eighth day, of the stock of Israel, of the tribe of Benjamin, an Hebrew of the Hebrews; as touching the law, a Pharisee; concerning zeal, persecuting the church; touching the righteousness which is in the law, blameless. *But what things were gain to me, those I counted loss for Christ. Yea doubtless, I count all things but loss for the excellency of the knowledge of Christ Jesus my Lord.* Chap. iii. 4–8. The other is a record of Luther's feelings by himself when he was first made to understand this doctrine. "Though as a monk," says he, "I was holy and irreproachable, my conscience was still filled with trouble and torment. I could not endure the expression—'The righteous justice of God.' I did not love that just and holy Being who punishes sinners. I felt a secret anger against him; I hated him because, not satisfied with terrifying by his law and by the miseries of life poor creatures already ruined by original sin, he aggravated our sufferings by the gospel. But when by the Spirit of God I understood these words—when I learnt how the justification of the sinner proceeds from God's mere mercy by the way of faith—then I felt myself born again as a new man, and I entered by an open door into the very paradise of God. From that hour I saw the precious and Holy Scriptures with new eyes. I went through the whole Bible. I collected a multitude of passages which taught me what the work of God was. And as I had before heartily hated the expression, 'The righteousness of God,' I began from that time to value and to love it as the sweetest and most consolatory truth. Truly this text of St. Paul was to me as the very gate of heaven." —*D'Aubigné.*

To a soul thus lost and ruined, this doctrine always has this power. To others it has neither power nor beauty, nor can we hope that it will make its way among men except where the soul is deeply aroused on the subject of religion. Then it is what it is so often said to be in the Scriptures,

"The power of God:" it is His mighty energy quickening the soul that was dead in sin to newness of life.

(2.) The second remark illustrating its bearing and importance, will be drawn from the contrast of this doctrine with the opposite. It has already been observed that there are, in fact, but two kinds of religion on the earth, that of self-righteousness and that of dependence on another for salvation; that in which man attempts to justify himself, and that in which he relies for justification on the merits of the Son of God. These systems divide the world; for, however numerous may be the methods by which men attempt to save themselves, they all have this essential characteristic, that they are systems of self-righteousness. What are the characteristics of these two systems? What would be the tendency of each of them? Let them be put in contrast, and what must be the effect of each of them? The effect of the one—of the plan of justification by faith—we have already in part seen. Its obvious tendency must be to produce humility, penitence, gratitude, a simple reliance on the Saviour, a disposition to make him all in all in religion. What are the effects of the opposite system? They must be such as these:—

(*a*) Pride. "God, I thank thee that I am not as other men are," is its language all over the world.

(*b*) A multiplication of forms, and a reliance on them. Religion becomes an *outward* thing, not a work of the heart. So it was with the Pharisees, the Greeks, the Romans; so it is now in the pagan world, among Mohammedans, and in all the perverted forms of Christianity. It matters little what the outward form is; but where the doctrine of justification is obscured or unknown, religion *must* degenerate into heartless forms. It makes up for its want of vital power by the multiplication of rites and ceremonies. It adds a new ceremony for every step of departure from the doctrine of justification by faith; it attaches an additional sacredness to them as this doctrine is obscured, and where this is wholly lost out of view, religion becomes merely a punctilious performance of imposing rites, a careful observance of forms. A man, when he thinks of death and the judgment, *must* have *some* righteousness on which to rely. If it be not that of the Saviour, and if it be the pretence of religion at all, it must be that consisting of a sacred reverence for forms.

(*c*) The denial of the doctrine of justification by faith will be always attended with superstition. There will be an attempt to merit heaven by reverencing dead men's bones, by pilgrimages, by bodily torture, by seclusion from the world, by garnishing the sepulchres of the righteous, and by imploring the intercession of departed saints. The world must make up its mind to have the doctrine of justification by faith held in its purity, or to have a religion of superstition substituted in its place. One or the other has prevailed always; one has always excluded the other; the suppression of the one has been the occasion of the introduction of the other; and one or the other will live to the end of time. The question is now before this country whether we shall cling to the great doctrine of justification by faith, or whether we shall go abroad and import all the superstitions of heathenism, whether original or baptized at Rome; whether we shall adhere to the grand truth which was the element in the Reformation, or take Christianity, so called, as it was in the days of Alexander VI. and Leo X.

(*d*) The system which denies this doctrine has been, from some cause, an exclusive and a persecuting system. To whatever this fact may be traced, of the fact itself there can be no doubt. The history of the world has confirmed it, and that history has taught us that if we would be free from the evils of an exclusive and a persecuting system, we must hold in its simplicity and its purity the great doctrine of justification by faith.

(3.) A third thing illustrating its bearing and importance, is the fact that it is connected with freedom of thought and the advancement of society. The fact here is more apparent than the reason of it. No one acquainted with history will dispute the fact that the doctrine of justification by faith has been held with the most simplicity and purity in the times when freedom of thought has most prevailed and in the lands most characterized for it. And no one can doubt that the denial of the doctrine, and the denial of the right of free inquiry, have gone together. It was the same system, which denied by all its arrangements the doctrine of justification by faith, which imprisoned Galileo. The Inquisition grew up in lands where this doctrine was denied, and has flourished there only, and could live nowhere else. The proclamation of this doctrine in Europe by Luther and his fellow-labourers unfettered the human mind and abolished the Inquisition; and nothing can be clearer than that no circumstances could ever arise in any land in which the doctrine of justification by simple faith in Christ is held in which such an institution could be established; and we may be certain that, as long as we can assert this doctrine in its purity throughout all our borders, we shall be free from thumb-screws, and racks, and *auto-da-fès*, and dark dungeons made to incarcerate the advocate of any religious belief. Whatever *else* we may be subjected to, this doctrine will be a palladium to us, not fabled as was the image of Minerva, but a reality to secure for us the protection of heaven.

The *reasons* of the fact which is now adverted to, would be found in such considerations as these:—That in this doctrine there is nothing which we wish to conceal; that it depends for its support on nothing which may not be fully examined; that it recognises everywhere the equality of men; that it asks no patronage from the state; that it relies for its advancement on its own simple power *as truth*—as commending itself to the conscience and the reason of mankind, and as finding a response in the soul of every man who feels that he is a sinner. The support of the other system is to be found in just the opposite of these things. It cloaks itself in mystery. It seeks to establish the claims of a priesthood composed of a superior order of men, and this *must* be done on arguments that will not bear the light. It is, and must be sustained by the power of the state. It loves a religion of *blind believing* rather than of *reasoning*. It is identified with all that human ingenuity can devise to substitute a righteousness in the place of that by faith in the Saviour. It is identified with interest—where the procuring of absolution becomes a matter of bargain and sale. And it is conscious that the free examination of its claims would show how baseless is the fabric on which it stands, and the worthlessness of all the devices which have been originated to enable man to work out a righteousness of his own. Without pursuing these thoughts further, one other remark may be added. It is

(4.) That the doctrine of justification by faith is connected with liberality in religion. We have seen what is the character, in this respect, of the opposite system. It is essential to every other system that it *be* illiberal and exclusive. The reason is this. According to every such system, grace is conveyed only through a certain channel. There are certain men who alone are appointed to dispense it; it is to be obtained only in union with a certain ecclesiastical connection, and in the performance of certain specified rites and ceremonies. But none of these things are essential to the doctrine of justification by faith. It is a direct concern between the soul and its

Saviour. It practically removes every human being from any participation in obtaining for the sinner the favour of God. However the ministers of religion may have been instrumental in arousing the attention of the soul to its guilt and danger, or in pointing the way to the cross, yet the transaction is one where all foreign agency and all human holiness of office are excluded. It is not essential whether the minister officiates with or without a surplice; whether in a plain "meeting-house" or a magnificent cathedral; whether he can trace his commission through the apostolic succession or not; whether his doctrines can or cannot be sustained by synods and councils; nay, whether there *be* any minister of religion at all, for the soul may be justified by simple faith in the Lord Jesus. The worshipper may be a Cameronian on the hills of Scotland under the open heaven; or a man who has strayed somehow into a conventicle; or a wandering savage who is made to listen, to attend, to be enraptured, till his eyes pour forth tears under the preaching of some humble missionary on whose head the hands of a mitred prelate have never been laid, and there shall be all the elements of the doctrine of justification. What has occurred to him on the hills, or in the woods, or in a school-house, or in a church, he feels *may* occur anywhere else in the same way. It will not become then *essential* to his view that the doctrines of religion should be preached *on* a hill, or in a valley; that the minister stands in front of a tent, or that he ministers at a certain altar; it will not be *essential* that he wear a certain vestment, or be able to trace his spiritual genealogy back to far distant times,—what he wishes to know is whether a man has experienced in his own soul what he has in his—the power of the doctrine of justification by faith in the blood of Jesus. If he has, that is enough. It is to him a question of comparatively no moment whether he thinks that baptism by immersion is the only method; or whether he regards John Wesley as the greatest and the best of men; or whether he believes that all human wisdom was embodied in the Westminster Assembly of divines; or whether he thinks that the ministry exists only in three orders. All these will be comparative trifles. The grand matter is, that the lost and guilty soul is justified by the blood of the "everlasting covenant;" and that settles every thing that is truly valuable in his view in regard to the salvation of the soul. Such a system, it is clear, must be essentially liberal. It cannot be a system which will be primarily concerned in "questions and strifes of words" about the externals of religion. It will recognise in every man, who has ever felt the efficacy of the blood of Christ, a Christian brother. It will regard all men by nature as essentially on the same level in reference to salvation. There will be, in the matter of religion, no favoured class, no holy order; none, by nature, nearer heaven than others, and none who shall have a right to prescribe to others what they are to believe or to do. One point—one grand doctrine distinguishes them, no matter of what sect, or country, or complexion, they may be—that they are redeemed by the blood of the same Saviour. They are of the same family. They have the same rights in the kingdom of grace. No one has a right, in virtue of blood, or name, or connection with outward forms of religion, to claim a superior nearness to heaven; nor, if the soul is justified by the blood of Jesus, has he the right or the disposition to withhold the name of Christian, or to say that a soul thus justified is left to "the uncovenanted mercies of God."

The doctrine which has been considered constitutes the peculiarity of the Protestant religion. Protestantism began in the restoration of the doctrine of justification by faith. This, more than any thing else, distinguishes the system.

All there *is* of Protestantism that is of value is in this doctrine; and all that we have of liberality in religion, and freedom from persecution, and purity of doctrine, is to be traced to this.

The whole discussion on the doctrine of justification may be closed by a personal appeal to those who may read this tract. There are but two ways conceivable on which you can be saved. One is, on the ground of your own righteousness; the other is, on the ground of the righteousness of the Lord Jesus. There is no middle way conceivable. It is the grand question, then, and one in which every individual has the deepest interest, What *is* the ground of your reliance? On which of these do you depend when you think of being admitted to heaven? If you rely on the former—on your own righteousness—it must be either because you can disprove *the facts* which are charged on you as sin, or because, if the facts are undeniable, you will be able to vindicate your conduct before the bar of the Almighty. Here, then, it may be solemnly asked, whether you are willing to rest your soul's interests on such a foundation? Are you prepared to abide the issue of such a trial? Can you calmly look forward to such an investigation of your life before God's bar, and feel secure when you think of the tremendous interests of the soul that are at stake? Are you prepared to go up to meet your Maker with the feeling that your only hope there is self-vindication? It may be permitted to the writer of this tract, in view of these reasonings, and of the truths that have been suggested, and in view also of the solemn fact that he, like those whom he addresses, is soon to stand before the tribunal where all will be judged, to say, "I AM NOT. I turn to the other system which I have endeavoured to set before you. I look away from all that I have done—the miserable rags of my own righteousness—to the white robe of salvation wrought out by my great Redeemer, and seek to wrap that robe around my guilty soul, and I feel that if justified by faith in his blood I shall be safe."

A guilty, weak, and helpless worm,
  On thy kind arms I fall;
Be thou my strength and righteousness,
  My Saviour and my all.

THE END.

STEREOTYPED BY L. JOHNSON AND CO.
PHILADELPHIA.

No. 4.

THE

ABRAHAMIC COVENANT AND THE NEW TESTAMENT CHURCH.

BY

JOSEPH C. STILES, D.D.

The Presbyterian Publication Committee.

DEPOSITORIES:

PHILADELPHIA: PRESBYTERIAN HOUSE, 386 CHESTNUT STREET.
NEW YORK: IVISON & PHINNEY, 178 FULTON ST.

No. 4.

THE

ABRAHAMIC COVENANT AND THE NEW TESTAMENT CHURCH.

THE covenant of God with Abraham under the old dispensation, and his covenant with men in these days of the Gospel, compose his great church arrangement for the salvation of the world.

In opposition to this statement, let it be observed, that the Church of God, as to its *origin*, was intimated to man at the moment of his fall, but found its first development in the Abrahamic covenant; as to its *essence*, the unity of the Church in earlier and in later times is established by identity of parties, relations, agencies, and objects; as to its *form*, it was encumbered by a multitude of observances, ceremonial and political, in ancient times, while its modern administration is marked by simplicity and spirituality; and as to its *force*, while the Abrahamic covenant worked as a temporal arrangement to the close of the first dispensation, it clearly carried at the same time a spiritual bearing, co-extensive with the general features of the Christian Church in the gospel dispensation.

We affirm, therefore,

THAT THE CHURCH UNDER THE ABRAHAMIC COVENANT AND THE NEW TESTAMENT DISPENSATION ARE SUBSTANTIALLY ONE AND THE SAME INSTITUTION.

We have two legitimate sources of evidence: Old Testament language of the covenant, and New Testament interpretation of it.

The Church of God in our day is based upon that permanent spiritual covenant between God and man, signed and sealed by a significant rite, whereby, through the atonement of his Son, and the agency of his Spirit, God offers and secures salvation to all that believe.

The New Testament Church embraces six particulars, and only six that are material: 1. Its dignity; a permanent covenant. 2. Its parties; God and man. 3. Its provisions; the Son and the Spirit. 4. Its great requirement of man; faith. 5. Its great promise by God; salvation. 6. Its appointed seal; a significant rite. If each of these particulars is fully embraced in God's covenant with the patriarch, then that covenant is the great gospel covenant; the constitution of the Church.

I. The Abrahamic covenant is a *permanent arrangement.*

It is universally conceded that the Church is a standing institution for all ages. If, therefore, the Abrahamic covenant is a temporary arrangement, it is not the gospel covenant. God's stipulation with the patriarch will be seen, however, to be an everlasting covenant, if we examine:

1. The language of the covenant itself; "I will establish my covenant between me and thee, and thy seed after thee in their generations for an everlasting covenant." Gen. xvii. 7. This covenant is not confined to Abraham, for it extends to his seed; nor to the patriarch's children, for it extends to his seed in their generations; nor to any limited number of generations, for it is established with Abraham and his seed, in their generations, for an everlasting covenant.

2. The multiplied and most solemn rehearsals of the covenant through all periods of the Old Testament dispensation, as an everlasting covenant.

In Abraham's day the Almighty said to the patriarch, "Sarah, thy wife, shall bear a son, and thou shalt call his name Isaac, and I will establish my covenant with him for an everlasting covenant, and with his seed after him." True to his word, God did renew this covenant with Isaac and with Jacob in their day. Nine hundred years after its formation, in the reign of David, this covenant was called up and confirmed in a most impressive manner. David said to Israel, "Be ye always mindful of his covenant, the word which he commanded to a thousand generations, even of the covenant which he made with Abraham, and of his oath unto Isaac, and confirmed the same unto Jacob for a law, and unto Israel for an everlasting covenant." Here is a covenant of eternal remembrance; a command to a thousand generations; to Abraham a covenant; to Isaac an oath; to Jacob a law; to Israel an everlasting covenant. In like manner, the Scriptures present frequent notices of this transaction as an everlasting covenant through all the days of the prophets, especially by Isaiah, Jeremiah, Ezekiel, and even by Malachi. Ps. lxxxix. 3, 4, 6; Is. xxiv. 5; lv. 3; lxi. 8; Jer. xxxii. 40; xxxvii. 26; Ezek. xvi. 60; Mal. ii. 10.

3. This institution survives the Old Testament dispensation, and acts in full force under the reign of the Gospel, as an everlasting covenant.

We shall be compelled to present a multitude of testimonies to this point under every successive head of investigation, and shall therefore mention very few in this connection.

In the Epistle to the Hebrews it is spoken of expressly as everlasting: "Through the blood of the everlasting covenant." We know that this passage refers to the Abrahamic covenant, because it includes Christ, and Christ a curse for us, as we shall abundantly show. Indeed the writer himself gives us satisfactory evidence of this in a parallel passage in the same epistle. The Abrahamic covenant is well known through all parts of the Old Testament by three marks: It is styled "an everlasting covenant;" carries the general promise, "I will be your God and ye shall be my people;" and usually annexes some special promise of spiritual regeneration.

In Jer. xxxii. 40, God holds out the everlasting covenant with the patriarchal promise, "I will be their God and they shall be my people," and then he adds, "And I will put my fear in their hearts, and they shall not depart from me." Now, in the eighth of Hebrews, Paul alludes to the Sinai covenant as an inferior abrogated one, and in contrast brings up that better, more enduring covenant which was established upon better promises. He gives us a sample of these better promises. One is, "I will be to them a God and they shall be to me a people." Another is, "I will put my laws within their minds and write them in their hearts." Here are the three marks of the covenant of Abraham: it is an everlasting covenant, securing to Israel Jehovah as their God, and putting his fear in their hearts.

Whatever ambiguity may sometimes arise from the limited use of the term "everlasting" in the Scriptures, if the spiritual and permanent nature of the subject in hand, its contrast with temporal covenants, its recognition in the gospel as a permanent institution, did not dissipate all doubt, surely the following testimony must settle the question forever. Under the New Testament dispensation, an inspired writer argues out the necessary perpetuity of the Abrahamic covenant, from its very nature as a solemnized compact. Such a transaction between men, says the apostle, is stable and binding; "Though it be but a man's covenant, yet if it be confirmed, no man disannulleth or addeth thereto." Gal. iii. 15. The Abrahamic covenant had been "ordered in all things and sure," and preceded the Sinai covenant more than four centuries, wherefore Paul continues, "Now this I say, brethren, that the covenant which was confirmed before of God in Christ, the law which was four hundred and thirty years after could not disannul, that it should make the promise of none effect." In substance this is Paul's reasoning: All the integrities of the Godhead had solemnly pledged certain blessings to Abraham and his seed forever. This covenant is immutable in its nature. Therefore the introduction of a new economy five hundred years after, in the days of Moses, could not destroy the covenant. By parity of reasoning, the introduction of another, two thousand years after, in the days of Christ, could not make the promise of none effect. Thus, with the strongest assurance, the apostle speaks of the blessings of God's covenant with Abraham as actually descending upon Gentiles in these days of the Gospel.

The Abrahamic covenant is therefore clearly a permanent arrangement for all periods of this world's history: because it is God's covenant with Abraham and his seed in their generations for an everlasting covenant; it was renewed in the persons of Isaac, Jacob, David, and all Israel as a covenant, an oath, a law, a word to a thousand generations, an everlasting covenant; was rehearsed as such by the prophets to the very close of the Old Testament dispensation; is still denominated in the New Testament an everlasting covenant, and marked by the well-known patriarchal promises; and is finally proved by the express argument of an inspired man to be essentially immutable.

So far as the first feature of the Church is concerned, permanency of obligation, is not the Abrahamic covenant identical with the Gospel? If the Gospel endures forever, the Abrahamic covenant also works through time and eternity.

II. Its *parties* are God and man.

All men know that the Church is not now confined to any one nation. Had the Abrahamic covenant, therefore, been limited to the Jews, this simple fact would have demonstrated its radical distinction from the Gospel. That the parties to the covenant with Abraham are the parties to the Church, not God and the Jews, but God and man, may be inferred:

1. From Abraham's titles.

The patriarch's first name, "Abram, high father," was changed to "Abraham, father of a multitude." The patriarch's descendants were numerous, and it might be objected that this appellation was ambiguous. He is styled again "father of many nations." It is difficult to confine this title to one nation. Again, "father of that which is of the law and that which is of faith." Should it still be said that there might be believers as well as legalists among the lineal descendants of Abraham, then let it be remembered, that Abraham is the "father of all them that believe," and "the father of the faithful." Surely these appellations transcend the boundaries of Judea to find the parties of the Abrahamic covenant. If there did exist one remaining doubt, it would be dissipated by his further designations, "heir of the world," "father of us all," Gentile as well as Jew.

2. From the descriptions of Abraham's seed.

Scripture furnishes two marks of the seed. Negatively: the promise of this covenant is not limited to the natural descendants of the patriarch; "neither because they are the seed of Abraham are they all children,"—all his descendants are not included. "They who are the children of the flesh are not the children of God,"—a part rejected. "For if they who are of the law be heirs, faith is made void, and the promise of none effect,"—this establishes the spirituality and consequent universal bearing of the covenant. Thus, they who are of the flesh, of the law, the seed of Abraham, naturally, are not the seed of the covenant.

Positively: the Gentile as well as the Jew is covered by the Abrahamic covenant. The condition of the promise was formed with an express reference to the universal bearing of the covenant. The promise of Abraham and his seed was not made through the law, but through the righteousness of faith. Had the promise been confined to the law, it would have been shut up to the Jews; but working through faith, all that believe are embraced, without limitation to time or territory. Indeed we are expressly informed by the apostle, that in this covenant with Abraham, there is neither Jew nor Greek, bond nor free, "For you, Galatians, believing, are Abraham's seed.' And of us Romans, believing, Abraham is the father." But this point is placed in the clearest possible light by one fact—Abraham believed before he was circumcised, expressly "that he might be the father of all them that believe, though they be not circumcised, that the blessing of Abraham might come upon the Gentiles."

The parties to the Abrahamic covenant, therefore, are clearly God and man, because Abraham, the representative of man's interest in the covenant, is styled the "father of many nations," "of all that believe," "of us all," and "heir of the world;" because the condition of the covenant being spiritual, one man is as near to the covenant as another, and all have access to it; because Abraham believed before he was circumcised, that the covenant might not be confined to the Jews, but extend to all mankind.

So far as the *second* feature of the New Testament Church is concerned—the *parties*—is not the Abrahamic covenant identical with the Gospel? Does the New Testament Church extend farther than to all who believe? Does the Abrahamic covenant fall short of that extent?

III. Its *provisions* are the Son and the Spirit.

All men know that the Gospel presents the atonement of the Son of God for justification, and the agency of the Spirit for sanctification. If, therefore, the Abrahamic covenant had not included the same divine provision, it would thereby have proved itself a distinct covenant.

That the Abrahamic covenant embraces *Christ* we are fully assured:

1. By the most explicit apostolic interpretation of its language. In his Epistle to the Galatians, (iii. 16,) Paul

says, "Now to Abraham and his seed were the promises made. He saith not, And to seeds, as of many; but as of one, And to thy seed, which is Christ." Christ was the natural descendant of Abraham, and was in that sense his seed. But we must not rest in that thought. The great idea is, that Christ is the only one of all Abraham's seed, the only being in the universe, with whom God could consistently covenant as a basis, a procuring cause, of blessings to men. Christ, therefore, on man's part is the capital, all-embracing, all-efficient party. How then do Abraham himself and all the rest of us become parties to this covenant? Here is the secret. The condition of the covenant complied with, identifies the party with the head of the covenant. Faith unites to Christ, so that all believers are in Christ. God therefore covenants with them, and promises to them, simply on account of their connection with him.

Who doubts that Christ is included in the Abrahamic covenant? In the seventeenth of Genesis, God covenants with Abraham and his seed. In the third of Galatians, Paul says explicitly that the seed of Abraham, in the eye of this covenant, is Christ. This fact places an irrefragable seal upon all that has been, and all that shall be advanced in this argument. For if Christ, in God's understanding, is indeed the seed of Abraham, then these six things clearly follow: The Abrahamic covenant is a standing covenant, not confined to the old economy, but extending to all generations; a universal covenant, not limited to the Jews, but opening itself to all the human family; a covenant, in its bounty providing the Son and the Spirit; in its authority, requiring faith on man's part; its reward, in promising salvation on the part of God; and in its designation, marked by a heaven-appointed seal.

2. This position is confirmed by other witnesses.

Zacharias, father of John the Baptist, testifies that the Abrahamic covenant includes the Saviour, and is at work in the times of the Gospel: Luke i. 68–74: "Blessed be the Lord God of Israel, for he hath visited and redeemed his people, and hath raised up a horn of salvation for us in the house of David, as he spake by the mouth of his holy prophets, which have been since the world began, to perform the mercy promised to our fathers, and to remember his holy covenant, the oath which he sware to our father Abraham." God raised up this horn—Christ, in performance of his covenant with Abraham. Does not that covenant include Christ? Mary, too, contemplating the birth of the Saviour, ascribes his coming into the world to the Abrahamic covenant: "He hath holpen his servant Israel, in remembrance of his mercy; as he spake to our fathers, to Abraham, and to his seed forever." Mary refers to the work of Christ, to God's fidelity to his covenant to Abraham and his seed forever. Does not that covenant include Christ?

3. This fact is still farther attested by the time and manner of the confirmation of the Abrahamic covenant.

Paul assures us, that long before the institution of the Mosaic economy the Abrahamic covenant was confirmed by God in Christ. Gal. iii. 17. If so, then, that covenant must have included the Saviour from its earliest inception.

4. This glorious truth is sealed by the declared end of Christ's sufferings and work on Calvary.

It is inspired language that "Christ hath redeemed us from the curse of the law, being made a curse for us." But why? "That the blessing of Abraham might come on the Gentiles through Jesus Christ." If the blessing of the Abrahamic covenant looks to Christ crucified as a channel,—as means to an end,—does not that covenant include Christ?

If Christ is the seed of the covenant; if he is a horn of salvation in performance of the covenant; if he is a helper of Israel in remembrance of the covenant; if he is God's confirmation of the covenant; if he is a curse for us to secure the blessings of the covenant; then, of a truth, the Abrahamic covenant embraces Christ, and was always a nullity without him.

The Abrahamic covenant provides *the Spirit* also.

It follows as a matter of course if the Son is embraced, that the Spirit is not excluded. It is the propitiation of the Son that opens the way for the dispensation of the Spirit. It is the Son who sends the Spirit. Nay, the Holy Spirit himself is the Spirit of the Son. If, therefore, the covenant of Abraham includes the one, it must include the other also.

But we have the express Scripture testimony on this head. We are told that Christ hath redeemed us from the curse of the law, being made a curse for us, "that the blessing of Abraham might come on the Gentiles through Jesus Christ; that we might receive the promise of the Spirit through faith." Gal. iii. 14. Here, in one inspired sentence, the blessing vouchsafed to Abraham and his seed in the covenant, includes in express terms both the Son and the Spirit. Christ works to secure the blessing of the covenant, and the Spirit is promised as a part of the blessing thus secured.

In this third feature—the provisions involved—is not the Abrahamic covenant identical with the Gospel? Does the Gospel provide more than the work of the Son and the Spirit? Does the Abrahamic covenant provide less?

IV. The great *requirement* of man is *faith.*

All men know that faith is the all-inclusive requirement of the Gospel. And if the Abrahamic covenant had satisfied itself with any thing less, it would thus have proved itself an entirely different institution. But the Abrahamic covenant, like the Gospel, works through the righteousness of faith, for—

1. The promise to Abraham was through faith.

We know that Abraham believed God before he was circumcised. We know, too, that Abraham's faith was counted to him for righteousness. We know by the Old Testament that the seal of the covenant was circumcision. And we know by the New Testament that the great import of circumcision was faith. For we have the testimony of an apostle, that Abraham received the sign of circumcision, "a seal of the righteousness of faith."

2. The promise of Abraham's seed required faith.

That the promise to the seed should be made on the same principle which carried it to the patriarch, needs no vindication. This the Scriptures assert: "For it was not written for his sake alone that his faith was imputed to him for righteousness, but for us also, to whom the same righteousness shall be imputed if we believe." Rom. iv. 23, 24. Therefore, as the apostle says, "the promise to Abraham and his seed was not through the law, but through the righteousness of faith." Rom. iv. 13. "Know ye, therefore, that they who are of faith, the same are the children of Abraham. So then they who are of faith, the same are blessed with faithful Abraham." Gal. iii. 7, 9.

Now if Abraham was justified by the righteousness of faith; if the promise to his seed is made only through the righteousness of faith; if it was recorded in the beginning that Abraham obtained his righteousness by faith, precisely that we might believe and obtain the same righteousness; if we who believe are the children of Abraham, and any other principle of acceptance, as the apostle says, would vitiate the promise; if the seal of the covenant is circumcision, and the scriptural meaning of circumcision is faith; and, finally, if the provisions of the covenant are, first, Christ a curse for us, the great object of faith, and, second, the Spirit of Christ, the great agent of faith,—what can be clearer than that in the covenant of God with Abraham, the great requirement of man is faith?

In this *fourth* feature—the *requirement of man*—is not the Abrahamic covenant identical with the New Testament Church? The Gospel calls pre-eminently for man's faith. The covenant with Abraham demands emphatically the same compliance.

V. The great *promise* by God is *redemption*.

All men know that the grand promise of the Gospel is salvation. If the Abrahamic covenant had promised less, it had thrown a gulf between itself and the Gospel. But that the Abrahamic covenant offers redemption to those who comply with its terms is proved,

1. By the language of the covenant: "I will give unto thee, and to thy seed after thee, the land of Canaan for an everlasting possession." The land of Canaan is a common type of heaven, and "given as an everlasting possession," would seem to enforce the propriety of this interpretation here. The accompanying promise, "And I will be their God," is frequently interpreted in Scripture, and always to imply salvation.

2. Spiritual and saving promises are perpetually and variously connected with the covenant as interpreted both by Old and New Testament writers. Among others the following may be found on record: "I will make an everlasting covenant with thee, even the sure mercies of David;" "My tabernacle shall be with thee;" "I will be with thee and will help thee;" "In thee and in thy seed shall the nations of the earth be blessed;" "Yea, I will be their God and they shall be my people;" "And I will give them one heart and one way, that they may fear before me forever;" "I will put my fear in their hearts, that they shall not depart from me;" "He hath clothed me in the garments of salvation and covered me with robes of righteousness;" "This is all my salvation and all my desire."

All this language evidently imports the salvation of the Gospel.

3. New Testament statements settle this point.

The duty required by the covenant—faith a righteousness—clearly shows that salvation is the reward. The provisions secured—the Son and the Spirit—clearly show that nothing less than salvation can be the offer of the covenant. The price of the blessing—Christ a curse for us—settles the fact that God's promise in the Abrahamic covenant is Christian redemption.

If the language of the covenant promises Canaan for a possession, and Jehovah for a God; if the prophetic interpretation of the covenant includes God's presence with them, and abode in them, and blessing upon them, clothing them with robes of righteousness and the garments of salvation; and if the New Testament teaches that the Abrahamic covenant requires faith, promises the Son and the Spirit, and needs the atonement to secure the blessing,—then, of a truth, the great promise of God in the Abrahamic covenant is salvation.

In this *fifth* feature of the covenant—its *reward*—is not the Abrahamic institution identical with the Gospel? The Church gives no more than redemption—the Abrahamic covenant no less.

VI. Its *appointed seal* is an *emblematic rite*.

Literal consummation consists in affixing oneself to the covenant by the act of signature and of sealing; spiritual consummation, in affixing the covenant to oneself by the solemn ceremonial act of appropriating its emblem.

Where interests of great magnitude are involved, it is a custom, sanctioned by the wisdom of the world in all generations, that engagements between men should be literally signed and sealed. Man's awful religious responsibilities, his inborn liability to unfaithfulness, and the deadly consequences of sin, demand all the moral help which can be secured. To meet the emergency, a spiritual covenant emblematically consummated is God's merciful contrivance. The moral bearing of a sacrament is invaluable. Sacraments address the senses, and summon them to give impressiveness to language. They address intellect, and emphasize upon it all the destroying and saving facts of man's case. They address conscience, and bring up distinctly before it the duty to be sworn. They address purpose and agency, and bring the soul to a deliberate and solemn self-commitment to God. When a man approaches a sacrament, all else is thrown off from the mind, and his very existence would seem to be shut up in the one deliberate act of forming and recording his vow to his Maker. Thus, in its first administration, the sacrament fixes on the mind a deep sense of final religious commitment, and through its every re-enactment or even remembrance, God looks in upon the soul and re-enforces obligation. It may be safely observed, therefore, of a sacrament, that by natural operation it combines strong moral influences to secure efficient moral action, and thus tends powerfully to sustain the fidelity of the subject.

Baptism, one of the two sacraments of our religion, is the sign and the seal of the great Church covenant in our day; and it is so in two senses. It operates an adoption of the covenant as by literal signature; and again, it solemnizes the act by an emblematic rehearsal of the covenant adopted. In baptism, God comes to man and covenants with his creature, and man comes to God and covenants with his Maker. By the authorized application of water and the pronunciation of the Triune name, Jehovah engages to be the God of the subject. By the voluntary reception of the sacramental water and name, the subject engages to be the servant of the Lord. Thus, baptism is both the signification and the signature, the expression and the execution of the great covenant of salvation, both on God's part and on man's.

The plan of salvation has always required on man's part repentance and faith, and pledged on the part of God, sanctification and forgiveness. All this baptism distinctly expresses. Baptism has a natural voice; it is purification from defilement. Man's voluntary application for God's holy water operates a confession of sin. God's application of it to sinful man expresses his promise of sanctification. Baptism speaks, too, by scriptural appointment, and expresses reliance upon Christ for remission of sins. The Master says: "He that believeth and is baptized shall be saved." He, therefore, who comes to God's minister to be baptized, professes to believe. The apostles summon men to be baptized for the remission of sin. He, therefore, who seeks baptism, applies for justification by faith in Christ; while God, in administering baptism, signifies his acceptance of the subject upon the righteousness presented. Thus, by natural import and scriptural teaching, the ordinance of baptism clearly expresses the whole religious transaction between God and man: on the one hand, both the repentance and the faith required of man; on the other, both the sanctification and the forgiveness promised by God. But baptism is not language merely, but conduct also. It executes the covenant. He who enters God's house and receives baptism at the hand of God's minister, thereby speaks out before heaven and earth his repentance toward God and his faith in the Lord Jesus Christ, and this with a view to a present and an eternal covenant with God for salvation. So when God, through his appointed representative, solemnly administers the ordinance upon the person of the applicant, he too, thereby, speaks out on his part, and closes the covenant with the believer by pledging the symbolized purification and forgiveness. But baptism goes still one step farther. By baptism, as through a door, the subject verily enters into the household of God; while through baptism, as by a personal embrace, God welcomes him to the adoption of a son.

What now is Christian baptism? It is neither more nor less than the great covenant of salvation between God and man expressed and executed, signed and sealed by both parties. Surely baptism is of God. The ordinance brings up every faculty of man's nature and every word of God's truth to impress upon man's soul the responsibility and the consolation of his covenant-stand at the moment when he first assumed it; and works to secure his final perseverance by solemnly renewing these impressions during every period of his subsequent life.

The final mark of the New Testament Church—what is it? It is this. The Church has its sign and seal in an emblematic ordinance appointed by God for this purpose. Now if the Abrahamic covenant had been established and administered without any such sign and seal, although scripturally identical with the New Testament Church, as all the world must see, in the five important preceding particulars, there would still have existed one important difference between them.

It is not enough to say that the Abrahamic covenant, like the New Testament Church, has its divinely-appointed sign and seal. More than this is true. Substantially the sign and the seal of the Abrahamic covenant is the sign and the seal of the Gospel covenant. This is true in a general sense. Each in its general nature is an outward sign of an inward grace. "Baptism is not the putting away of the filth of the flesh, but the answer of a good conscience toward God." 1 Peter iii. 21. "Neither is that circumcision which is outward in the flesh, but circumcision is that of the heart, in the spirit, and not in the letter." Rom. ii. 29. Each, too, in its general office, is the covenant of a purity required of man, (Gen. xvii. 11,) and promised by God. Deut. xxx. 6. But the similitude between baptism and circumcision is not confined to their general features; it is exact in every important particular. Four things define Christian baptism: 1. By its nature, baptism expresses purification from defilement. So does circumcision. Jer. iv. 4. 2. By scriptural appointment, baptism stands for faith a righteousness. So does circumcision. Rom. iv. 11. 3. By baptism the subject speaks out his repentance and faith, covenanting with God, and God pledges purification and pardon, covenanting with the subject. Precisely this is the operation in circumcision. Gen. xvii. 11. 4. In the very use of baptism the subject literally enters into God's family, and is received by him. Exactly so was it with him who was circumcised of old. Phil. iii. 3.

Respecting this last feature of the New Testament Church—the appointed seal, an emblematic rite—is not the Abrahamic covenant identical with the New Testament Church? The covenant of the Church in our day carries a sign and a seal appointed of God, and embodying the substance of the covenant, both on God's part and on man's. The covenant of the Church in Abraham's day employed a sign and a seal equally appointed of God, and descriptive of the respective pledges of the parties.

It follows that the Abrahamic covenant and the Gospel economy, or New Testament Church, are one and the same institution.

It will be readily granted, if we separate from any given institution a permanent character; or from it its parties, God and man; or from its provisions, the Son and the Spirit; or from its requirements, faith a righteousness; or from its promise, eternal salvation; or from its consummation, a divine seal emblematic of the covenant; we thereby prove that it is not the New Testament Church. But if we show an institution of which these six things are true:—first, it is a divine arrangement as durable as the world; second, its parties are God and man; third, its provisions are the Son and the Spirit; fourth, its requirement is faith a righteousness; fifth, its promise is final salvation; sixth, its consummation is a divine rite embodying the covenant,—is not that institution the Gospel economy? —the New Testament Church? If any man denies this proposition, what can he say? Certainly such an institution fills up the definition of the Church precisely. What is lacking? Here is the Founder of the Church! And the permanency of the Church! And the parties of the Church! And the provisions of the Church! And the requirement of the Church! And the reward of the Church! And the seal of the Church! And what of the Church is *not* here? If any man will do himself the justice to study out what he means by "The Church," we are persuaded he will find every constituent of it in the patriarchal economy.

We present two brief confirmations of this doctrine:

1st. The necessary identity of the Church in the two dispensations.

The Church must be the same in all ages, because the foundations are the same. What is the Church? The body through which is accomplished the plan of God for saving lost man, through Jesus Christ. What are the foundations of the Church? The great governing foundations are twofold—God's nature and relations on the one part, and man's nature and relations on the other. These are always the same. On the one hand, God's perfect character, and his creating, preserving, blessing, and governing relations, are always one and the same to all men. Man's accountable nature, fallen state, and infinite dependence, are certainly one and the same in all ages of the world. Clearly, therefore, the plan of mercy growing up out of these elements can never essentially vary. Now if the nature of things, the history of the Church, and the word of God assure us that the two *dispensations* are not two *religions*, then the unity of the Church in both makes it certain that our interpretation of the Abrahamic covenant is correct. For the Gospel properties ascribed to the Abrahamic covenant must be found somewhere in the Old Testament. Can we find them in the Decalogue? Can we find them in the covenant of Sinai? Where are they if not in God's gracious covenant with the patriarch?

2. Express Scripture declarations.

It is the word of Paul: "If ye be Christ's then are ye Abraham's seed, and heirs according to the promise." Gal. iii. 29. If you are Christ's, you are as closely identified with the Gospel, with our New Testament Church, as you can possibly be. But if you are Christ's, if you are in the Gospel, if you are of the Church, this very fact makes you the seed of Abraham, connects you this day with that covenant which God of old made with the patriarch. Settle this fact, that you are a Christian, and you have settled another fact, that you are under the Abrahamic covenant. You cannot be in Christ and out of Abraham. For an apostle says: "If ye are Christ's, then are ye Abraham's seed, and heirs according to the promise." This is just saying, if you cannot tear away the Gospel from Christ, you cannot tear it away from the Abrahamic covenant.

Again, Paul opens his way to the previous text by this announcement: "The Scripture foreseeing that God would justify the heathen through faith, preached before the Gospel unto Abraham, saying, In thee shall all nations be blessed." Gal. iii. 8. This, in substance, is the summing up of the Abrahamic covenant. The first thought, justification by faith, and the second, the blessing of the nations in the seed of Abraham, make up its ordinary description. This passage identifies itself with the Gospel in two ways. The apostle's description of the Abrahamic covenant is an exact description of the Gospel. What is the Gospel? Christ for man; and justification by faith. The Abrahamic covenant includes them both. First, "In thy seed—Christ—shall all the nations be blessed." Here in the Abrahamic covenant we have Christ for man. Again: "Foreseeing that God would justify the heathen through faith," as well as Abraham the chosen. Here in the Abrahamic covenant we have justification by faith. Thus the Abrahamic covenant is the Gospel,—that is, it is a system of salvation by Jesus Christ, which of old justified Abraham by faith, and is now justifying the heathen on the same principle. But this passage involves express as well as argumentative testimony to the identity of the New Testament and Abrahamic covenant. The New Testament name is given to the Old Testament covenant. The apostle expressly affirms this covenant with Abraham to be "*The Gospel.*" God of old made a covenant with Abraham. In so doing, the apostle says, "He preached the Gospel unto Abraham." If the Scripture, or the Scripture's God, knows what the Gospel is, the Abrahamic covenant is the Gospel: nor can mortal deny it, save at the expense of being wise above what is written.

INFERENCE.

If the doctrine advanced be true, then CHRISTIAN PARENTS ARE BOUND TO PRESENT THEIR CHILDREN FOR BAPTISM.

It is a remarkable fact, that there is one duty enjoined by the Abrahamic covenant which is not only styled the keeping of the covenant, but in one form or other is frequently repeated in the language of the covenant. This is the *application of the sign and the seal of the covenant to the person of the seed.* God says to the patriarch: "Ye shall circumcise the flesh of your foreskin, and it shall be a token of the covenant betwixt me and you." He whose alone right it was to limit or extend the covenant and its token, of his own good pleasure, has placed on record this additional emphatic language: "*This is the covenant* which ye shall keep between me and you and thy seed after thee, *every male child among you shall be circumcised.*" The Abrahamic covenant is the New Testament Church. What right has any member of the Gospel Church to violate a principle so strongly taught in the covenant with Abraham?

I. Our brethren respond, *the Abrahamic covenant belonged to the old dispensation, and is not binding in the new.*

We now respectfully inquire, Where is there the shadow of an argument to establish this assumption?

1. Where in *reason?* Do not the nature and the relations of the parties, God and man, necessarily define true religion? This will not be disputed. Are not the nature and the relations of God and man at all times the same? This will not be denied. How, then, can we escape the inference that in all essential particulars God's religion in the day of Abraham must be God's religion in the day of Christ, and consequently binding upon this generation? Again: Can we form any idea of the New Testament Church apart from that permanency, those parties, those provisions, that requirement, that promise, and that seal, recorded above as constituting the Church of God in the Christian dispensation?

2. In the *Scriptures*, where do we find the slightest countenance of this opinion?

God's great church arrangement in the days of Abraham, as we have shown, stands and works in our day. The New Testament tells us that there were two covenants in the old dispensation. The one a covenant of law, the other a covenant of grace. The former was styled the "Sinai," the "Hagar," the "bond-woman" covenant. This law-covenant "gendered to bondage," and was cast out. In strongest antithesis the apostle brings up the covenant of the "free-woman," the "Sarah," the Abrahamic covenant. Of this he makes a singular and decisive averment: this is "the covenant which was confirmed before of God in Christ," and therefore a covenant essentially immutable. For who can reason more clearly than this: If a man's covenant, being confirmed, must stand—God's covenant, confirmed, cannot fail?

But God has said, "This is my covenant," that ye apply the token thereof to your child. If the Abrahamic covenant works in our day, and if the Abrahamic covenant commands the parent to apply the sign and seal of the covenant to the person of his child, why is not every Christian bound to present his child for baptism?

We have been rejoiced, though not surprised, to hear that some of the most excellent and learned of our brethren who are not considered to hold our doctrine in the premises, do yet preach from the pulpit the present obligation of the Abrahamic covenant. Sooner or later, the whole Church of God, it would seem, must come to this faith. But why then do they not enjoin the baptism of children? Because they hold with their brethren,

II. *That the sign and the seal of the Abrahamic convenant is laid aside in the New Testament dispensation.*

Our brethren must bear with us while we respectfully renew the inquiry, where can evidence be found to sustain such a conviction?

1. What dictate of *reason* calls for the preservation of the covenant, but the abandonment of its sign and seal? During a long period of the world's existence, Jehovah subjected every male on earth who followed his counsels, to strong physical pangs, that through the bloody rite of circumcision, mankind might derive two important advantages: First, that they might impressively learn, on the one hand, their helpless depravity and condemnation; on the other, his gracious promise both of purification and of pardon.

And again, that through the same appointed sign and seal, mankind might be led to a solemn covenant-dedication of themselves and of their families to God's service, and be strengthened and comforted in the discharge of covenant obligations by God's emphatic assurance of seasonable co-operation. Now, if the generations of the old world in the service of God derived so much light and strength and comfort from the appointed sign and seal of the covenant, why do not we of this generation in the same service equally need its seasonable help? If a wise and merciful God did thus attribute so much importance to this sign and seal of old, as to style it "his covenant," and the neglect of it the rejection of his covenant, (Gen. xvii. 10, 14,) why should he order its abandonment in these days?

2. What *word of Holy Writ* suggests the thought that God is administering his covenant without a sign and seal in our day? Are we reminded that circumcision is abolished? Very true! But recall another fact; circumcision, in its outward nature, never was the sign and the seal of God's great Church covenant, but the sign and the seal of only one dispensation of it. A dispensation of a covenant has respect simply to the outward form of its administration, and may be changed a thousand times without touching the integrity of the covenant, even in its sign and seal. The setting aside of circumcision, therefore, may be nothing more than the exchange of one sensible form of representation for another more suitable to the genius of the new administration. The form of the sign and seal of God's great covenant with man is changed with the dispensation, but so also has the form of the passover been changed, and the form of public worship has been changed, and the form of the ministry, and the day of the Sabbath. And this is all that can be changed, the *forms* of things essential to the Church of God. For if religion is and must be the same in all generations, then the great leading principles of reli-

gion at one time must prevail at all times. Was it necessary to the cause of religion that there should be a Sabbath in ancient times? Then we must find a Sabbath in the present dispensation, and we do. Was it necessary that there should be public worship in ancient times? Then we must find public worship in the present dispensation, and we do. Was it necessary that there should be a ministry to represent God among men? Then we must find a ministry in our day, and we do. Now was it necessary that there should be an appointed *sign and seal* to impress man's mind through his senses; to rouse man's conscience by a sacramental commitment of himself and family to God; and to encourage man's heart by God's signed and sealed assurance of gracious co-operation? Then we must find such a sign and seal at work in our day, and we do. Baptism is the refreshing sign and seal of the gracious Christian dispensation of the great covenant, as circumcision was the painful token of the Old Testament dispensation of the same covenant.

It is said that baptism does not come in the place of circumcision. If it does not, we will show our brethren a marvel. Baptism utters every word and works every end of circumcision perfectly. Circumcision, as to its nature, is heavenly language of spiritual things through a sensible sign,—so is baptism, precisely. Circumcision in its natural import declares, "I am defiled and must be cleansed," on man's part; "you are defiled and I will cleanse you," on God's part. This is the natural language of baptism, precisely. Circumcision was set up to signify faith on man's part, and its imputation to him for righteousness upon God's part. So, too, baptism was instituted to express faith on man's part, and remission of sin on God's part, precisely. In circumcision man says, "I covenant with thee, O God, repenting of my sin, and looking through faith to offered righteousness;" and God responds, "I covenant with thee, my believing child, and will wash your impurity and accept your righteousness." So does baptism speak out the very same voices of the parties, precisely. Finally: Circumcision carried the party into the visible family of God, and brought the arms of the father round his adopted child. Here, too, baptism accomplishes the very work of circumcision, precisely.

Circumcision touched three things only: God, man, and the covenant between them. Baptism touches only three things: God, man, and the covenant between them. Every bearing of circumcision upon God, man, and the covenant, baptism carries out toward God, man, and the covenant, with precisely the same spirit, thought, and intent. In a word, by God's appointment, circumcision expresses and executes the great covenant of grace between God and man in ancient times. So, by God's appointment, baptism expresses and executes the great covenant of grace between God and man in modern times. What then can that man mean who says that baptism does not come in the place of circumcision? And what can Paul mean when he makes baptism follow circumcision in the same sentence, and pronounces baptism the circumcision of our dispensation? "In whom also you are circumcised with the circumcision made without hands, in putting off the body of the sins of the flesh by the circumcision of Christ—buried with him in baptism." Col. ii. 11, 12.

The argument may be summed up in a word. The Scriptures assure us that the Abrahamic covenant works in our day. The Scriptures assure us that one integral element of the covenant is this: its deliberate and solemn consummation by the parties respectfully in and through their own personal act of signing and sealing the covenant. Now since no voice of reason or Scripture indicates its repeal in the Gospel dispensation, like every other part of this standing covenant, the sign and the seal of the covenant stands also, and is of obligation in our day.

But the covenant itself distinctly requires that its appointed sign and seal should be applied to the child of the believer. Why then does not every believer present his child for baptism?

The third and last objection of our brethren is this:—

III. *Baptism is indeed the sign and the seal of the Gospel Church, but it is to be applied to the believer only, and not to his children.*

Permit us once more respectfully to inquire, Where in all revelation to reason or to faith can man find authority for this limitation? A covenant of mercy with guilty man it belonged alone to God to make. A sign and a seal to this covenant it belonged alone to God to affix. The application of this sign and seal it belonged alone to God to determine. What has God done? By the very language of institution, as well as by the uniform administration of the covenant, God commands that the token of the covenant shall be extended to *two* parties—to the believer and to *his seed.* What right has man to restrain the application of this sign and seal to *one* party only?

1. What in *reason?*

What is the *foundation* of the covenant? The natures and the relations of God and man are alike unchanged in the old dispensation and in the new. If, therefore, the foundations of the covenant called for the application of the token to the child of the believer in the early periods of the Church, the same foundations call just as strongly for the application of the token to the child of the believer in the later periods of the Church. Does it not seem an outrage upon the basis of the covenant to hold that it suggests the limitation of the sign and the seal to the parent only?

What in the *spirit* of the covenant? Without the child's consent the parent brings him into the world, places him under law, imparts to him his own corruption, and opens upon his soul the assaults of the world, the flesh, and the devil; and there the child is, largely by his parents' act, a helpless, hopeless immortality! Bear in mind, God made the heart of the parent to love the child almost as himself. When, therefore, the parent's mind has been enlightened, his heart circumcised, his sin forgiven, his soul adopted, and, in testimony of all this, when his very person has been solemnly signed and sealed by God's appointment,—what an agony must ever wring the heart of that considerate parent, as he looks out from the bosom of God's family upon his unsealed and excluded child, and feels that there is no hope of relief on earth! Here let us inquire, what is the spirit of the covenant on God's part? Surely it is the richest, strongest sympathy with the adopted soul! God feels for him in all the state of his nature, and gloriously relieves him there. God feels for him in all the state of his relations, and gloriously relieves him there. When our sympathizing God sees the parental feeling of this father, agonized deeply by the exclusion of his child from the family of heaven, intensely by the conviction that his own hand had largely wrought the mischief, and desperately by the assurance that creation can lend him no help, shall He feel for this father everywhere, save where his heart is swelled to bursting by the marked disinherison of his own child by his own father, and there shall God leave him unpitied, unrelieved? Rather is it not just like the spirit of our heavenly Father in all other parts of the covenant to cry out to the smitten, desperate parent, "Come! bring your child to me. Put him in my arms. If creation cannot help you, I will. I will place him in my family by your side. I will even fix the sign and the seal of my covenant upon his person; and he shall stand or fall largely according to your fidelity or unfaithfulness?" The spirit of the covenant on man's part, what is it? The Christian loves his child as he loves his own soul. He has been toiling, by God's help, to throw off his own corruption; why should he not seek God's grace to wash the heart of his beloved child? He had been struggling, by God's help, to bring his own sins to the blood of Jesus; why should he not struggle, by God's help, to bring the blood of atonement to sprinkle the soul of his child? He had sought for his own soul the counsels, sympathies, and prayers of God's people; why should he not desire these same blessings for his child? He had accepted God's overtures, and through the appointed sign and seal dedicated himself to his Maker. In every other matter, without exception, he acts for his child; why should he not in this contingency also act for him who cannot act for himself, and in like manner dedicate his child to the God of his salvation? Surely it would seem in strong accord with man's spirit in all other parts of the covenant, nay, but a fair expression of his faith in God, that he should surrender to him his child also under a sealed covenant of religious education. Does it not seem, therefore, an outrage upon the spirit of the covenant, both on God's part and on man's, to affirm that it suggests the limitation of its sign and seal to the believer only?

What in the *object* of the covenant? The great object of the covenant is to glorify God in the salvation of men. In renewing and sanctifying the heart of man, the Spirit presents truth on the page of Holy Writ, by the voice of the preacher, and signally in the use of sacramental signs. These religious rites were appointed of God expressly to emphasize saving truth, enforce it upon the wayward mind, and thus bring the soul to swear to God under all the advantages of aroused thought, settled conviction, and fixed purpose. In the day of the revelation of all things it shall be seen, that the sacraments of the Church wrought powerfully, and especially in keeping man faithful to covenant. But where in all human society is the strong moral influence of a sacrament more needed than in this very relation of parent and child? Where would it accomplish more for human salvation? Only let any one generation of parents be faithful, and the world is converted. Fix your mind upon this capital fact in the ancient covenant. In the presence of God, to secure parental fidelity, circumcision imposed upon the parent a vow of faithful family education. This is indicated by the *act* of the parent. Circumcision was the seal of a vow. What was that vow? When Abraham circumcised himself, he cut off defilement from his body, and applied to it the symbol of purity. Thus he vowed that he would put away sin and live holy to the Lord. When Abraham's child was circumcised, a vow of holiness to the Lord was recorded upon his person, and Abraham's hand had placed it there. Surely by this act Abraham stipulates that he will do what he can to make the child holy. God's *command* teaches the same lesson. God said to Abraham: "Every male child among you shall be circumcised." By God's direction, Abraham took his children and circumcised them with his own hand. Thus God commanded Abraham to do that which vowed the holiness of the child. Of course, God bound the parent to educate the child to holiness. God's *interpretation* of his interview with the patriarch settles this point. The Abrahamic covenant is recorded in the seventeenth chapter of Genesis. In the eighteenth chapter, God alludes to the covenant, and proceeds to say of Abraham: "I know him that he will command his children and household after him, and they shall keep the way of justice and judgment, *that the Lord may bring upon Abraham that which he hath spoken of him.*" The instruction is palpable. The promise of the Abrahamic covenant was in part conditioned upon the fidelity of the patriarch in the religious education of his children. Thus, by the act of the parent, the direction of God, and God's interpretation of both, we do assuredly know that the circumcision of a child under the ancient form of the great

Church covenant, imposed upon the parent a solemn vow to train him up for God.

Now, if the great object of the covenant is to bring the world to holiness, and if a religious sacrament is so well adapted to secure fidelity to the vow recorded, would it not greatly facilitate the design of the covenant if all the parents of the Church were summoned into the sanctuary there to record their sacramental vow, that they will faithfully co-operate with God to educate their children for the kingdom of heaven? Does it not seem, therefore, an outrage upon the object of the covenant to limit the application of its sign and seal to one party only, and thus absolve all the Christian parents of future generations from the solemn church-vow of religious education which was imposed upon all the parents of the church in generations past?

What in the *administration* of the covenant? In the world of nature God placed the child in the family with its parent. In like manner in the spiritual world, under the *old* economy, God placed the child in his own family with its parents. What imaginable change has passed upon the relation of parent and child in changing generations? If through all the ages of the Church's history anterior to the advent of Jesus, heaven and earth saw the children of the faithful abiding with their parents in the visible family of God, is it not an outrage upon the spirit and principle of the old dispensation to change the relation of parent and child so violently as to limit the ordinance to one party only?

The *spirit and bearing* of the *new dispensation* is still more unfriendly to the exclusion of the children of the Church from the seal of the covenant. Under the ancient administration gracious things were faintly shadowed through types and prophecies; under the new, the great Antitype himself is come, and a clear light shines forth on every hand. Under the old, the laws, moral and ceremonial, sounded out their condemnations of sin, and the whole economy largely gendered to bondage; but grace and truth came by Jesus Christ, and now promises and mercies everywhere abound. Under the old, worship was largely limited to one spot of the earth; the covenant was preached to one nation under heaven; the badge of salvation was affixed to one sex of the race. But under the liberalities of our most glorious day, every blessing is enlarged without limitation. All manner of worship is open to every foot of earth's soil where the spirit of man will come to God in spirit and in truth; the gospel is preached to every creature under heaven, Gentile as well as Jew; and the baptismal badge of salvation is extended to the whole race—to the female as well as to the male.

Now, when every other great and noble blessing, circumscribed and tied up under the first economy, breaks out into boundless development in our day, is it not an outrage upon the broad and liberal genius of the Gospel, to suppose that this very year of jubilee, which strikes to the earth all checks and hinderances to God's redeeming mercy, should strike from the persons of all the children of the Church that strengthening, comforting sign and seal of God's covenanted adoption which all the narrowness of the early dispensation could not deny them, and should cast our offspring out of God's family unsealed, to wander among the cursed heathen? The sign and seal of God's covenant, so comfortably pledging God's gracious and necessary help, —why should it be granted to the children of our fathers in the old dispensation, but denied to our children amid the abounding philanthropies of the Gospel? What shadow of a reason for this forbidding conclusion do we find either in the *foundations*, or in the *spirit*, or in the *object*, or in the *administration* of the covenant? What one thought can reason allege for this chilling limitation?

2. What in *Scripture* do we find to countenance this assumption? First, it is affirmed that *Christ the Master does not expressly teach the doctrine of infant baptism, and, therefore, refutes it.* We answer, first, that Christ, the Master, does not formally repeal the doctrine of the Church membership of infants, and, therefore, establishes it.

Christ, it is said, does not announce the doctrine. Why should he utter one word upon the subject? The Abrahamic covenant! Is it not the Christian Church? Is it not the primary law of the kingdom of Christ? *There* is the doctrine. There—in the very first record of the Christian Church. There—in the very constitution of the kingdom of Christ. There is the principle laid down with preeminent distinctness, that the token of the covenant shall be affixed to the children of the covenanting party. Why should he call up the doctrine in language? *There* it is, in the faith of every member of the Church of God,—every member without exception! There it is, within the knowledge of every man who is not a member! Where is the necessity of one word of further instruction? Who denies it? Who doubts it? Who is ignorant of it? Why should he open his lips upon the subject? *There* is the doctrine practically embodied before every man's eyes! There are all the children of the Church, round about in every direction, every one of them wearing the sign and the seal of the great Church covenant, and all the world consenting both to the authority and the benignity of the arrangement. This recorded command to apply the sign and the seal of God's saving covenant to the seed of the believer, if Jesus Christ did not purpose to repeal it, why should he waste one breath to teach it? Why, when the fundamental law of the Church clearly enjoins it? When the faith of every friend and foe of the Church strongly embraces it? When the practice of every member of the Church publicly expresses it? and when not a solitary tongue on earth is lifted up against it? Who can fail to see the force of this appeal? Here, for example, is a Presbyterian pulpit which does not publicly disclaim the doctrine of infant baptism. Then its silence teaches the doctrine. For there is nothing now to gainsay the standards of the Church; nothing now to oppose the avowed faith of the Church; nothing now to set aside the uniform practice of the Church.

Brethren! Christ held your doctrine or ours,—that children should not, or should be baptized. If he held *your* doctrine, necessity is upon him, and he must speak out. For the standards of the Church, and the faith of the Church, and the practice of the Church, and universal public sentiment are all against him; and to put down this mighty testimony of God in the past, and set up an opposite sentiment and practice for the future—nothing can avail short of an express and authoritative *countermanding* of all prior teaching. But this Christ did not do, and you acknowledge it. Then he does *not* hold *your* doctrine. If he held OUR doctrine, there was no necessity for the utterance of a word. His silence leaves unsilenced and operative upon the world, all the fundamental, well-known, and well-received teachings of God in the prior dispensation.

Again: On various occasions the language and conduct of Jesus are such, that he will certainly be understood to teach the doctrine of infant baptism, if he does not expressly disclaim it.

When pious parents of old brought their infants to Jesus, however plausible the interpretation, that their little children were presented simply to be touched and to be prayed for, certain other things in the history were unquestionably true, and doubtless contributed to make up the mind which impelled them to visit the Saviour. 1. John and Jesus had solemnly testified to Judea, that the old dispensation was passing away, and that the kingdom of heaven was at hand. These parents believed the proclamation, for, had they deemed Jesus an impostor, they never had sought his blessing upon their children. The changes! The changes that are to take place! What are these changes? How will God's people be affected by them? What disposition will they make of our children? These, these are the things which God has emphatically commanded the people to lay to heart and expect. Doubtless the serious and pious of the land did think and feel deeply concerning the great coming change. Nor is it possible to conceive, at such a time as this, that these parents should have been indifferent to the dispositions and purposes of the acknowledged Head and Founder of the new order of things respecting themselves and their children. Though the new forms were not yet introduced, still it was a perfectly natural effect of the preaching and miracles of the Saviour and his forerunner, that these individuals should bring their children to Jesus with a view, by some simple method, and if it was a custom, as some say, to bring children to eminently pious persons to be touched and prayed for, then by this step, to seek the Saviour's blessing upon their offspring, and learn the temper of the new economy toward them. 2. The religion of these parents, it must not be forgotten, had scarcely furnished them the very faintest conception of spiritual blessings unsealed. It is highly probable that they had never seen nor heard of any human beings whom they judged to possess one spiritual favour from heaven, who did not carry in their person, or in the person or persons of representatives, the mark, the appointed outward mark of God's adoption. The children in their arms bore the sign and seal of covenant mercy, and this, doubtless, encouraged them to anticipate his gracious consideration in their behalf. As they had no conception of holy blessings corporeally unsealed, of God's favours dispensed to those who did not carry the mark of God's adoption, they would naturally infer if their children did receive spiritual favour at the hand of Jesus, in the proper time and way, they would also receive the appointed mark of connection with his people. Thus the whole drift of their sentiments and of their circumstances would powerfully expose these parents to misunderstand the teachings of Jesus, if he favoured their application, but did not distinctly apprize them, that their children, under his dispensation, would have no visible connection with God's kingdom. 3. Jesus knows all their mind. Now, if he knew that the kingdom of heaven would soon strike the seal of God's covenant from the persons of all the children of the Church, and to the dismay of every parent in Judea publicly amalgamate them with the children of the heathen, is it not highly probable that he will undeceive these applicants by direct explanation upon the subject? If he has such a message from God, is not this the very time and place to deliver it? Is it not certain that he will at least carefully avoid all such language and conduct as is calculated to awaken the very slightest expectation of any sensible connection between their children and the kingdom of heaven? What does he do? Does he utter one word designed to instruct these anxious parents, that, in the dispensation of his favours, they must not expect their children to receive any such mark of God's acceptance as shall visibly distinguish them from the children of the heathen? Not a word! On the contrary, all his conduct and language assure them that the same comfortable testimonies of heavenly favour which had always constituted so essential a part of their very idea of divine blessing they and their children should certainly receive. Mark the interview! Some would throw discouragement upon the hopes which were swelling in the breasts of these parents. The conduct of the disciples would fain indicate that there would exist no very strong sympathy, no very close connection between the Founder of the new economy and the children of

God's people. But how promptly did Jesus come to their relief! He substantially responded, "I am the Founder and Head of the kingdom of heaven. Little children are not to be separated from the kingdom hereafter, any more than they have been heretofore. Suffer little children to come unto me, and forbid them not, for of such is the kingdom of heaven." Matt. xix. 14. It is scarcely plausible to say, that the last words of the Saviour teach that the kingdom of heaven consists of persons who possess child-like dispositions. What had this to do with the spirit and object of these parents? This construction violates two most important rules of interpretation. It forces the *language* of the speaker. The phrase, "child-like dispositions," is not found in the passage or the context. "Little children" is the clear antecedent of the term "such," "of such little children," is the language. The very first law of interpretation requires that words be understood in their most known and usual signification. The Greek term τοιούτων signifies, "these and the like." What Jesus said, therefore, is clearly this: "Of these little children, and their like, is the kingdom of heaven composed." Again: This construction forces the *sense* of the speaker. Only give the words of the Saviour their plain, simple meaning, and they express a clear thought. Little children are component parts of the kingdom of heaven, and should be brought to Christ, because the members should be connected with their head. Nor need it be denied that it might also have been in his mind, that there was a peculiar impropriety in excluding little children, because they, and those like them, are especially in character near to the kingdom of heaven. As thus: These are members of the kingdom; of all persons, do not exclude these little ones, and those like them. But concede that the language of Jesus does not, of itself, teach the doctrine of infant baptism with absolute clearness, yet his failure to repeal the teaching of the Abrahamic covenant does. Place the history before you. The children of believers have always been members of the kingdom of God; and the thought of their possible exclusion may never have entered the mind of a Jew. The Jewish world are summoned to prepare for a new dispensation of this kingdom. These parents bring their children, wearing the mark of present membership, to seek for them the blessings of the Head of the new administration. He proclaims, in their hearing, to all who surround him: "Suffer little children to come unto me, and forbid them not, for of such is the kingdom of God." If the language of the Saviour, apart from its connection, did not incontrovertibly establish the doctrine of infant membership, the circumstances of the case more than supply its lack of explicitness. It is a rule in the construction of language, that words are always to be understood in the sense in which the speaker knows that the hearer will understand them. These parents! consider the customs of their country and their religious education on the one hand, and their state of anxious inquiry concerning the prospects of their children, which the spirit of the times called for, on the other, and what possible interpretation could they have put upon the Saviour's conduct and language, other than this: "Whereas your children have been hitherto distinguished from the children of the heathen by visible adoption into God's family under the Abrahamic covenant, so shall it be with them in the kingdom of heaven?"

Shortly anterior to the ascension of the Saviour, he delivered to his disciples the memorable apostolic commission in this language: "Go ye, therefore, and teach all nations, baptizing them in the name of the Father, and of the Son, and of the Holy Ghost." Matt. xxviii. 19. By this commission, who are the subjects of baptism? Clearly those who are taught. Go teach the nations—baptizing them; baptizing—the taught. What is the teaching here commanded? The meaning cannot be mistaken. The Greek word μαθητεύσατες expresses this idea precisely,—"Causing to be discipled." The general idea is involved in the common Gospel address, "Believe and be baptized;" "Repent and be baptized," for repentance and faith are marks of discipleship. There are other terms, however, which more precisely express the import of the word *teach* in this passage. From Judaism and heathenism go *convert* the nations to Christianity. There is still another word, if possible, more exactly synonymous with the capital term in the commission, "Go ye, therefore, and *proselyte* the nations, baptizing them," &c., "Go bring them over to the spiritual and practical adoption of my religion." It may be advanced, therefore, as an incontrovertible truth taught in this passage, that Christ required his apostles to baptize those whom they had discipled—those whom they had proselyted. The question returns upon us with increased responsibility. What exactly in this commission did Christ mean that his apostles should do when he commanded them to disciple—to proselyte the nations? A well-established principle of interpretation settles with perfect precision the proper reply to this question. Language is always to be understood in view of the sentiments and usages of the party speaking and the party addressed. Jesus and his apostles were Jews. The opinions and the practices of the Jews in regard to proselyting, must, therefore, fix decisively the meaning of this passage. Who doubts this? Every man knows that things are not formed to fit words, but words are chosen to express things. The word *proselyte,* therefore, must come to the then prevalent practice of the Jews for its signification. For certainly we perpetrate the most violent absurdity, if we attempt to force the ancient practice of the Jews into conformity to any independent notion which we may choose to entertain of the meaning of the word. The matter of proselyting among the Jews, what was it? What did they do when they proselyted the stranger to Judaism? The answer is this,—they proselyted him by the act of circumcision. Who were the parties circumcised when proselytism was practised by the Jews? The answer is at hand. The parties circumcised were always *the children with the parents*, and this was an every-day fact with which Jesus and his apostles and all the Jews were perfectly familiar. Jennings lays down the doctrine thus: "In proselyting, two things are observable—1. That when a man becomes a proselyte all his males were to be circumcised as well as himself; whereby his children were admitted into the visible church of God on his right as a father."* So say all the authorities. The idea of including the parents, in teaching the nations, but excluding the children, for aught we know, never once entered the mind of speaker or hearer.

Concede that this text does not establish the doctrine of infant baptism with unquestionable certainty, still the Saviour's omission under these circumstances to guard his apostles against the baptism of infants, affords, in connection with the words themselves, a strong argument. The history of the nation, the practice of the heathen, the universal opinions and habits of men in their day, imperatively constrained the apostles, in the absence of the slightest countermanding word from Christ, to carry out baptism in the new dispensation precisely as they had carried out circumcision in the old. That is, they must baptize the children as well as the parents.

Once more. Does not the silence of the Jews, concerning Christ's doctrinal treatment of their children, constitute of itself a standing triumph over all objections to our faith and practice?

---

* Jewish Ant., vol. i. 132.

Call up Jewish faith respecting the position and the prospects of their children. They believed that God's hand had placed them in the bosom of the Church. The evidence was this. They saw their children by divine authority wearing the sign and the seal of God's covenanted adoption. They felt of course assured of their salvation. Once convince the Jews, therefore, that this divine mark had been obliterated from the persons of their children by God's command, and you have forced into their minds the further conviction, that God had thrown out their children unsealed among the heathen, and doomed them to a common destruction with his enemies. Such a proclamation from the lips of Jesus would have inflicted a sudden and frightful shock upon the very deepest feeling that slumbered in the land of Judea. It would have struck a blow upon the heart of the nation, which must have roused and heaved the people, as no other movement within the compass of created agency could have done. It would have waked up an outburst which had stormed up and down that land with continually augmenting violence and vengeance. But who ever heard the very first lisp of an objection by any Jew against the Saviour's doctrinal treatment of the children of the Church? Oh, our brethren may rest assured, that Christ never uttered such a faith as theirs in the land of Judea. No, never!

Call up the heart of the Jew toward the Son of God; the moment Christ stood up on earth the mediator between God and man, he assumed a stand exactly, inexorably fatal to all the political, ecclesiastical, and spiritual claims and prospects of the Jewish nation. His teaching, character, and agency never failed to reach their souls in precise and deadly antagonism to all they nationally thought, felt, and hoped. The Jews, therefore, deeply realized one thing, that to put down Jesus was vital to the rescue of their polity from impending destruction. Jesus, too, had such power in his countenance, spirit, and speech; such authority in all their history, prophecy, and types; such witnesses in saints, angels, and devils; such coworkers in his own miracles, their own consciences, and the spirit of God, that, to destroy him they felt to be their only refuge against an embodied terrific foreboding, set up by righteous wrath to appal their spirit before the time. Nor must we forget that the Jews were sick unto death of the multiplied, unavailing, humiliating, agonizing conflicts with the Son of God. His calm and lucid teachings had triumphantly vindicated all God's assaulted words and ways, and laid before their own eyes and the world all their own irreverence, injustice, and hypocrisy; all their perversions, abominations, and rebellions. Exasperated to the last degree by this terrible discipline, the governing mind of Judea could now bear him no longer. They thirsted for his blood. They resolved to shed it. They sought again and again to do so. They were chafed to distraction by their failures. They could not sufficiently destroy his popularity with the people. At length, lashed to desperation, in solemn conclave they upbraid each other and cry out, "What do we? We prevail nothing. The world is gone after him. If we let him thus alone, the Romans will come and take away our place and nation." Had that eminent personage, who ever carried about him such dread testimonies of God's present authority, but once solemnly exclaimed, "Henceforth the sign and seal of God's covenant of adoption, in all the children of this land, by God's authority, I cancel forever," who, who can imagine the explosion that must have instantly followed! Parental affection from one end of the land to the other—oh, how sincerely agonized! how vindictively, fiercely, fired! What would not such a feeling have done? *Jewish frenzy*, too, to put down the power of Jesus—for years to its wit's end, it had toiled, and plotted, and menaced, and failed to lay hold of one solitary charge that could avail to turn the tide of popular vengeance against him; with what an agony of relief and triumph they had instantly seized this teaching of the Son of God and proclaimed it to the people. Are we now to be told that the heart of the Jewish nation could have listened to the authoritative abolition of the most precious provision of the Abrahamic covenant from the mouth of its mortal foe, without one faint note of remonstrance? without one feeble murmur of opposition? without one single effort to turn it to his disadvantage? without one solitary syllable of response? If, in all the story of their fault-finding, there is not one sentence, not one word, projected against the abrogation of their children's bill of rights in the Abrahamic covenant, rest assured of it, that bill of rights has never been repealed! Rest assured of it, Jesus never taught your doctrine—never held your faith! No, never!

Secondly, It is affirmed that the face of the Scriptures discountenances the doctrines of infant baptism.

The subject of baptism, it is alleged, is repeatedly brought up in the Gospel, the party to be baptized is frequently spoken of, but it is written nowhere either that infants were baptized, or that they should be.

The objection, analyzed, will be found to advance nothing new. We respond, however, that the face of the Scriptures is just what it should be to teach our doctrine.

If an examination be made, it will be seen that the impressions upon this subject arise from an oversight of this one great truth—the unity of the Church in both dispensations. Rather depreciating the Old Testament, and considering the Gospel very much as a new religion, our brethren have refused to receive the doctrine of the baptism of infants, for this reason mainly, because it is not laid down in the Gospel with that distinctness, which, in their judgment, should mark the bearing of a new ordinance. But to suppose that there can be two religions is the grandest error mind can commit. All that makes up religion is always the same. Indeed the practice of Jesus and the apostles, to refer to the Old Testament as the grand depository of all instruction and authority upon questions of New Testament doctrines, clearly establishes the unchangeableness of the Church through all dispensations. Now the nature of the Church, once understood, decides the interpretation of the Scripture, in regard to it.

If the Gospel is indeed a new religion, we have a right to require that infant baptism shall stand out clearly revealed on its pages. But if the Church is one in both Testaments, then we are not permitted to discard a doctrine, simply because a certain portion of the word of God does not seem to set it forth with unquestionable clearness. The fact is, that the tenor of God's word, wisely examined, both in the Old Testament and in the New, will be found to teach our doctrine precisely as we should have expected.

If the church is one, then

1. *Foundations lie in the Old Testament; republication, explication in the New.*

Every element of the constitution of the Church of God we have found grouped together in the Abrahamic covenant. The Gospel, therefore, is not a laying down of new foundations. The old, the eternal, the immutable foundations had been put down long before. So far as its novelties are concerned, the Gospel is but the new weather-boarding of the old fabric, the new dress of the old body. In view of this truth, how perfectly natural is the face of the Scriptures! The new edition of the old covenant does indeed republish and explain with more or less clearness and fulness, every essential element of the Church; but it takes care to keep us apprised that these are matters already made known in the prior revelation.

Now, if foundations lie in the old economy, how unreasonable it is to interpret New Testament statements concerning the frame-work of the Church, as though nothing had been settled upon the subject before?

2. Much of the teaching of the New Testament touching the essentials of religion, we should expect just such as would be addressed to a party supposed to have been previously pretty fairly instructed.

If the Church, of necessity, must be one and the same in both dispensations, since the Old Testament has already laid down first principles, the language of subsequent exposition will very naturally be sometimes sententious—by allusion—incomplete. In a word, it will be such teaching as presupposes that there are things pertinent to the proper understanding of the words of the teacher already in the mind of the party addressed; such teaching as will expect the pupil to interpret things spoken in the light of things previously taught. The face of the New Testament, it will not be denied, abounds in just such presentations of truth. How unreasonable it is, therefore, to interpret an apparent lack of fulness of teaching in the Gospel, as deciding a question respecting the structure of the Church, without consulting what had been previously revealed upon the same point in its original organization!

3. On all points radical to the structure of the Church, we should be satisfied to find the Gospel a fair reflection of the old economy.

On some points, New Testament expositions will be fuller and clearer; on others, they will rely more largely upon the foundations previously established. On the whole, the New Testament Church, with greater or less distinctness, will carry out in every particular the essential stipulations of the Abrahamic covenant. So that he who has seen the face of God's religion in the Old Testament, will recognise its image in the New. Certainly the face of God's word bears out this last inference from the unity of the Church.

What difference do we find between the features of the

Old Testament and the New, respecting the precise point under discussion? What was the Church of God of old, in *composition?* Of old, the kingdom, in part, was obviously composed of little children. "Of such" little children, says the Saviour, "is the kingdom of heaven" in our day. Matt. xix. 14. In *covenant description of the parties?* Of old, the covenant promise was addressed expressly "to you and to your children." In our day, Peter says, expressly, "The promise is to you and your children." Acts ii. 39. In general *description of the seed?* Of old, an uncircumcised child was styled *unclean*—a circumcised child, *holy*. In the New Testament, also, the child of the unbeliever is called *unclean*—the child of the believer, *holy*. 1 Cor. vii. 14. In the *visible process of introduction?* Of old, church-members were often introduced by families. "Thou and thy seed, and he that is born in the house, and he that is bought with thy money." Gen. xvii. 10–12. So in the New Testament. Though the recorded cases of baptism are few in number, and greatly abbreviated in history, yet a part of them were by household. Acts xvi. 15. "And when she (Lydia) was baptized, and her household." Acts xvi. 33. "And was baptized, (the jailor,) he and all his, straightway." 1 Cor. i. 16. "And I baptized, also, the household of Stephanas." Finally, one thing preeminently marked the child of the believer under the old dispensation: he received in his person the sign and the seal of the covenant which his father made with God. Baptize the child of the Church in our day, and we complete the parallel between the teachings of the Old Testament and the New on this subject. Where, then, is the argument founded on the face of the Scriptures? In the light of the oneness of the Church in both dispensations, does not the word of God teach the church-membership of infants in the most natural manner conceivable?

Thirdly, it is said, that faith is the scriptural pre-

requisite of baptism, and therefore the ordinance should not be administered to infants.

It impairs the force of this assumption to reflect that there is no such essential peculiarity in faith as constitutes a special fitness for the ordinance. Baptism is the badge of Christianity; and since the nations must turn from some form of false religion to reach it, it is natural that faith should present itself as the representative of that Christianity which the ordinance demands. Let it be recollected, too, that the Scriptures express qualification for the ordinance in the use of other terms: "Then said Peter, 'Repent and be baptized every one of you.'" Acts ii. 38. Again: "Can any man forbid water, that these should not be baptized which have received the Holy Ghost as well as we." Acts x. 47. Nor should we forget that the Abrahamic covenant is substantially the Christian Church. Nothing can be more unreasonable, therefore, than to attempt to settle the membership of the Church without the slightest reference to its constitution.

But we remark more directly, that it overthrows this objection to examine the prominent scriptural authority upon which it is based. It is said, that the very sentence from the lips of the Saviour, which originated the ordinance of baptism, confines its administration to those who believe: "Go ye into all the world, and preach the Gospel to every creature; he that believeth and is baptized, shall be saved; he that believeth not, shall be damned." By this interpretation of the text, of every creature, those only who believe are to be baptized. The pertinency of this Scripture is a little ambiguous. There are two classes of the human family—the adult and the infant. The preaching of the Gospel is applicable to the one—not to the other. The common sense of the passage would rather seem to be this: "Of every creature to whom I send you to preach the Gospel, he only that believes shall be baptized." The irrelevancy of the text, however, is not the principal difficulty. The structure of the passage is fatal to the interpretation advanced. Here are two parts of one sentence, addressed to the same person. If the first part of the sentence is addressed to the infant, so is the second. If it is held, therefore, that the infant's lack of faith, by the first section, unfits him for baptism, it must be held, also, that the infant's lack of faith, by the second section, fits him for damnation.

But, surely, this is not divine teaching. Behold the child! He has great natural interests, but cannot look to them. God, in nature, appoints the parent the trustee of the child. He has great social interests, but cannot protect them. Here, too, universal human consent permits the parent to do for the child what he cannot do for himself. He has still more important spiritual interests, and we know that God often requires the parent to represent the child here also.

But bend your thoughts upon this remarkable historical fact. In the formation of the Church, God himself did set apart the parent to act for his child. *Circumcision* was the act whereby faith was expressed in the first Church covenant. Therefore God commanded Abraham to circumcise himself. He did so, and thus expressed his faith. *Circumcision* must, of course, express the faith of the child under the same covenant. But the child cannot circumcise himself. What is to be done? God settles this question. He commands the parent to act for his child and circumcise him. Accordingly, as by the circumcision of himself, Abraham expressed faith for himself, so by the circumcision of his child, Abraham expressed faith for his child. The Abrahamic covenant is the New Testament Church! If God, in the former, required the parent to act for the child and express his faith, God, in the latter, requires the parent to do the same.

Should there still hang about the mind an impression that the faith of the subject should be personal, there is a teaching in the Scriptures which should satisfy it. Baptism expresses faith, it is true, but circumcision also expresses faith, for God built this ordinance purposely, that it might be a distinguished sign of faith. Rom. iv. 11. If then, scripturally, faith is necessary to baptism, scripturally, faith was just as necessary to circumcision. Yet circumcision, "a seal of the righteousness of faith," was scripturally administered to the infant. Where lies the very slightest scriptural difficulty in the last case which was not scripturally removed in the first? If the incapacity of the infant to believe did not, in ancient times, prevent his being circumcised on the strength of his father's faith, why should the incapacity of the infant to believe, in modern times, forbid his being baptized on the same basis; especially in view of the fundamental fact, that, in founding his Church, God commanded the parent to act for the child?

If our readers will attend to two points, they will see how the Almighty addresses the conscience of parents on the basis of the Abrahamic covenant:

I. *The Abrahamic covenant, in its substance, is a valid covenant in our day.*

We shall not go over the arguments already adduced to establish this truth. The apostle's climax is all we shall repeat: "Though it were a man's covenant, it should not be disannulled, yet this is the covenant that was confirmed before of God in Christ."

II. *The application of the sign and the seal to the children of believers in the Abrahamic covenant is not matter of form, but of substance.*

"This is my covenant. Every male child among you shall be circumcised." What is important in a covenant beyond parties, obligations, influence?

1. *Parties.* You covenant with a hundred men. If we so interpret your deed as to throw out fifty of the parties, is this an unimportant modification of your contract? Have we left the substance of your deed untouched? On the contrary, is any thing more important in a covenant than its parties? Put some other person in the place of Him who so kindly covenants with man in the patriarchal interview, and have you not substantially altered the covenant? The parties to the Abrahamic covenant, on man's side, you know, are believers and their seed. Abolish the application of the sign and seal to the seed of the believer, and you throw out of the covenant more than half of its original parties. Whatever may be our opinion of the matter, we apprehend that both the world above and the world below adjudge this a very serious change in the substance of the covenant.

2. *Obligations.* You affect the obligations of the parties just as seriously. Obligation relates to two things—the act to be performed, and the moral force which impels to the performance. The Scriptures command all parents to bring up their children in the fear of the Lord; and all children to honour and serve their Maker. The application of the sign and seal of the covenant to the seed of the contractor does not affect the obligation of the parties, so far as respects the services to be rendered. But it greatly augments their obligation, in view both of the kind and of the degree of the moral force which binds to the duty. Surely God's general word, enjoining upon

parents the pious education of their children, creates the most solemn obligation. But when God calls the parent before his very face; spreads before him his solemn duty to his children; makes him solemnly swear that he will be faithful; compels him to affix both his signature and his seal to the vow; and, finally, dismisses him, well-assured that he leaves all this upon record in God's house until the day of reckoning,—who will dare to say that such a transaction contributes no additional obligation? Again: When God, as it were by his own hand, writes on the very body of the child a solemn oath,—that this person is sacred to God, and that he will serve him forever,—ere long, when time makes known to his adult years, that it was God himself who had caused that oath of consecration to be religiously inscribed upon his person,—who will dare to say that the party is, nevertheless, authorized to consider this whole procedure as a senseless formality, and that respect for God does not require him to take the slightest notice of that personal claim to his heart and service so emphatically asserted by the God who made him?

3. *Influence.* If there is one additional thing important to a covenant, it is this: *It should possess dignity enough to influence the parties to do their duty.* The application of the token to the children of the Church, is well calculated to wield a vast power in securing fidelity to the covenant. That solemn act of all the good men and women of the world, whereby they enter God's house, and there sign and seal, in God's presence, their solemn vow that they will be faithful to their children,—who can believe that this religious vow will exert no influence over their parental fidelity? That merciful act of God, whereby he meets them with his own signed and sealed pledge of gracious countenance and co-operation in their most arduous, anxious

task,—who can believe that this sacred pledge will never encourage them in moments of despondency, nor rouse them to renewed prayer and toil when faith had almost failed? Who can believe that the well-educated children of the Church will neither feel that their solemn dedication to God, by his direction, lays them under obligation to serve him; nor take encouragement, in the hour of honest struggle, from God's formal pledge of saving assistance? In a word, the application of the token of the covenant to the seed of the pious, levies contributions upon every power of every parent and child of God's Church, and calls out the combined strength of all, through every moment of life, to build up God's kingdom in the world. Assuredly there will be a vast shortcoming of universal, adequate response to this appeal, but it is just as certain that this very appeal will secure a vast increase of holy power to the cause of Christ in the world.

And, now, we expect our brethren, in Christian integrity, to stand by us and say, If there is any one thing in the Abrahamic covenant which is matter of substance, and should stand and be enforced in our day, *it is the obligation to do now what God commanded to be done of old, even the infixing of the blessed token of divine adoption upon the child, as well as upon the parent.*

Under the administration of early times, such a spectacle was scarcely ever seen in the Church of God, as a parent whose child did not carry the sign of God's covenant of adoption. Whenever such an unhappy object was found, that child was instantly cut off from God's family. But the Abrahamic covenant is the Christian Church. The Abrahamic covenant is in full force. We leave it a question for the consciences of our brethren,

How is it that your children are wandering abroad upon the earth without the mark of God's covenant of mercy? How is it that you, as Christian men, have never recorded your vow in the temple of the Lord, to do a parent's part by them?

THE END.

STEREOTYPED BY L. JOHNSON & CO.
PHILADELPHIA.

www.ingramcontent.com/pod-product-compliance
Lightning Source LLC
LaVergne TN
LVHW010253110826
845151LV00004B/1461

* 9 7 8 1 4 2 5 5 2 2 6 5 0 *